Immigration and the American Ethos

What do Americans want from immigration policy and why? In the rise of a polarized and acrimonious immigration debate, leading accounts see racial anxieties and disputes over the meaning of American nationhood coming to a head. The resurgence of parochial identities has breathed new life into old worries about the vulnerability of the American Creed. This book tells a different story, one in which creedal values remain hard at work in shaping ordinary Americans' judgments about immigration. Levy and Wright show that perceptions of civic fairness – based on multiple, often competing values deeply rooted in the country's political culture – are the dominant guideposts by which most Americans navigate immigration controversies most of the time and explain why so many Americans simultaneously hold a mix of pro-immigrant and anti-immigrant positions. The authors test the relevance and force of the theory over time and across issue domains.

MORRIS LEVY is Assistant Professor of Political Science at the University of Southern California.

MATTHEW WRIGHT is Assistant Professor of Political Science at the University of British Columbia.

Cambridge Studies in Public Opinion and Political Psychology

SERIES EDITORS

Dennis Chong, *University of Southern California and Northwestern University*
James H. Kuklinski, *University of Illinois, Urbana-Champaign*

Cambridge Studies in Public Opinion and Political Psychology publishes innovative research from a variety of theoretical and methodological perspectives on the mass public foundations of politics and society. Research in the series focuses on the origins and influence of mass opinion, the dynamics of information and deliberation, and the emotional, normative, and instrumental bases of political choice. In addition to examining psychological processes, the series explores the organization of groups, the association between individual and collective preferences, and the impact of institutions on beliefs and behavior. Cambridge Studies in Public Opinion and Political Psychology is dedicated to furthering theoretical and empirical research on the relationship between the political system and the attitudes and actions of citizens.

Books in the series are listed on the page following the Index.

Immigration and the American Ethos

MORRIS LEVY
University of Southern California

MATTHEW WRIGHT
University of British Columbia

CAMBRIDGE
UNIVERSITY PRESS

University Printing House, Cambridge CB2 8BS, United Kingdom

One Liberty Plaza, 20th Floor, New York, NY 10006, USA

477 Williamstown Road, Port Melbourne, VIC 3207, Australia

314–321, 3rd Floor, Plot 3, Splendor Forum, Jasola District Centre,
New Delhi – 110025, India

79 Anson Road, #06–04/06, Singapore 079906

Cambridge University Press is part of the University of Cambridge.

It furthers the University's mission by disseminating knowledge in the pursuit of
education, learning, and research at the highest international levels of excellence.

www.cambridge.org
Information on this title: www.cambridge.org/9781108488815
DOI: 10.1017/9781108772174

© Cambridge University Press 2020

This publication is in copyright. Subject to statutory exception
and to the provisions of relevant collective licensing agreements,
no reproduction of any part may take place without the written
permission of Cambridge University Press.

First published 2020

A catalogue record for this publication is available from the British Library.

Library of Congress Cataloging-in-Publication Data
NAMES: Levy, Morris, 1982– author. | Wright, Matthew, 1979– author.
TITLE: Immigration and the American ethos / Morris Levy, Matthew Wright.
DESCRIPTION: Cambridge, United Kingdom ; New York, NY : Cambridge University Press, 2020. |
    Series: Cambridge studies in public opinion and political psychology | Includes bibliographical
    references and index.
IDENTIFIERS: LCCN 2019037308 (print) | LCCN 2019037309 (ebook) | ISBN 9781108488815
    (hardback) | ISBN 9781108738873 (paperback) | ISBN 9781108772174 (epub)
SUBJECTS: LCSH: United States–Emigration and immigration–Public opinion. | Group identity–
    Political aspects–United States. | Fairness–Political aspects–United States.
CLASSIFICATION: LCC JV6456 .L48 2020 (print) | LCC JV6456 (ebook) | DDC 325.73–DC23
LC record available at https://lccn.loc.gov/2019037308
LC ebook record available at https://lccn.loc.gov/2019037309

ISBN 978-1-108-48881-5 Hardback
ISBN 978-1-108-73887-3 Paperback

Cambridge University Press has no responsibility for the persistence or accuracy
of URLs for external or third-party internet websites referred to in this publication
and does not guarantee that any content on such websites is, or will remain,
accurate or appropriate.

Contents

List of Figures		*page* vii
List of Tables		ix
Preface		xi
Prologue		xv
1	What Do Americans Want from Immigration Policy, and Why?	1
2	Civic Fairness and Group-Centrism	25
3	Functional Assimilation, Humanitarianism, and Support for Legal Admissions	61
4	Civic Fairness and the Legal–Illegal Divide	86
5	Civic Fairness and Ethnic Stereotypes	125
6	Assimilation, Civic Fairness and the "Circle of We"	142
7	Conclusion	169
Notes		185
Bibliography		209
Index		227

v

Figures

3.1	Mean support for policy to increase immigration from Mexico by 100,000 annually, by treatment condition	*page* 68
3.2	Effect of functional assimilation cue by individualism and humanitarianism	70
3.3	Effect of family and refugee treatments by individualism and humanitarianism	71
3.4	Response to the "Green Card Experiment"	75
3.5	The Green Card Experiment, version 2.0	77
4.1	Effect of egalitarianism on opinions about level of legal immigration versus legalization for illegal immigrants, ANES 2008, 2012, and 2016	90
4.2	Legalism and egalitarianism across the legal–illegal divide, SSI 2013	93
4.3	Legalism and admissions preference across the legal–illegal divide	100
4.4	Egalitarianism and admissions preference across the legal–illegal divide	101
4.5	Humanitarianism and acceptance probability across statuses	103
4.6	Ethnocentrism and acceptance probability across statuses	104
4.7	Categorical judgments (positive and negative) across statuses	106
4.8	Probability of acceptance and individual immigrants' functional assimilation and human capital	108
4.9	Probability of acceptance and ethnoreligious traits	110
4.10	Penalties for norm violation, by immigrants' national origin	111
4.11	Feelings toward Asians and Latinos and support for immigrants from Germany, China, and Mexico	113
4.12	Feelings toward Asians and Latinos and support for immigrants from Germany, China, and Mexico by legal status	115

viii *List of Figures*

4.13	Support for illegal immigrants versus support for illegal immigration policy by national origin	120
5.1	Ethnic bias with and without functional assimilation cues	132
5.2	Ethnic bias, information, and party identification	134
5.3	Ethnic bias and information, groups rather than individuals	136
5.4	Groups versus individuals by respondent ethnicity	137
5.5	Attitudes toward Latinos and Asians and support for immigrants in the vignette experiment	139
6.1	Distribution of dependent variable scales overall and by official status	153
6.2	Influence of cues about immigrant patriotism and naturalization on perceived fit in community and support for benefits eligibility	155
6.3	Legalism and egalitarianism predict differentiation between citizens' and legally resident noncitizens' eligibility for public benefits	157
6.4	National attachment and the influence of support for functional and formal assimilation on immigration policy opinions	163

Tables

2.1	Elements of civic fairness	*page* 39
2.2	Summary of hypotheses	59
3.1	Summary of treatment conditions	65
4.1	Ethnic group affect and policy opinions in the American National Election Studies	95
6.1	Determinants of horizontal attachment and public opinion about eligibility for benefits and political right	150
6.2	Norms of American identity and immigration policy opinions	161

ix

Preface

This book would not have been possible without the support and assistance of a great many people. No acknowledgment can convey how blessed we are to be Jack Citrin's students, collaborators (including in earlier phases of this project), and above all dear friends. Jack is a pioneer and a giant in this field of scholarship. His intellectual imprint is everywhere in this volume. We will always be honored to have been the final two products of the Citrin Academy of Political Science, which has launched so many productive academic careers. We hope to have made some small contribution to its mission of understanding what binds mass citizenries to a political community.

Under Jack's stewardship, the Institute of Governmental Studies (IGS) supported a number of the surveys that provided some of the key findings described in these chapters. IGS was also a scholarly home base for us as we developed these ideas and a place where we could frequently consult with fellow graduate students and faculty members. John Hanley, Ruth Bloch Rubin, Greg Elinson, Jason Anastasopoulos, Rob Van Houweling, Laura Stoker, Rodney Hero, and Irene Bloemraad, among very many others, have been helpful (and indulgent) sounding boards for these ideas over the years.

In addition, we received a great deal of support throughout the project from American University (AU) and its School of Public Affairs. One of the first surveys we conducted as a part of this project, which supplied some of the results that make up this book and inspired subsequent studies, was funded by an AU Faculty Research Support Grant back in 2012. More recently (in Fall 2017), AU's School of Public Affairs generously supported a workshop devoted to our in progress manuscript.

We are also indebted to numerous others who read, discussed, insightfully critiqued, and otherwise assisted us with parts or all of the manuscript: Debbie Schildkraut, Dan Hopkins, Leonie Huddy, Stanley Feldman, John Sides, David Barker, Danny Hayes, and Jen Lawless all played major parts in the American University book workshop. Jane Junn, Jeb Barnes, Jeff Sellers, Dowell Myers, and Dennis Chong at USC all gave valuable suggestions, some generously taking hours on multiple occasions to talk through possible revisions. Jeremy Ferwerda, Sara Goodman, and Nick Valentino also read and provided useful feedback on some of our draft chapters. Youssef Chouhoud and Emily Bello Pardo provided skilled research assistance at various stages of this project.

We have benefited from presenting portions of this book at various conferences and workshops over the past several years, including the Workshop on Immigration, Race, and Ethnicity at Harvard's Kennedy School of Government and the Research Workshop in American Politics at the University of California, Berkeley's Institute of Governmental Studies. We received valuable comments from several presentations over the years at the workshop "Comparative Approaches to the Study of Immigration, Ethnicity, and Religion" – at Massachusetts Institute of Technology in 2013, at Stanford in 2014, at University of North Carolina-Chapel Hill in 2015, and at Yale in 2016. We thank Jens Hainmueller, Karen Jusko, Rahsaan Maxwell, and Maggie Peters for hosting these events. We are also grateful for the opportunity to present parts of this research at various workshops around the District of Columbia area and greater northeast, including the New York Political Psychology Meeting (in 2016), the National Capital Area Political Science Association's biannual American Politics Workshops, and smaller workshops held at the University of Maryland and American University. Finally, we were fortunate to have opportunities to present aspects of the book at Oxford University and the University of Copenhagen in the summer/fall of 2016 at workshops hosted by Gina Gustavsson and David Miller, and Nils Holtug (respectively). We are deeply indebted to all those who engaged with us at them, even though they are far too numerous to name here. We would like, however, to single out our various formal discussants at these venues, including Rafaela Dancygier, Gina Gustavsson, David Miller, Cecilia Mo, Efrén Pérez, and Cara Wong.

Cambridge University Press has been wonderful to work with from start to finish. We are extremely grateful to Sara Doskow and everyone else at Cambridge who worked under her capable leadership. Sara managed an unfailingly clear, responsive, prompt, and constructive process that improved the book by leaps and bounds. It was our extremely good fortune as well to receive two most thoughtful and incisive anonymous reviews and to have the support and oversight of series editors Jim Kuklinski and Dennis Chong.

We dedicate this book to our families, without whose confidence, patience, and encouragement it would never have come together. Our families also had a thing or two to say about the manuscript. In addition to deftly assembling the book's appendix, Julia Salvatore asked probing questions about the book's broader lessons that fueled productive discussions about revisions and

Preface xiii

additional studies. Daniela Levy helped identify and improve parts of the manuscript where the argument was unclear and took us to task for numerous stylistic infelicities. John Pineda provided ever-thoughtful reactions at various points in the process. Dan Levy read portions of multiple drafts of the manuscript and commented insightfully almost line by line.

Prologue

America is a creedal nation. Classical works on the country's political culture portray individualism, equality of opportunity, and the rule of law as foundational values that set the terms of public debate and shape beliefs about the proper means and ends of political action.[1] But in a diverse nation stratified since its inception by race and ethnicity, observers have long seen parochial group identities and animosities as profound threats to American ideals. Witnessing the enslavement of blacks and decimation of Native Americans in the early 1830s, Alexis de Tocqueville prophesied that American democracy would be engulfed by race war and genocide.[2] In the aftermath of the Civil Rights movement, Harold Isaacs cast the "convulsive ingathering of people into their numberless groupings of kinds"[3] as an existential challenge to the individualist "bedrock of the whole American system."[4] A quarter century later, Rogers Smith depicted ideologies of ethnic, sexual, and religious hierarchy and exclusion as co-equal traditions in American political culture that continue to subvert their liberal and republican counterparts. He attributed the persistent appeal of these "ascriptive" traditions to a human craving for belonging that belief in abstract principles alone cannot sate.[5] In our own era, conflict over mass immigration has breathed new life into old worries about the vulnerability of creedal aspirations to chauvinism, prejudice, and balkanization.[6] "Tribalism" is the word on everyone's lips.[7]

Is a resurgence of group identity undermining Americans' fealty to their creed? Alongside the historical record, the last half century of research on public opinion, much of it inspired by sociopsychological theories of group relations, suggests so. While scholars continue to see values as important organizing principles for mass opinion, nagging doubts remain about the solidity of people's commitment to the ideals they profess to believe in.[8] Principles that Americans widely endorse in the abstract – the right to free expression, limited government, and equality of opportunity, for example

xv

xvi   *Prologue*

– often seem to fall by the wayside when people face questions that bear on the status and interests of salient social groups.[9] Study after study finds that group identities and attitudes are pervasively linked to issue opinions and electoral choice.[10]

This idea that group identifications, attachments, and animosities play a dominant role in structuring mass political choice has rapidly gained influence in the study of public opinion.[11] One prominent assessment of mass democratic capabilities recently called for a thoroughgoing corporatization of politics in which "identity groups," rather than individual voters, would become the official units of democratic decision making.[12] Setting aside the question of who, then, would speak for the identity group, the authors reason that decades of research on mass opinion and voting behavior point to group identities and interests as the most reliable bases on which people make political choices. If citizens really regard politics as an arena in which identity groups compete for status and wealth, why not set up the political system accordingly?

We label accounts of mass opinion and political behavior that trace political choices to ingroup favoritism and outgroup derogation "group-centrist."[13] As we will elaborate in the coming chapters, group-centrist theories differ in many respects. Some maintain that people assign intrinsic value to relative group status and material well-being.[14] Others emphasize the instrumental value that group resources and position carry for people who believe their personal fortunes to be so tethered to the collective's that they put its welfare before their own.[15] Some see group-centrism as "primordial" – hard wired into the psyche during the millennia in which our forebears depended for survival on their membership in small, tight-knit communities. Others focus on the political "construction" of group ties and boundaries – their malleability, manipulation by elites, and strategic deployment by individuals in all walks of life.[16] And, as if things weren't complicated enough, group-centrist accounts highlight a wide array of overlapping and often intertwined group memberships, from "imagined communities"[17] such as the nation and the ethnos, to inherently political identities such as partisanship, to economic strata such as class.[18] Yet, for all that, what group-centrist accounts of mass politics have in common is the view that ordinary citizens' political choices are rooted predominantly in considerations about how the alternatives affect the interests and status of salient social groups.

Not all group-related influences on mass opinion qualify as "group-centric" in our definition. This is because not all such influences stem from concerns about group status and interest per se. Information about how a policy affects social groups can instead influence people's political choices by drawing their attention to the values at stake in a policy choice. Otherwise staunch supporters of free expression, for example, may favor censoring "hate speech" against minority groups because they believe that such speech deprives individual minority group members of equal opportunity in schools or workplaces rather than because they are invested in these groups' collective prosperity and

Prologue   xvii

esteem.[19] Nevertheless, the dominant interpretation of citizens' tendency to conceptualize political issues in terms of group interest[20] is that it reflects the worth people assign to their collective identities.

The coming chapters examine the relative influence of political values and group-centrism in American mass politics using an extended case study of contemporary public opinion about immigration. This is a hard test for values and a seemingly easy one for group-centrist theories that emphasize ethnic and national identities. Immigration policies define and bind a political community, determining who can join and on what terms. Such questions, by their nature, touch off a process of social categorization that unleashes the ethnocentric instinct to favor "us against them."[21] Immigrants start, virtually by definition, as outsiders relative to the national community. Most hail from racial, religious, and cultural backgrounds that differ from the American majority and mainstream, presenting what some citizens see as an acute threat to their nation's traditional way of life.

In the rise of polarization and acrimony in the country's immigration politics, leading scholarly accounts see long-festering racial anxieties and disputes over the meaning of American nationhood coming to a head. The titles of recent books that attend primarily or in part to the causes and consequences of public reactions to immigration loudly announce their group-centrist bent – *White Backlash*, *The Politics of Belonging*, *Us against Them*, *White Identity Politics*, and *Identity Crisis*.[22] And while most scholars would accept that values play some role in determining Americans' opinions about immigration, it is commonly argued that appeals to principle are rationales constructed post hoc to defend opinions that really stem from ethnic and national attachments.[23]

This book tells a different story, one in which creedal values remain hard at work in shaping ordinary Americans' judgments about immigration. It makes a case for the influence of mass perceptions of *civic fairness*, which we define as a set of normative beliefs about what the political community owes to its aspiring members and what they owe in return. We show that values that influence perceptions of civic fairness are the dominant guideposts by which most Americans navigate immigration controversies most of the time. Headlining the account is a multifaceted but "thin" modern incarnation of liberal assimilationist norms that are rooted in the value of individualism and beliefs in the importance of rigid adherence to the rule of law. But the values of egalitarianism and humanitarianism temper the application of these assimilationist norms to many immigration policy controversies.

These values have long been central to the country's political culture. The coming chapters demonstrate that they remain so today even in a sphere of politics that is commonly thought to be dominated by group-centrism. In so doing, they illustrate that value conflicts arising within the liberal tradition of American political culture continue to shape mass politics. We define political culture similarly to Herbert McClosky and John Zaller in their classic *The American Ethos*: "a set of widely shared beliefs, values, and norms concerning the relationship of citizens to their government and to one another in matters affecting public affairs."[24] Many of these beliefs, values, and norms, we argue, are also applied to opinions about relationships that involve resident noncitizens and others who aspire to live in America or join the political community.

Taking stock of how these values shape public opinion sheds light on empirical puzzles that earlier research has by and large overlooked and that existing theories cannot adequately explain. First and foremost, why do the great majority of Americans hold some mixture of "pro-" and "anti-immigrant" issue positions? We will show that these patterns are functions of the distinct sets of competing values that different facets of immigration policy evoke and the diverse ways that individuals prioritize them. Though ambivalent and complex, American public opinion about immigration does have a discernible structure, one that is rooted more widely and deeply in creedal values than in group-centrism. Going further, we will show that the centrality of values in American public opinion about immigration helps explain other little-noticed anomalies in group-centrist theories as well. The importance of competing values illuminates, for example, why ethnic cues influence opinions about immigration in some contexts but not in others and why feelings of communal solidarity with immigrants often fail to translate into support for "pro-immigrant" policies.

To illustrate the power of a particular set of values associated with the American creed is not to gainsay or ignore other influences, including economic self-interest, the national interest, and rival traditions of American political culture.[25] Our account pays particular attention to ideologies of ascriptive hierarchy that have promoted race, ethnicity, and religion among other virtually immutable circumstances of birth as barriers to full membership in the polity.[26] As we shall see, group attachments and prejudice do hold sway at times in American public opinion about immigration. Racial stereotyping is pervasive. Stigmas attached to some groups are resistant to information. Feelings of obligation to help "one's own" are sometimes strong enough to supersede abstract beliefs about what is fair. Yet on the issues we examine, when group loyalties and prejudices collide directly with abstract values that shape public conceptions of civic fairness, the latter tend to carry the day. What the economist Gunnar Myrdal called "the American ethos" – a distinctly American moralistic and rationalistic outlook that bristles at flagrant inconsistency between creedal values and the base prejudices that are fundamentally antithetical to them – maintains its place in ordinary citizens' hearts and minds.[27]

Before delving into our main subject, which is to characterize and explain public opinion about immigration policy, we think it is worthwhile to highlight the political relevance of our topic to those whose main interest lies in understanding immigration politics and policy making. This would have been harder for us to do a quarter century ago. As recently as the early 1990s, political leaders gave scant public attention to immigration policy except to celebrate the

Prologue xix

country's storied past. Not a single State of the Union Address between 1966 and 1994 so much as mentioned it.[28] On the rare occasion that the issue surfaced, it elicited little intense public conflict. Asked about illegal immigration in their final primary debate in 1980, George H. W. Bush and Ronald Reagan agreed that current policy erred in criminalizing so many "strong people" whose presence in the country was an economic boon and a strategic asset.[29] As late as 1992, Pat Buchanan's formidable antiglobalization primary challenge to the incumbent President Bush failed to penetrate the general election: three presidential debates featured not one question about immigration.

This was not for want of things to talk about. Landmark reforms drastically overhauled the nation's immigration policies during this period and forever changed the nation's social fabric.[30] With national origins quotas abolished, an admissions policy that liberally allotted visas to relatives of US citizens in place, and an unofficial policy of salutary neglect toward illegal immigration punctuated by a large-scale amnesty in 1986, the country's foreign-born population skyrocketed from 4% in 1970 to 14% in 2017, rivaling its pre–World War I apex. Over the same period, its Latino and Asian populations quadrupled to a combined 22% of the total.[31]

Yet these developments remained on the periphery of public debate. Pollsters rarely asked ordinary Americans what they thought of all these major reforms and the momentous demographic changes they were ushering in. When they began to do so more regularly in the early 1990s, far more Americans said they wanted to decrease immigration than increase it. This restrictive bent seemed so thoroughly disconnected from the direction of public policy that scholars widely dismissed the diffuse objections of an unorganized citizenry as a sideshow in the politics of immigration. Policy making, they argued, was dominated by ethnic lobbies that thrived on immigrants' votes and industries that profited from their labor operating in an insular world of cloistered expert commissions and iron triangles.[32]

Before the ink had dried on these scholarly profiles, a populist insurgency forced the politics of immigration into full public view. The opening salvo was California Governor Pete Wilson's campaign to restrict immigrants' access to public benefits, which culminated in California's Proposition 187 in 1994 and new federal limitations on immigrants' access to federal services in 1996.[33] As the illegal immigrant population exploded and spread to "new destinations" in the South, the Midwest, and the suburbs, grassroots restrictionists trained their fire on "amnesty" for unauthorized immigrants. Bipartisan efforts at comprehensive immigration reform repeatedly buckled in the face of furious populist headwinds.[34] As conservative opposition to illegal immigration raged on the airwaves and found a home in the Tea Party, immigrants and their allies countermobilized.[35] Millions of immigrants, co-ethnics, and sympathizers took to the streets to demand legal recognition and rights, an unprecedented show of force by America's noncitizen population.[36]

xx *Prologue*

Polarization intensified as moderate voices were drowned out or scared off by hardliners. Republican rising stars such as former House Majority Leader Eric Cantor and presidential hopefuls Jeb Bush and Marco Rubio learned the hard way about the perils of defying an inflamed party base.[37] Meanwhile, few Democratic elected officials had the gumption to face down activists' demands for rapid and comprehensive legalization with few strings attached – by executive fiat if necessary.[38] Then Donald Trump descended the gilded escalator of Trump Tower to kick off his campaign with a barrage of anti-Mexican invective, and the rest is unfolding before our eyes.

These events make it clear that no credible account of immigration politics can leave the public on the sidelines. The recent history of immigration politics is unintelligible without taking account of the public pressures that policy makers have faced. However, the underpinnings of these public pressures remain sketchy and the relationship between what the public wants and what politicians have said and done about immigration is poorly understood. If immigration policy making is now so manifestly susceptible to popular pressures, why do scholars continue to see deep disconnects between public opinion and public policy, much as they did during the bygone era in which policy making was carried on at a safe distance from the mass public? Why do reforms to legal and illegal immigration policy that most Americans say they want consistently fail to pass legislative muster, despite the pervasive belief that the country's immigration system is "broken?"[39]

Taken together, the coming chapters indicate a resolution to this puzzle. In brief, for all the handwringing about the need for immigration reform, the status quo enjoys what V. O. Key termed a "permissive consensus," wherein many Americans prefer less immigration, more enforcement of immigration law, and some move to normalize the status of illegal immigrants, but few are strongly enough animated by these aims to spur legislative action. Moreover, the concrete policy changes that would be required to achieve these aims often run up against the liberal assimilationist, egalitarian, and humanitarian values that are central to Americans' conceptions of civic fairness. Where people's commitments to these values are inflexible, as in the case of much opposition to what is derided as "amnesty" for illegal immigrants, they lead to what Key referred to as "opinion dikes" that check and channel the course of policy making. These intense pockets of opinion can undermine softer majority support for change. Since it is easier in the American system of government to retain than alter the status quo, a new grand bargain, or "comprehensive immigration reform," has been elusive even when the individual components of these proposals have been popular and backed by powerful interests.[40] We develop this idea in our concluding chapter. But first, to elucidate the key contours of mass opinion about immigration and their underpinnings, we must turn to the central question that this book addresses.

I

What Do Americans Want from Immigration Policy, and Why?

What does a nation of immigrants want from its immigration policy, and why? The evidence from decades of public polling defies simple answers. Scholars and journalists reflexively label people as "pro-immigrant" or "anti-immigrant" and seek to situate them along a spectrum running between these two poles. But most Americans hold seemingly idiosyncratic mixes of "pro-" and "anti-immigrant" opinions across the range of controversies that make up contemporary immigration debates. Their opinions about specific policies routinely deviate from their more general feelings about immigrants and immigration and confound familiar explanations based on "economic" or "cultural" threat. Their views about different facets of immigration policy diverge to the point that the great majority of Americans at once endorse some policies that would greatly expand immigrant admissions and rights and others that would sharply curtail them.

Two general observations help make the point. First, *people tend to be conflicted between abstract policy goals and the specific policies that might bring them about.* Gallup polls conducted since 1965 consistently find that far more Americans prefer to decrease immigration than to increase it. But majorities nowadays also reject major cuts to the admission of refugees, skilled workers, and close relatives of US citizens, categories that account for 95% of green cards that the government issues each year. Most Americans express negative views about illegal immigrants and support efforts to crack down on unauthorized border crossings and hiring. But strong majorities – in some polls approaching 90% – support giving millions of illegal immigrants a way to become US citizens and oppose mass deportation.[1]

A second observation is that *a great many people hold seemingly divergent – and often perplexing – mixes of opinion as we move from one policy area to the next.* Consider three fairly common poll questions about immigration: how many immigrants should be admitted, what to do about illegal immigrants

What Do Americans Want from Immigration Policy, and Why?

residing in the country already, and whether legal immigrants who have not become US citizens should be eligible for political rights and social benefits available to citizens. In the 2016 American National Election Study (ANES), about one-quarter of respondents said that the level of immigration should be decreased "a great deal." More than one-half of these respondents nevertheless said that illegal immigrants should be given a path to US citizenship instead of temporary work permits or deportation. On the other hand, many people who are comfortable with large-scale legal admissions draw the line at illegal immigration. Fifty-six percent of the ANES sample thought the level of immigration should be kept about the same or increased, but more than 20% of this group rejected even a limited legalization program. In the 2014 General Social Survey (GSS), the 57% of Americans who wanted to maintain or raise the level of immigration also supported ratcheting up enforcement against illegal immigration by 48–35%. Still others are generally supportive of legal admissions but would deny equal rights to legal immigrants who have not become citizens. Fewer than one-half of those who wanted to preserve or increase immigrant admissions believed that legal immigrant noncitizens should have the same rights as citizens: 39% rejected this idea, with another 13% undecided. Perhaps even more surprisingly, a substantial minority of those who favored reducing legal immigration levels nonetheless supported extending more expansive rights to legal immigrants already here. Twenty-seven percent of Americans who wanted to reduce immigration supported equal rights for legal immigrant noncitizens with another 12% unsure about this.[2]

All of these poll questions cover terrain well within the mainstream of public debate. None of them is especially confusing or opaque. They are not the kinds of questions that a person with overridingly strong positive or negative feelings about immigration should struggle to answer consistently. And yet only 25% of the 2014 GSS sample took even a weakly restrictive position on all three issues put to them – agreeing that immigration should be reduced at least a little, disagreeing (not necessarily strongly) that noncitizens should have the same rights as citizens, and agreeing (again, not necessarily strongly) that more effort should be made to stop illegal immigration. Combining them with the 11% who took at least a weakly "expansionist" position on all three issues leaves nearly two-thirds of the public exhibiting substantial inconsistency on these three items alone.

Another way of summarizing this inconsistency is that measures of attitudes about immigration are poor predictors of one another. Of the forty-eight bivariate correlations that could be calculated from questions about immigration included in ANES surveys since 1992, all of which we have catalogued in the Online Appendix, ten are below .3, eighteen fall between .3 and .4, fifteen between .4 and .5, and only one is slightly greater than .5. Attitudes in the GSS are even more weakly inter-correlated. Of the twenty-seven possible bivariate correlations between items about immigration included in the 1994, 2004, and 2014 modules on national identity (again, see the Online Appendix for details)

Prevailing Accounts Do Not Explain These Complex Patterns 3

fifteen were below .3, nine ranged from .3 to .4, and only three were .4 or higher. Correlations of this magnitude are generally considered weak to moderate. Indeed, they are comparable to the correlations between a standard ANES item about whether the government should spend more on services even if it means higher taxes or reduce taxes even if it means cutting spending on services and a battery of questions about whether to increase or decrease spending on a variety of public priorities. These weak associations are often invoked as evidence that few citizens' opinions about specific spending priorities are highly constrained by abstract left-right ideology. Similarly, the evidence suggests that most citizens' opinions about specific immigration policies are little constrained by generalized positive or negative orientations toward immigrants or immigration.[3]

PREVAILING ACCOUNTS DO NOT EXPLAIN THESE COMPLEX PATTERNS

That so many Americans' opinions about immigration run the gamut poses a challenge to leading accounts of mass immigration politics circulating in and out of the academy. It undercuts the idea, popular among public intellectuals, that public opinion about immigration boils down to general reactions toward ethnic change and globalization. Few Americans show any trace of the sunny cosmopolitan outlook of historian Michael Lind's prosperous, coastal "Densitarians." Neither do they resemble his dispossessed working-class "Posturbians," who cling to an inflamed nationalism as a bulwark against the twin menaces of immigration and free trade.[4] They are not like moral psychologist Jonathan Haidt's "globalists," who celebrate the borderless utopia described in John Lennon's "Imagine" as a "vision of heaven." But neither do they seem hunkered down in an authoritarian reaction against a "human tidal wave" that threatens his "nationalists'" way of life.[5] There is value in characterizing and seeking to explain the public fissures that globalization has created, but the reality is that while *some* Americans might reliably think about immigration in terms of these clash-of-worldviews narratives, most do not.

Perhaps the "warring tribes" portrayal of a nation of immigrants divided against itself should always have been taken with a grain of salt. Most Americans' opinions about immigration *even in the abstract* manifest ambivalence, moderation, and uncertainty. Here we provide only a brief illustrative summary, but more extensive discussion is provided in the Online Appendix. Paralleling the tenor of contemporary media coverage,[6] few people hold uniform views about whether immigration is a good or a bad thing. Asked five agree-disagree items about the impact of immigration on crime, culture, the economy, job competition, and "new ideas" in the 2014 GSS, only 21% of the sample gave a pro-immigrant response to all five and only 3% gave across-the-board anti-immigrant responses, while 42% gave at least one positive and one negative response. On none of the five items did more than a combined 16% agree or disagree strongly.[7] Another indication of uncertain views about immigration in general is that a very large number of Americans answer differently about how much of it they want from survey to survey.[8] The 2006–2010 GSS panel, for example, solicited respondents' preferences about the level of immigration in 2006, 2008, and 2010.[9] In each wave of the panel, about one-half wanted to preserve or increase the level of immigration and one-half wanted it decreased at least "a little." Aggregate stability masks considerable individual instability, however. Between each wave, one-quarter to one-third switched sides, and only 61% consistently stayed on the same side in all three waves; 28% would have been expected to do so by chance alone.[10] All in all, only 9% of the sample took the hard-line position in all three interviews that immigration should be reduced "a great deal," and only 4% consistently wanted immigration increased at least "a little." In other words, most of the public exhibits no stable commitment to the kinds of clearly expansionist and restrictionist positions that are common among elites.[11]

Leading scholarly perspectives on public opinion about immigration fare little better than public intellectual accounts in accounting for the admixtures of "pro-" and "anti-immigrant" policy positions most Americans hold. Consider first the school of thought that puts rational economic calculation center stage. *Homo economicus* reacts to immigration on the basis of beliefs about how it affects his wages, tax burdens, or cost of living – material well-being in the narrowest sense.[12] This can help explain hostility to immigration among blue-collar workers at risk of being put out of work, or why native-born workers in high-tech industries often oppose the H1b visa program, which allows highly skilled foreign workers to work temporarily in the United States. But mere pocketbook concerns do not explain why tens of millions of Americans want less immigration but also support legal status for undocumented immigrants, or why they reject deportation but still support spending more on enforcement measures that would curtail new illegal immigration. They cannot tell us why over one-quarter of those who want to reduce immigration would not restrict legal immigrants' access to costly public benefits. Indeed, most citizens may eschew self-interest as a guide to forming opinions about immigration policy because they regard the effects of immigration on their own personal well-being as remote, uncertain, or unlikely to be large.[13]

As the evidence has mounted that most Americans' views do not align with a pure, narrow pocketbook calculus, economic explanations have come to focus instead on "sociotropic motivations" – the idea that people judge immigration on the basis of whether they believe it is good for the national economy. There is still a good deal of theoretical ambiguity in these claims – do sociotropic concerns reflect enlightened self-interest, a concern for the well-being of one's fellow Americans, or what? How do people acquire clear beliefs about the economic consequences of immigration when experts disagree on the order of hundreds of billions of dollars on both sides of the ledger?[14] How can "it's the

Prevailing Accounts Do Not Explain These Complex Patterns 5

economy, stupid" explain the fact that, at any given time, large numbers of Americans want to naturalize illegal immigrants already living in the United States while repelling new influxes at the border, or to reduce immigration but accept the most destitute of refugees?

While economic explanations still have their supporters, by far the most common explanations of immigration attitudes are social-psychological, and the leading paradigms are fundamentally group-centrist.[15] These theories, which we introduce briefly here but develop at length in Chapter 2, tie immigration policy opinions to social categorization and the tendency to favor "ingroups" over "outgroups." They assert that people will support policies that help groups they identify with or feel attached to or that harm groups they dislike or feel threatened by.

These accounts vary in emphasis and mechanism. They alternately focus on racial, religious, and ethnic divides or civic or assimilationist understandings of American national identity.[16] Those that highlight prejudice and ingroup solidarity also vary on multiple dimensions. One dimension concerns whether prejudice is "generalized," as in an ethnocentric preference for one's own group over any and all outsiders, or "group specific" or targeted at a particular group. Similarly, ingroup solidarity may be mono-ethnic, pan-ethnic, or cross-ethnic. The line between these categorizations blurs, however, as group identifications expand or contract. Latin American immigrants generally come to the United States as Mexicans, Cubans, Puerto Ricans, and so on, and discover or are ascribed a "Latino" or "Hispanic" identity in this country. A smaller minority adopt a broader "people of color" identity. The rising recognition of plural identities and multiracialism introduces further complexity into the meaning of group labels and attachments. A second dimension concerns the degree to which group-specific prejudice, in particular, is acknowledged, out in the open, reflexive, and fused with normative considerations. Borrowing from a large literature on the nature of antiblack prejudice in post-Civil Rights America, scholars have identified white prejudice against Latinos that is explicit, implicit, and symbolic, concepts we will develop in the next chapter and test for throughout the book.[17] Finally, group-centrist accounts cite different psychological underpinnings of ingroup favoritism and outgroup derogation, ranging from the "minimal group" paradigm of social identity theory, with its emphasis on how the "positive distinctiveness" of one's group yields self-esteem,[18] to the zero-sum competition of realistic group conflict theory, to the group hierarchies of sociostructural theories that emphasize group position, and many other variants of these ideas.[19]

Whatever group-centrist perspectives illuminate about people's immigration attitudes, they do not, in isolation, explain much of the attitudinal ambivalence and complexity we identified earlier. Generalized ethnocentrism and xenophobia cannot explain why so many Americans at once support some policies that obviously benefit a great many foreigners and "outsiders" and staunchly oppose others. This is true regardless of whether the relevant "us" and "them"

6 *What Do Americans Want from Immigration Policy, and Why?*

are defined on the basis of ascribed attributes or others. Unless different policies prompt Americans to redraw the boundaries of their subjectively defined communities or ingroups in a variety of ad hoc ways – an idea that lacks theoretical parsimony – these theories cannot explain the divergence between people's opinions about whether to admit legal immigrants and furnish them with benefits. Nor can they explain why dislike of illegal immigrants coincides with many Americans' support for permitting them to become US citizens.

At first glance, theories that emphasize group-specific (rather than generalized) prejudice seem better equipped to explain mixes of pro- and anti-immigrant policy opinions. Perhaps people associate different policies with different racial groups, some of whom they like or dislike more than others. For example, people might associate "illegal immigration" more readily than "legal immigration" with Latino ethnicity.[20] If so, someone who dislikes Latinos would favor a more restrictive policy in the former domain than the latter. We investigate this possibility in the following chapters and find little corroboration. But even without additional exploration, it should be clear that group-specific prejudice cannot explain all of the variability we observe because people make distinctions even between policies that call to mind the same group. Illegal immigration is again a case in point. Illegal immigrants elicit more "cold" than "warm" feelings, and there is strong public support for more enforcement on the border (as long as you don't call it "The Wall") along with overwhelming support for enforcement on the interior in the form of programs such as E-Verify that seek to prevent employers from hiring illegal immigrants.[21] Yet strong majorities also support normalizing the status of illegal immigrants and giving them full political membership provided they meet certain conditions such as learning English and undergoing a background check. Positive attitudes toward Latinos cannot explain cold feelings toward illegal immigrants and support for strong enforcement, and negative attitudes cannot explain strong support for legalization and opposition to deportation, yet a broad cross-section of the American public simultaneously holds both sets of views.

Strikingly, ambivalence persists even when we shine the light on individuals who should be especially prone to various group-centric outlooks. Take, for example, the immigration policy opinions of a group that is unambiguously and explicitly ethnocentric: whites who *openly* rate their own racial group more highly than they do blacks, Latinos, and Asians.[22] These are precisely the kinds of people whom group-centric theories would expect to react in a consistently negative way to immigrants and immigration. Yet their immigration policy opinions in the 2016 ANES, well into the rise of Donald Trump, were modestly *less* intercorrelated than those of unprejudiced whites. Only 18% of *explicitly prejudiced* whites supported both deportation for illegal immigrants *and* wanted to reduce immigration a great deal. Only one-third of this group both opposed a path to citizenship for illegal immigrants (instead favoring deportation or temporary work visas) *and* wanted to reduce immigration *even a little*.

Prevailing Accounts Do Not Explain These Complex Patterns 7

Even among the 10% of whites who expressed outright "cold" feelings toward Latinos, only 38% supported building a wall on the southern border *and* opposed a path to citizenship – two policies that are quite manifestly associated with Latino ethnicity in public debates.[23]

On the other side of things, it seems reasonable to assume that Latinos and blacks, two ethnic minority groups that have long faced discrimination in and exclusion from American society, would see immigration through a sympathetically group-centric lens founded on co-ethnic, pan-ethnic, or cross-ethnic solidarity.[24] Yet Latinos and blacks hold *less* uniform and constrained opinions about immigration than do whites on the whole. The average bivariate correlation among the six immigration items in the 2016 ANES – the level of immigration, feelings about illegal immigrants, birthright citizenship for children of illegal immigrants, what to do about illegal immigrants already in the country, a wall on the US–Mexico border, and whether to send back children apprehended at the border to their home countries (see the Online Appendix for more detail) – for example, is .43 for whites, .41 for Hispanics, and .25 for blacks. Even when the context is ripe for group-centric thinking and the policies clearly connected to one's own group, individuals take different positions on different policies. Only 58% of Latinos, for example, supported a path to citizenship *and* opposed the construction of a border wall, despite the salience of Trump's anti-Latino rhetoric in the 2016 presidential campaign. Greater ethnic consciousness among Latinos does work against supporting restriction but does not come close to producing blanket support for expansionary policies. Among the 34% of Hispanics who said that their ethnicity was "extremely important" to their identity, only 28% supported both a path to citizenship and increasing immigration even "a little." The modal position, taken by 34% of Hispanic respondents who report the highest level of ethnic consciousness, is to keep the level of immigration "about the same" and to support a path to citizenship with conditions and restrictions. Among the 57% of blacks who said their race was extremely important to their identity, only 14% supported both these positions, so there is little basis for supposing that high racial consciousness among blacks makes for uniformly pro-immigrant views out of sympathy for another marginalized group.

It is not only that people who express ethno-racial identity and high levels of group consciousness fail to espouse consistently pro- or anti-immigrant *policy* positions. Beyond this, they are no less ambivalent, no less moderate, and no more consistent about how much immigration there should be, or whether it is on balance a good or bad thing for the country. For example, prejudiced whites hold *less* stable opinions on standard measures of immigration attitudes than unprejudiced whites. The same is true of whites, blacks, and Latinos who report that their race or ethnicity is very important to their identities, compared to those who say their racial identity is less important to them.[25] Part of the reason for these surprising patterns is that these groups also tend to be less educated and politically attentive. Such citizens' issue opinions are on average less crystallized than those of others. Still, group-centric accounts would suggest that immigration is the sort of "easy" issue that politically disengaged citizens could construct consistent and constrained opinions about easily, without sweating the details.[26]

To summarize, much of the debate in the literature on egocentric, sociotropic, and group-centric sources of public opinion about immigration has focused on general positive or negative valence. These leanings surely exist and can be measured and, in many cases, are tied to group identities of various kinds. But they only modestly constrain Americans' opinions about the many immigration policy controversies that comprise contemporary debates. Whatever the true weight given to economic and group-centric considerations in citizens' abstract feelings about immigration, they give us surprisingly little ability to predict which side of a given immigration policy issue citizens will take. There is a very small minority of people whose views on these issues are uniformly "pro-" or "anti-immigrant" or close to it, and we leave it to others to sort out whether they are preoccupied about racial change, the integrity of the nation, or their own wages, the state of the economy, crime, and other material considerations such as traffic, pollution, and overpopulation.

Instead, our point of departure is that the great majority of Americans must be weighing *something* else beyond their feelings about immigration in general and beliefs about its consequences. Whatever that something is, it must be powerful enough to derail what is manifestly the simplest way to decide on these issues – consistently taking positions that increase immigration and expand immigrant rights or ones that decrease immigration and diminish immigrant rights. It need not be coherent or systematic, however. In this regard, public opinion about immigration may be much like the standard portrayal of public opinion about many other topics – ambivalent, temporally unstable, little constrained by any overarching ideology, and flexible in the face of information that affects whatever happens to be at the top of people's heads at the time.[27]

What is surprising in the present context is that public opinion about immigration shares these characteristics *despite* its supposedly strong group-centric moorings. But to this point we can only conclude that group-centrism imposes weak constraint. It is not clear that much should be read into the *particular ways* that opinions about different immigration policies deviate from one another and from more general attitudes about immigration and immigrants. The majority of citizens who lack strong and clear positive or negative general views about immigration may simply be responding idiosyncratically to the way that different questions are worded, superficially glomming on to particular phrases they find appealing or unappealing and constructing "doorstep" opinions that are for all intents and purposes random. Some may find common poll questions confounding or unclear. We might simply adduce that Americans' general orientations toward immigrants and immigration are too mixed, uncertain, or simply muddled to structure public opinion about

Civic Fairness 9

immigration policy. If so, most Americans' opinions about immigration policy may simply be what Philip Converse called "non-attitudes" – weak, unstructured, and highly volatile opinions about political objects that citizens tend to find remote or arcane, a matter of indifference, ignorance, or confusion.

CIVIC FAIRNESS

On the contrary, in the coming chapters, we will demonstrate that much of the complexity and ambivalence in citizens' opinions about different immigration policies is systematic and structured – nuance, not statistical noise. This nuance can be explained by the salience and prioritization of a set of values that are deeply ingrained in American political culture. These values powerfully shape the opinions that citizens form about specific immigration policy issues. They do so by informing people's conceptions of *civic fairness*, which we define as a set of normative beliefs about what current and aspiring members owe their political communities and what these communities owe them in return.

We will have much more to say in the next chapter about the norms and values that shape public conceptions of civic fairness. To preview, however, liberal assimilationist norms set the criteria by which, in principle at least, anyone can become American. The public widely endorses a pluralistic and limited version of liberal assimilation. One of its two requirements is that immigrants become functional, self-sufficient members of American society by earning their keep and learning to speak the country's dominant language (*functional assimilation*). Support for functional assimilation is strongly tied to the value of economic *individualism*. Its other requirement is that immigrants follow formal rules and procedures for becoming American as a condition for obtaining the perquisites of membership (*formal assimilation*). The emphasis people place on formal assimilation is linked to their abstract support for a value we term *legalism*, or a belief in the strict and rigid enforcement of rules and laws. Each of these values, and the norms of assimilation that they undergird, is deeply rooted in American political culture. But they often conflict with other values that Americans cherish, among them the belief in equal opportunity and the responsibility to help alleviate humanitarian distress. In such instances, many people who are strongly committed to *egalitarian* and *humanitarian* values relax or abridge the norms of functional and formal assimilation out of an aversion to enduring status inequalities or a desire to combat the suffering of innocents.

Citizens' values, and their beliefs about how these values relate to political choices, are often conflicted.[28] Opinions about immigration policy will therefore vary not only based on how citizens balance competing values but also as a function of these values' salience and perceived relevance to the issues at hand. Salience and perceived relevance, in turn, vary with the type of policy information that is available and the degree to which frames link that information to individuals' values and specific policy alternatives. Simply put, the informational cues and frames embedded in public debates about different types of immigration policies make different sets of values salient. Americans choose between the alternatives at hand based on their prioritization of the values they discern to be at stake. Since this mode of choice commonly overrides their mixed or uncertain general feelings about immigration, they wind up on the "pro-immigrant" side of some issues and the "anti-immigrant" side of others.

Much of our inquiry examines how the influence of values fares relative to the tug of ethnic and nationalistic group-centrism. What happens when people's values compel them to accept immigrants they view as social "outsiders"? What if, on the other hand, their values lead to the implication that one of "us" must be left out in the cold? What takes priority – a group-centrist impulse to bolster "us" and exclude "them" or the norms and values that Americans claim to prize? It is precisely because the values we highlight often predominate over group-centric impulses that they help explain the diffuseness of individuals' opinions about immigration policies – why, to preview some of the topics we probe in the coming chapters, opinions about specific admissions policies depart from generalized attitudes about immigration, views about legal immigration diverge from views about illegal immigration, and beliefs about whether immigrants should qualify for rights and benefits differ from both of these.

We also illustrate that the civic fairness framework explains other anomalies in group-centrist accounts. For one, the degree of ethnic bias in Americans' immigration policy choices varies markedly across studies in ways that group-centrist perspectives cannot explain. But this variation is well anticipated by automatic stereotyping and heuristic information processing about the norms and values that are at stake in a policy choice. For another, some dimensions of assimilation that engender powerful feelings of group loyalty and shared identification only marginally influence policy choice. And norms of formal and functional assimilation that strongly influence policy choice often play a limited role in shaping subjective boundaries of communal solidarity and attachment.

SUMMARY OF THEORETICAL CONTRIBUTIONS

We are of course not the first to examine how values influence public opinion about political issues, including on immigration and others that are freighted with racial, ethnic, national, and other group identities.[29] The values associated with the American creed and its liberal and civic republican traditions antedate Tocqueville and have been featured in classic studies of American political culture ever since.[30] Accounts that relate immigration to conceptions of American national identity have emphasized assimilationist norms and their relation to liberal, republican, and multiculturalist values.[31] Adrian Pantoja has demonstrated that individualism, egalitarianism, and humanitarianism predict

Where Civic Fairness Stands

opinions about immigration and, anticipating our focus here, notes some differences in their influence across different aspects of immigration policy.[32] More recently, researchers have illustrated that humanitarian appeals can override the influence of threatening primes on opinions about immigration policy[33] and that they are tied to public opinion about refugee policy in Europe.[34] In the United States, appeals to family unity are found to resonate in conservatives' judgments about illegal immigration policy.[35]

We advance this research in four principal ways. First, we show that these values not only play a role in public opinion about immigration but that they are more potent than group-centric influences predicated on racial and national identities for *most* Americans, *most of the time*. Second, we illustrate that distinct sets of values have come to structure different facets of the immigration debate. This attests to the influence of political values on public opinion about immigration issues and also explains the ambivalence and mixtures of pro- and anti-immigrant policy positions that most Americans hold, a feature of public opinion about immigration that prior research has largely overlooked.[36] Third, we demonstrate instances in which group-centrist perspectives have overstated their case by claiming to account for empirical patterns that are not intelligible without taking stock of values. Fourth, we provide a much more comprehensive account of the values and norms that are at work in shaping opinions about immigration than most previous research has done, explaining how and why different sets of values are distinctively tied to different aspects of public controversy over immigration.

WHERE CIVIC FAIRNESS STANDS VIS-À-VIS VARIETIES OF GROUP-CENTRISM

In advancing this argument, we by and large maintain that existing accounts of American public opinion about immigration are incomplete – though substantially incomplete at that – rather than incorrect. By focusing heavily on shared identity and prejudice, some group-centrist accounts can give the impression that ingroup favoritism and outgroup derogation dominate mass opinion about immigration to the exclusion of anything else. Political scientist Victoria M. De Francesco Soto, for example, has summarized the discipline's insights into the sources of American public opinion about immigration as follows: "Anti-immigrant sentiment is about Latinos. Negative feelings toward this group drive anti-immigration stances."[37] A major conclusion of this book is that views of this kind misread the evidence in numerous ways. They drastically overstate the influence of racial identity on American mass opinion about immigration. They ignore the overriding power of values for most people in most contexts. And they overlook a crucial distinction between deep-seated racial animus and the discriminatory effects of automatic stereotypes that are responsive to information routinely made available in public discourse about immigration. To a considerable extent, these same critiques apply to the view that opinions about immigration policy are predominantly an outgrowth of feelings of solidarity and kinship toward a national "we" and hostility or indifference to a foreign "they."

We are also at odds with a subset of the literature that explicitly questions Americans' ability and willingness to apply the values they claim to care about in a racially neutral way. This claim has surfaced in recent research tying white Americans' immigration policy opinions to "symbolic racism" and implicit prejudice against Latino immigrants. On this logic, people's professed commitments to abstract values about fairness, equality, and the rule of law, are at least somewhat disingenuous and disparately applied across racial groups. It is clear that no small number of whites exhibits substantial bias against Latinos in settings where information is sparse or muddled and automatic stereotypes often go unchecked. However, we will show time and again that they apply civic fairness criteria equivalently irrespective of immigrants' ethnic background, and that they update their views evenhandedly as new information becomes available. We find no evidence, for example, that whites exact a special penalty on Latinos who are believed to have violated norms of civic fairness, or that they fail to credit Latinos who live up to them; European and Asian immigrants are equally held to account. When exposed to clear information that clarifies the values at stake and counteracts prevailing stereotypes, ethnic biases fade substantially. Our studies show again and again that the great majority of the public forms opinions about immigration policies primarily on the basis of cues about civic fairness, even when explicit group cues are provided. This is true not only of the public generally but also, to a surprising degree, of segments of the public that hold strong and politicized ethnic identities or express prejudicial views toward the ethnic groups that most immigrants belong to.

Our account is, finally, irreconcilable with a smaller body of scholarship that holds many or most Americans' opinions about immigration to be almost all about racism, with norms serving only as disingenuous rationales for discrimination. In this view, modern support for restricting immigration or immigrant rights is a direct heir to the legacy of Know-Nothings, Chinese Exclusion, racist restrictions on citizenship, and eugenics. Hostility to Latinos, America's largest immigrant group, catalyzes opposition to comprehensive immigration reform, opposition to birthright citizenship for the children of illegal immigrants, and efforts to crack down on immigrants' access to public assistance.[38] The particular pariahs and scapegoats have changed, as has the discourse. Anglo-Protestant America is no more. Euro-Christian America has taken its place. Many Americans whose ancestors were maligned as unassimilable racial or religious "others" have come into the fold. But they have done so only to turn against the next group of unlucky "outsiders" at the gates, succumbing to the same kinds of dogmas and hysterias that have long animated American nativism.

Immigration and the American Ethos 13

These kinds of accounts allege – often on the basis of analogy to the sins of the nation's past – that commonly articulated rationales for opposing liberal immigration policy are smoke screens. Liberal norms proscribe the open expression of racial prejudice – or at least did – so restrictionist politicians couch their appeals in the language of liberal values and principles: getting ahead through hard work, respecting the rule of law, learning English. But this is asserted to be merely a veneer – a "dog whistle" or "code" whose psychological essence is the same as it has ever been.[39] People may genuinely care about assimilation on some level, but these appeals *really* resonate because they tap into the public's unacknowledged anxiety about nonwhite or non-Christian immigrants, fueling xenophobic "backlash" that has metastasized all the way to the Oval Office.[40]

Of late, these narratives have gained currency outside the academy. The *Washington Post*'s Jennifer Rubin concludes that the evidence from "study after study" so definitely upholds the upsides of large-scale immigration that "the excuses for opposing immigration or for deporting illegal immigrants en masse no longer pass the smell test .... Strip away the fallacious arguments, and you arrive at an uncomfortable truth: This is largely about plain old bigotry."[41] Notably, Rubin's indictment is not that *some* people are motivated primarily by old-fashioned bigotry in *some* contexts. It is a general indictment of public opposition to immigration as it might be expressed in precisely the sorts of contexts where people encounter mainstream arguments about the issue. The results we describe in the coming chapters will establish that this cynical and sweeping view is without merit. Of course, prejudice of various kinds continues to be an important force in American public opinion about immigration, and our studies will attest to this and clarify its role. But the evidence that we present refutes the idea that values are simply a façade and shows that they are by and large genuinely held, salient in a wide range of contexts in which people contemplate immigration policy alternatives, and applied to "us" and "them" alike. The centrality of these values in American public opinion about immigration explains both the popularity of many of the "anti-immigrant" policies that Rubin derides and the simultaneous popularity of the "pro-immigrant" policies she presumably supports.

IMMIGRATION AND THE AMERICAN ETHOS

Our inquiry speaks to a defining debate over what kind of a nation America really is. Gunnar Myrdal's 1944 classic *An American Dilemma* asserted that the rationalistic and moralistic "American ethos"[42] would force the public to reckon with the inconsistency between their racial prejudices and their higher commitments to liberty and equal opportunity.[43] This conflict, he maintained, would resolve in favor of the latter. Writing more than fifty years later, Rogers Smith countered that the country's long-standing and evolving racist and nativist "ideological tradition" of ascriptive hierarchy continues to compete against, fuse with, and on occasion supersede, its venerated liberal and republican traditions. These ascriptive traditions persist not only because they confer material benefits and political power but because they imbue American identity with "meaning" and "inherent and transcendent worth, thanks to nature, history, and God."[44]

Smith's depiction of American political culture as an endless churn of competing liberal and ethnoracial traditions unfolds on a societywide stage with the evolution of policy and elite discourse. But political culture is above all about norms, shared assumptions, and behavioral expectations,[45] and Myrdal's thesis speaks to the nature and resolution of the conflicts that prejudice engenders in ordinary citizens' hearts and minds. Its force depends on the degree to which ordinary Americans' political opinions are marred by racism and ethno-nationalism.

The ensuing chapters explore whether Myrdal's confidence was well founded or misplaced. In an era of rapidly rising ethnic diversity, "identity politics," and burgeoning racial resentments, does the American ethos elevate moral precepts above base group loyalties when the two conflict? Our inquiries generally support Myrdal's conviction that creedal values would gain the upper hand. When it comes to public opinion about immigration, civic fairness predominates in Americans' judgments. But our account also underlines the importance of recognizing what Lawrence Fuchs described as Myrdal's "too optimistic conclusion that if Americans applied their creed consistently they would overcome racism."[46]

On a practical level, this raises an intriguing question about whether the American public could be engaged by an immigration debate that eschews identity politics and elevates appeals about how best to balance the conflicting values that immigration policy dilemmas inevitably raise. Indeed, some political leaders have been involved in such a debate for decades. But the temptation has often proved too strong to cater to hard-line constituencies by discrediting opponents' motivations as fundamentally group-centric or by making racist or racially tinged appeals. Do such appeals and recriminations reveal the public's true priorities? Or would many be open to listening to, even persuaded by, debates that focus squarely on how policy alternatives further widely held values and dispense with appeals to prejudice and parochialism. If an immigration debate focused on values could resonate with the public, perhaps this is true of other seemingly group-centered issues as well.[47]

CAVEATS AND CLARIFICATIONS

Before outlining the chapters that follow, a few caveats are in order:

Norms and Social Identities Are Intertwined

With good reason, norms, values, and group identities are often treated in the scholarly literature as interlocking components of "sociological" perspectives on public opinion. Norms and values are created, packaged, imparted, and

Caveats and Clarifications

reinforced by social groups. They evolve and are maintained in part to facilitate coordination among group members and to bolster the group's position relative to others. Particular "modules" of social values may be hardwired into human beings,[48] but their cultural adaptation into systems of belief that activate some and deemphasize others is attributable in part to people's multiple and overlapping group memberships. They are enforced through sanctioning by fellow group members. In the United States, values such as individualism, equality, and the rule of law are often regarded as "American values" that define the nation's moral spirit. They have also been enmeshed in the country's history of racial stratification and oppression and can serve as tools of social control and conformity. In short, norms are seldom "identity free." And while ethnic and national identity groups are by no means the only sources of value commitments and priorities in the political realm, they are clearly important ones.

It is therefore important to clarify that when we ask whether values or group-centrism predominates in public opinion about immigration, we mean a very particular form of group-centrism. Specifically, we mean that policy choices stem from immediate concerns about relative group status and interests. This excludes cases in which people remain faithful to a given set of values because they feel that to do otherwise would be to betray the moral precepts and customs of their social group. To be animated, for example, by the idea that "as an American" one has a duty to respect individual liberty is clearly not the same as selectively invoking concerns about individual liberty to justify rights for dominant groups while explaining away arbitrary subjugation of subordinate group members. It also excludes what might be termed "enlightened group-centrism" – the idea that the long-run well-being of one's group is best pursued by conforming to existing norms no matter how much this benefits "them" at "our" expense in the short run. We have no empirical basis for believing that many people think in this way, but we also know of no way to rule it out. What we can examine is whether people remain consistent in their application of values even when they are at odds with *narrow* and *immediate* group-centrism.

Analogous qualifications are routinely made in the large literature that considers the relative strength of self-interest and sociological influences on public opinion and political behavior. The two are in many ways intertwined. People may construe self-interest broadly to include the satisfaction that comes from moral action or group loyalty. Or their political choices may hew to values, general orientations, and group identifications because they believe that doing so is in their longer-term personal interest. Indeed, every defining component of sociological perspectives, even those that emphasize automaticity, can be tied to rational choice and individual instrumentality: there are selfish bases for compliance with norms, maintenance of norms, coordination with other group members, valuation and salience of group identity, and the process of inculcating group identities and conditioning the young to value norms and learn to behave, as a matter of habit, in accordance with them.[49] The existence of these connections clearly bears on the utility of rational choice, symbolic politics, and other paradigmatic accounts of political attitudes. But it does not preclude a more modest examination of the role that narrow and immediate material self-interest plays in shaping political attitudes in most contexts.[50]

Accordingly, most research that considers *homo economicus* and *homo sociologicus* as rival theories of public opinion and political behavior in effect examines situations in which narrow, material self-interest pushes in one direction while group identity, values, and other symbolic orientations push in the other. What happens, for example, when ideologically liberal homeowners would benefit from a cap on property tax assessments?[51]

By the same token, our main approach is to examine and construct scenarios where group-centrism and values are theoretically expected to work at cross-purposes. In such scenarios we can observe whether cues about civic fairness or group cues prevail and under what circumstances. Instead of asking *why* values are important generally or why particular values are employed evenhandedly or seeking to understand the ultimate basis for values-driven behavior, we ask the more modest question of *whether* a particular set of values, whatever their origins, are now applied sincerely and evenhandedly. Asking *whether* rather than *why* sidesteps questions about the social origins and functions of human compliance with social norms. This limits the scope of our inquiry but not its force. Whatever their origin, the values that undergird mass conceptions of civic fairness exert a profound influence on the way that people think about immigration policy. More "pro-immigrant" Americans do not jettison them when they support policies that would restrict immigration, and more "anti-immigrant" Americans do not discard them even when it means expanding immigration. These patterns are not anticipated by the types of group-centrist theories that predominate in the literature, but they are well explained by civic fairness.

Civic Fairness Cuts Both Ways

In claiming that people tend to arrive at judgments about civic fairness in a race-neutral manner, we are not implying that Americans would become devoted cosmopolitans if only they knew enough. Indeed, both "pro-" and "anti-immigrant" views flow from the application of civic fairness values. Sometimes people include on the basis of their values, and sometimes they exclude. So, unlike Myrdal's account of race relations, which could more straightforwardly take racial discrimination to be manifestly at odds with the liberal creed, our account of public opinion about immigration policy allows that liberal values can promote restrictive or expansionary policy preferences. There is a lively debate among normative theorists over which sorts of restrictions on immigration, if any, are permissible in a liberal state.[52] We take no normative position on the right of the state to regulate the flow of people across its borders, or what is owed to those allowed to come. Our criterion for what

Caveats and Clarifications

counts as a "liberal" value here is one that applies equally regardless of race, ethnicity, religion, and other "ascriptive" attributes and stems from creedal commitments to individualism, equality, and the rule of law.

Facts about Values versus Value Judgments about facts

This is a book about the powerful role of norms in structuring public opinion about a set of issues that evoke deep-seated group loyalties and animosities. It is not a normative assessment of those norms or the way that people prioritize competing values. The fact that Americans are widely applying normative considerations to immigration policy issues could be thought of as "good news," if the alternative is that they are simply and inflexibly bigoted. On the other hand, consistent application of norms and values can produce, sustain, and reinforce sharp disparities in status and wealth between groups, and some types of "identity politics" have often been instrumental in promoting equality and human dignity. One can at once identify a central role for values and be critical of them or the way they are applied, just as classic accounts of American political culture have often pointed out that the uncritical embrace of the liberal tradition has at times led to closed-mindedness and repression.[53]

Scope Conditions

This book contends that the civic fairness framework explains what most Americans think about immigration policy most of the time, including, somewhat surprisingly, many of those who evince strong predispositions to group-centrism on conventional measures. But no theory explains everyone's choices in all circumstances. Some people's opinions are likely to be better explained with reference to narrow economic self-interest or some type of group-centrism than civic fairness. Workers faced with job competition from immigrants, employers whose bottom line depends on a steady supply of immigrant labor, and American citizens who wish to sponsor their relatives for green cards are probably poor cases for the civic fairness framework.[54] So too are dedicated white supremacists. The kind of inflamed and overt bigotry on display at "alt-right" rallies and marches may be less prevalent in contemporary mass opinion than extensive media coverage of these phenomena makes it appear.[55] But a small minority of the public in relative terms is still large enough in absolute terms to be politically relevant.

The yardsticks that most Americans apply to evaluate immigration policy can also change dramatically across individuals and with context. Economic and cultural strain can lead to perceptions of threat that heighten the importance of ethnocentrism relative to the values we highlight.[56] War, depression, and other threats to security and well-being can intensify ingroup loyalty and lead to scapegoating of outsiders. Sociopolitical context – ethnic and linguistic diversity in people's surroundings, media coverage of the immigration issue, the

18   *What Do Americans Want from Immigration Policy, and Why?*

threat of terror, and so on – explains why latent ethnocentrism can be dormant at one moment and active the next. Our own era is one of relative peace and prosperity but plagued by episodic terrorism, working class wage stagnation, and worries about lost political and economic status.[57] Malaise is widespread even if full-blown alarm is limited. But things could change.

Even in happier times, we find pockets of the public brooding about foreign influence and how it undermines the American way of life. John Higham certainly says as much about the so-called "Age of Confidence" (1860–1880) and "Rebirth of Confidence" (spanning from the turn of the twentieth century to WWI). Richard Hofstadter, writing at the height of the nation's post-WWII prosperity, situates the contemporary right's obsession with anti-Communism and foreign influence within a long tradition of "heated exaggeration, suspiciousness, and conspiratorial fantasy."[58] And, during an era where immigration was the last thing on most Americans' minds, Paul Ehrlich's *The Population Bomb* and follow-up *Golden Door*, published in 1968 and 1979, respectively, sensationalized the threat of overpopulation and the particular threat of Mexican immigration and sparked a movement devoted to these issues.[59] When such nativist hysteria is concentrated in a single party, even a relatively small number of adherents can have a profound influence on the course of politics. The civic fairness framework may not describe these kinds of attitudes as well as group-centrist perspectives.

Looking ahead, the studies we describe in the coming chapters may also fail to capture some contexts in today's politics in which group-centrism seems likelier to dominate people's thinking about immigration – a raucous political rally, perhaps, or the experience of reading a dyspeptic presidential tweet. On the other hand, there may just as well be other important real-world contexts – the sober atmosphere of the voting booth and other settings where civic responsibilities are exercised – in which group-centrism is an even weaker force than our research suggests and principled judgment an even stronger one. As we will show in Chapter 2, however, the experimental and observational designs we use mimic the information and cues provided in mainstream coverage and public discourse about immigration. Moreover, our research uses the same survey-based techniques as the rest of the largely group-centrist literature (and the public opinion literature more broadly) to examine competing theories of what is and is not on people's minds when they think about a given political issue. Whatever limitations of external validity these designs face in describing the full range of public opinion about immigration, our research challenges the conventional scholarly wisdom on its own terms.

Which Varieties of Group-Centrism?

Our main goal in this book is to juxtapose civic fairness and group-centrism. Although we will continue to use the term "group-centrism" as shorthand, it is important to clarify that our focus in this regard is specifically on theories that

Caveats and Clarifications 19

privilege *two particular kinds of group-centrism* as the dominant influences on public opinion about immigration. These are racial and ethnic attachments and animosities (Chapters 3–5)[60] and also attachment to the national ingroup that promotes favoritism for subjectively defined members of the national community and indifference or hostility toward "strangers" (Chapter 6).[61] These jointly dominate the literature on public opinion about immigration. Other group loyalties also surely matter. One example is partisanship. We do not probe the role of partisanship because its profound influence on public opinion, including about immigration,[62] is already well known, deeply explored, and richly documented. It has heretofore played a marginal role in the literature focused on immigration, most of which argues for the primacy of ethnic and national ties. Indeed, one of the only substantial works to address this question, Abrajano and Hajnal's *White Backlash* – which we discuss at length – treats partisanship as a consequence of ethnic threat, not as a cause of immigration attitudes.

Public Opinion or White Public Opinion?

Recent work on public opinion about immigration has argued, persuasively in our view, that there are important differences between how whites and nonwhites view immigration and immigration policy.[63] Clearly, one must be cautious about generalizing from survey samples that are dominated by non-Hispanic whites and attuned, as much as the data allow, to the possibility that the salience and prioritization of the values we highlight may differ across groups. This is true even if the values themselves are pervasively endorsed among virtually all groups in American society.[64] Our studies were not designed, by and large, to test for these sorts of group differences, and we are limited in our ability to do so. Moreover, one of our major questions – to what extent does anti-Latino prejudice anchor restrictive opinions about immigration policy – pertains in large part to whites, or at least to non-Latinos. However, inasmuch as the data allow, we do test for differences in the emphasis that whites and nonwhites place on the values that we highlight and also for differences in the way those values are applied to the policy choices we examine.

We see little evidence of differences in the way that whites and nonwhites respond to the experimental treatments we administer, with a few exceptions we discuss as they arise. Of course, this does not rule out that future research will turn up additional important differences. Provisionally, however, we have no reason to believe that the kinds of perceptions of civic fairness and conflicts of value that we describe here are unique to whites. They seem to illuminate the way that a great many nonwhites think about immigration policy as well, which helps explain why the two largest racial and ethnic minority groups in the country – blacks and Latinos – show no less ambivalence and complexity in their opinions about immigration than do whites.

What about Group-Centric Appeals?

Readers may naturally wonder about how the apparent rise and resonance of group-based appeals and racial demagoguery in American political discourse squares with our account. On this point, we assume that most readers will have in mind a profusion of right-wing anti-immigrant appeals rather than appeals to co-ethnic or cross-ethnic solidarity that are common among immigrant advocacy groups.

It is important to be circumspect about just how prevalent and resonant naked group-based appeals are in American political discourse about immigration – even nowadays. When such appeals are made, they tend to get a great deal of attention precisely because they are *not* the norm. This attention will tend to make people believe they are more common than they really are, an example of what psychologists term the "availability heuristic" – a tendency to inflate the frequency of phenomena that can easily be brought to mind. More-over, appeals that are widely derided as racist are seldom *simply* group-based appeals and contain significant content related to civic fairness. The contro-versy over President Trump's travel ban is a case in point. Though the ban was obviously designed to appeal to widespread prejudice against Muslims, most of its supporters did their level best to *avoid* overtly group-centric appeals (rejecting the term "Muslim ban," for example) and to amplify values-based rationales for the policy. This is one example of a broader pattern we illustrate in a media content analysis in Chapter 2: group cues seldom appear in discus-sions of immigration in isolation of cues about civic fairness. Civic fairness cues might, as is often alleged, be a "dog-whistle" addressed to prejudiced segments of the public, in effect functioning as a racial appeal. But this is an empirical question, and the results of our studies will show that considerably larger segments of the public take civic fairness cues at face value, not simply as group-based appeals shrouded in socially acceptable language.

Of course, there are some naked group-based appeals in discussions of immigration, and their prevalence, or at least their salience, seems to have increased in the last few years. An important takeaway from our analyses is that politicians will often have an incentive to use these types of appeals even when speaking to a public that is broadly more concerned with civic fairness than group-centrism. There are at least three reasons that this is so.

First, and most obviously, such appeals will resonate with a deeply preju-diced and xenophobic minority of Americans that our studies bring into relief, by activating deep-seated group loyalties and hatreds in the most basic group-centric sense. Their impact in this regard is narrow but potentially deep. Second, ethnic cues can also influence a broader swath of Americans whose opinions about immigration policy harbor negative stereotypes about particu-lar immigrant groups. This segment of the public is not strongly invested in the well-being and status of racial ingroups and outgroups per se but reads infor-mation about civic fairness into cues about racial or ethnic identity. The effect of these cues is therefore greatly attenuated in the presence of more directly pertinent information about the values at stake – information that is routinely available in public discussions about immigration. But in some sparse or muddled information environments, group-based appeals can go unchecked and therefore influence segments of the public whose underlying concerns about immigration policy are rooted in beliefs about civic fairness rather than in group-centrism. Third, for an even broader segment of the public and in a wider set of contexts, ethnic appeals may be disregarded but not *repudiated*, conferring no political benefit but also exacting no cost. In this sense, our theory of civic fairness contrasts with the implicit-explicit model of racial priming.[65] The implicit-explicit model of racial priming maintains that although Americans are widely moved by implicit or subtle racial appeals, these same individuals tend to turn against policies framed in explicit racial terms that conflict with egalitarian values.

On the other hand, egalitarianism plays a major role in structuring many other Americans' views about immigration policy, and recent events suggest that the more naked variety of group-centric appeals can backfire with broad segments of the public. Republican rhetoric in the run-up to the 2018 midterm elections about an "invasion" by migrant caravans is widely credited not only with energizing minority voters but also turning off moderate, well-educated suburbanites, many of whom had reliably backed the GOP in previous elections. Putting this speculation on firmer footing, research by Loren Collingwood and colleagues found that attacks on Trump's "travel ban" as a violation of egalitarian norms about race and religion successfully mobilized public opinion against it.[66]

In short, group-based appeals will encounter a highly varied reception in the court of public opinion – resonating powerfully with a narrow but consequential minority of voters whose perspective on immigration is largely group-centric, influencing a broader segment of voters who process these appeals heuristically in particularly sparse information environments, being ignored by many of these same voters in richer information contexts and by others in any context, and alienating voters most attuned to the way that such appeals breach prevailing norms of racial equality. The use of such appeals is therefore most likely where politicians face little sanction from other elites for violating antiracism norms, pertinent information is unclear or in short supply, and target audiences are composed of few strong egalitarians and relatively large numbers of old fashioned racists. Even in a public whose opinions about immigration are predominantly shaped by civic fairness, such circumstances are not aberrant.

THE EVIDENCE

The main source of evidence throughout this book is public opinion surveys. We make use of a full compendium of all publicly available poll questions, both commercial and academic, about any aspect of immigration policy since 1992. As in this chapter, we draw heavily on the ANES and GSS, which provide high-quality data about public opinion concerning immigration going back to the early 1990s. To dig deeper than these surveys allow, we turn to data gleaned from multiple surveys that we fielded, some nationally representative and some on California voters. We designed these surveys for the specific purpose of teasing apart the competing influences of group-centrism and civic fairness. Surveys furnish us with large and systematically gathered interview data that represents the views of millions of Americans. Not all of our surveys perfectly represent the public. But they all speak to the opinions of broad swaths of the public, a major advantage over some of the in-depth interview-based socio-logical work[67] and political "memoirs"[68] on related topics that have gained in prominence as the commentariat puzzles over the rise of Trump, though these types of approaches certainly have their advantages.

The surveys we report on not only canvass opinions about distinct facets of immigration more comprehensively than publicly available data. They also make use of an array of cutting-edge experimental techniques such as conjoint analysis and other multifactor designs that allow us to zero in on the sources of variation in Americans' opinions about different immigration policy questions. These techniques can also help allay concerns about social desirability response sets that could lead people to distort their true attitudes about immigration in order to avoid appearing prejudiced. We provide nontechnical explanations of these techniques in the ensuing chapters.

SPECIFIC CLAIMS AND CHAPTER OUTLINE

Chapter 2 develops the model of public opinion that we test in the subsequent chapters, elaborates on the values that predominate in public conceptions of civic fairness, and describes the informational context that accompanies Americans' exposure to immigration controversies. It then develops six hypotheses that adjudicate between group-centrism and civic fairness.

Chapters 3 and 4 focus on testing the civic fairness framework by examining cases where civic fairness and group-centrism collide. In so doing, they also illustrate how conceptions of civic fairness help explain why citizens' opinions about different facets of immigration policy so often diverge from one another and from their generalized attitudes about immigration. Chapter 3 asks why, when it comes to legal immigration, many Americans profess both "abstract restrictivism" about immigrants and immigration and "operational openness" to policies that allow ever more of them into the country. We argue that two civic fairness values – functional assimilationism and humanitarianism – encourage Americans to support liberal immigration policy even when they favor reducing immigration in the abstract. In Chapter 4, we focus on another major distinction in public opinion, that between legal and illegal immigration policy. Our main focus is on the importance of legal status per se, which

Specific Claims and Chapter Outline 23

corresponds to the aspect of civic fairness we call formal assimilationism, a norm that is tied to legalistic values but powerfully counteracted by egalitarianism.

Chapters 5 and 6 take a close look at empirical patterns that are pervasively interpreted as evidence for group-centrism, revealing anomalies that are well explained by civic fairness. Chapter 5 scrutinizes the role of stereotyping in shaping Americans' opinions about immigration, focusing on white Americans' bias against Latino immigrants relative to European and Asian immigrants. We examine how anti-Latino bias varies as a function of individuating and policy-specific information about functional assimilation. If anti-Latino bias often reflects the application of automatic stereotypes about lack of assimilation, it should dissipate in the face of clear information that counteracts these widely propagated beliefs. We show in two different experiments that it does.

Chapter 6 assesses whether the assimilationist thread of civic fairness can be boiled down to feelings of solidarity with those immigrants who are regarded as part of the national community. The idea that the real importance of civic fairness is in its delineation of a national "we" and hostility or indifference to others is a group-centrist interpretation of the findings we describe in Chapters 3–5. Proponents of this view would accept the explanatory limitations of ethnic group-centrism and the importance of values. But they would argue that assimilation matters *because* it engenders almost familial feelings of loyalty and affinity directed at those who are seen as fellow members of the national community, or ingroup. However, we show in a variety of ways that identifying with immigrants in a social sense does not matter very much to people when they are asked whether they support extending government benefits and political rights to immigrants. Formal assimilation, by contrast, powerfully influences these policy opinions without much influencing feelings of group solidarity and shared identity with immigrants. This suggests that adherence to the values associated with common public conceptions of civic fairness does not arise simply because Americans wish to benefit immigrants they see as part of the national ingroup over those they perceive as "outsiders."

Once we get out from between our survey respondents' ears, these patterns raise intriguing questions: how does what we have learned from survey evidence help explain the broader politics of immigration reform and what does it portend for the future? How does the "information context" created by media treatment of immigration and political rhetoric map onto the personal and media-driven environment that confronts people in the real world, and how might things be different if these contextual influences were to change?

We return to these questions throughout the book and then offer a synthesis, however tentative, in Chapter 7. There, we also consider some of the broader implications of our argument. More broadly, we consider how the applicability of civic fairness might vary across immigrant groups. We also probe how it informs questions about the nature of prejudice and identity, as well as the implications of our findings for those who write about solidarity, "cohesion," and redistribution in an era of "deep diversity." We speculate about the interplay between social identity and civic fairness in countries outside the United States, with different historically rooted norms about the nature of political community. One question, which this book can only consider but not resolve, is to what extent the way that most Americans think about immigration and immigration policy is "exceptional" and to what extent it is similar to citizens in other advanced democracies that host large and growing foreign-born populations. Most research to date has been skeptical that Americans' opinions about immigration are distinctive.[69] Our analysis provides a foundation for richer explorations to come. Finally, we return to consider what our study can illuminate about the elusive relationship between mass opinion and immigration policy.

2

Civic Fairness and Group-Centrism

In this chapter, we develop a framework for understanding how Americans' opinions about immigration policy issues emerge from their conceptions of civic fairness. We then review leading theories of immigration attitudes that are premised on group-centrism, with an eye to considering (1) what questions they leave open about the relative influence of considerations rooted in political values and group allegiances and animosities, (2) what challenges they pose to the civic fairness framework, and (3) where they lay claim to empirical phenomena that could also be explained by conceptions of civic fairness. Finally, from this discussion we derive several hypotheses that guide the empirical tests in the chapters that follow. These hypotheses apply to situations where values collide with group loyalties to race and nation, which is to say instances in which the civic fairness and group-centrist perspectives make distinct predictions about what immigration policy alternatives Americans will choose.

WHAT IS CIVIC FAIRNESS?

Main Claims

The civic fairness framework advances two central claims about how citizens choose between immigration policy alternatives, each of which stands apart from prevailing group-centrist accounts that we elaborate at length in this chapter. The first claim is simply *that* a particular set of values influences the way people think about immigration policy alternatives. By values, we refer to beliefs about what means are acceptable and what aims are desirable in the political realm.[1] Research on values in American public opinion has tended to focus on freedom and equality,[2] both traditional components of the liberal creed. We highlight a broader set of values that includes notions of individual freedom (individualism) and political equality (egalitarianism)   but also

25

encompasses more general regard for the welfare of others (humanitarianism) and insistence on rigid adherence to rules and law (legalism). The last of these is related to values of obedience and conformity[3] but more conceptually focused on formal process and law-abiding behavior and empirically distinct, we show, from standard measures of authoritarianism.[4]

These values are deeply held and sincerely invoked by people when they think about immigration policy. Some of them are nearly consensual, though people assign them quite different priority.[5] These values guide beliefs about what immigrants owe their adopted lands, what the host country owes in return, and more generally, what goals public policy ought to promote and how. They are imparted and reinforced through familial, personal, and formal relationships and institutions,[6] and they are widely understood to be among the primary standards by which the fairness of public actions ought to be judged. As such, they can impose a kind of "psychological constraint" on people's political attitudes that may coincide with or cross-cut the "packages" of policy positions advocated by political parties.[7]

Because these values are important to people emotionally and accessible cognitively, elites will seek to frame their preferred policy alternatives as consonant with them in order to win public support.[8] Elites of course appeal to self-interest and group-centrism as well. The theory of civic fairness assumes only that appeals to values will be prevalent enough in political communications to reinforce citizens' commitments to values and habituate them to relating these values to the alternatives at stake in immigration policy controversies.

The second claim pertains to *how* values-based fairness judgments are formed in particular instances. Specifically, when people encounter immigration policy controversies, they use the way these controversies are presented and framed to make inferences about the values at stake. They then choose between the alternatives posed according to which values matter more to them. While people will seldom deliberate deeply about these choices, they do take stock of clear, easily digestible, and manifestly relevant information about how policy alternatives further or compromise the values they hold most strongly, and update their policy judgments accordingly.[9] We make no claim that any large number of citizens will be motivated enough to seek out any of this information on their own when the available information is absent or ambiguous. As is well known in the study of mass politics, most people are able and willing to allocate only a small portion of their leisure time to public affairs.

In assessing fairness, people will therefore often rely on whatever considerations are mentally available to them in the moment that they are confronted with a choice.[10] Judgments about civic fairness will consequently vary as these considerations change. They may be strong and rigid in some cases. But they also may be volatile in others, changing depending on what arguments and information citizens have been recently exposed to and evolving as they deliberate the alternatives. As we noted in Chapter 1, people's ideas about "what is fair" or right in the political realm are usually inchoate, with a range of

What Is Civic Fairness?

conflicting values often seeming applicable and important all at once.[11] Immigration policy is no exception. Differences in the applicability, accessibility, and priority accorded these values account for the striking variability – even seeming inconsistency – in individual Americans' opinions about immigration policies. They are the fundamental reason that specific policy opinions are only loosely connected to more general orientations toward immigration and to one another, the puzzle we developed in the previous chapter.[12]

An important corollary to this second claim, about information processing, concerns the interrelationship between civic fairness values, prejudice, and stereotypes. Stereotypes help people make sense of the world by reducing complex judgments about individuals to simpler beliefs about the categories they belong to.[13] As Walter Lippmann notes, "[t]here is economy in this. For the attempt to see all things freshly and in detail, rather than as types and generalities, is exhausting, and among busy affairs practically out of the question."[14] Some of these are "misleading fictions" (to use Lippmann's terminology), whereas others might be "workable ideas."[15] Regardless of their basis in truth, their influence arises because they are *believed to be* true.

The ubiquity of stereotyping in immigration is a given, and ethnic stereotypes are clearly among the most prevalent. In the civic fairness framework, stereotypes come into play instrumentally rather than as the product of deep-seated racial antipathy. Ethnicity is strongly correlated in people's minds with beliefs about assimilation and human capital. Mass media coverage of immigration amplifies and sometimes grossly exaggerates and distorts these patterns.[16] This gives rise to and sustains ethnic stereotypes, many (though not all) of which are negative. These stereotypes, in turn, stand in for deeper information about civic fairness in some contexts, even for people who care little about race per se and, in the civic fairness framework, are not at root motivated by an ideology of racial supremacy or acute feelings of racial threat. This is to say that where people lack direct or clear information about immigrants' personal attributes or the requirements that a given policy imposes, automatic stereotyping will often unconsciously "fill in the blanks" despite consciously held values that proscribe ethnic discrimination.[17] The civic fairness framework therefore expects ethnic biases in Americans' immigration policy choices in many contexts. But, as we will see, it also makes strong claims about how those biases will respond to information that supersedes group cues as a guide to the values at stake in a policy choice. These claims distinguish the civic fairness and group-centrist perspectives on the interpretation of such biases.

It is worth emphasizing that the theory of civic fairness postulates the importance of sincerely held values to political choice generally and the salience of certain values to Americans' political choices in particular. It does not take a position on *where* values come from, *why* they matter, or why American society came to embrace and continued to espouse the distinct set of values that undergirds mass perceptions of civic fairness. As noted in Chapter 1, the origins of values and the source of their importance are clearly multiple and varied, ranging from evolutionary pressures, to socialization and conditioning, to their tie-in with personal and social identities, to the selfish instrumentality of rational choice. The particular values we emphasize have their origins in and owe their persistence to influences as diverse as religious faith, the absence of a feudal period in American history, their association with economic success, and their contrast with the values of foreign adversaries. While these foundational issues lie well beyond the scope of our account, a justification of the particular values we highlight and consideration of their relevance to public opinion about immigration is well within it.

The Elements of Civic Fairness

Liberal Assimilationism

The foundation of civic fairness is the venerable liberal assimilationist tradition, which represents a "social contract" between America and its aspiring new members or, put another way, the rules for joining the political community.[18] This idea traces back to Crèvecoeur's *Letters From an American Farmer* and its image of "the American, this new man" as an alloy of all nations and foreign traditions. In its modern incarnation, liberal assimilationism rests on *subjective* assessments about whether immigrants have made sufficient effort and followed the appropriate procedures to become both *formal* and *functional* members of the American political community.[19] Becoming *functionally* American is understood to mean learning English and working hard to become self-sufficient. Becoming *formally* American means obtaining official status and American citizenship as a condition of living in America and gaining equal rights. Each norm plays its own role in the psychology of immigration attitudes. When citizens see immigration policies as upholding these precepts, they tend to support them. When they see them as abrogating these precepts, they tend to oppose them.

These norms are liberal because they are, in principle, achievable by anyone – not to say everyone. Only in the nation's folklore has the Golden Door opened to all who were willing to accept the creed and love America. Earnest belief and sincere emotion never secured a visa, spared a quarantine, or stamped a naturalization certificate. Crucially, however, while both types of assimilation have been conflated with race and ethnicity throughout US history, neither is *intrinsically* tied to race.

These modern-day strains of assimilationism have evolved from a much thicker norm of assimilation that prevailed in earlier periods of American history.[20] Assimilation American-style has never been as demanding of sameness as the continental version. But a "hard assimilation" that expected immigrants to discard other identities, loyalties, sentimentalities, and practices – even in private – once had more currency. This hard assimilationist view reached its apex during the Progressive Era, where scholars and practitioners came to understand social problems as stemming from immigrants' difficulty

What Is Civic Fairness?

adopting the American way of life. It resulted in crusades for the "Americanization" of immigrant groups (and the denunciation of "hyphenated Americans") in the shadows of WWI and the "Red Scare."[21] Hard assimilationism of this sort lives on in the country's political rhetoric. Former Louisiana Governor Bobby Jindal, himself a child of immigrants, stated in a summer 2015 interview during his moribund presidential campaign that he was "done with all this talk about hyphenated Americans."[22]

But the zeitgeist has become more pluralistic. The "salad bowl" supplants the "melting pot" in schoolchildren's civics lessons. Diversity is in vogue, and "Americanization" is out.[23] Gone are the legions of settlement house workers hounding the tenement dwellers to lay off the garlic and breastfeed the American way. The core of Teddy Roosevelt's famous dictum continues to apply: "if the immigrant who comes here in good faith becomes an American and assimilates himself to us, he shall be treated on an exact equality with everyone else." It is the additional proviso – "But this is predicated upon the person's becoming in every facet an American, and nothing but an American ... There can be no divided allegiance here"[24] – that is no longer a clear assimilationist norm.[25]

This is no mere elite-level paradigm shift, and it may reflect a distinctively American laissez-faire attitude about cultural assimilation. In the 2013 national identity module of the International Social Survey Program (ISSP), only 5% of Americans agreed strongly and 28% agreed at all that "it is impossible for people who do not share America's customs and traditions to become fully American." This is a good deal lower than the level of agreement in any European country surveyed save Iceland and about half the number that agreed in France, Germany, and Britain.[26] Many Americans wish that immigrants would blend in more with a variety of aspects of mainstream culture,[27] but relatively few insist on it.

Functional Assimilation

Still, Americans insist on a substantial degree of functional assimilation as a practical matter and brook no Tower of Babel multiculturalism or exceptions to the nation's by-the-bootstraps credo.[28] Ninety-four percent of Americans surveyed in the 2014 General Social Survey said that learning English is either "very" or "fairly" important to making someone "truly American," a near consensus that has barely budged since the General Social Survey started paying attention in 1996. Immigrants themselves agree: 90% of foreign-born respondents interviewed in the 2006 Latino National Survey rated speaking English as very important. Similar numbers consistently say the same about "working hard to get ahead." More of the world's huddled masses make a new life here than anywhere else, but the land of rugged individualism still spurns those "Paupers, Idiots, Lunatics, and likely public charges"[29] deemed unfit for the American Dream.

The expectation that immigrants will blend in enough to become functioning members of American society is related to the liberal tradition's valuation of economic individualism. Working hard (and renouncing decadence and sloth) are at the heart of Weber's idea of the "Protestant ethic" and have always figured centrally in debates about American political culture. Americans believe more than the citizens of most other countries that hard work is the primary determinant of economic success and that failure reflects lack of effort rather than discrimination.[30] As a result, they are uniquely tolerant among the world's liberal democracies of inequalities in economic outcome so long as everyone has a "fair shot" at getting ahead and more reluctant to support government efforts to address economic inequality.[31] Immigrants are therefore expected to embrace the creedal value of individualism and to live it. Individualism has both economic and political components. Of course, one can work hard and sustain oneself in America without knowing English. But it is also clear that the great majority of people continue to see proficiency in English as critical to upward mobility. Learning English is itself widely seen as an exertion in the direction of making one's way in the new country.

It is difficult to disentangle language's instrumental function from its more ethnic and cultural connotations.[32] Those who oppose language tests for immigration often see them as a latter-day literacy test, meant to exclude immigrants from backgrounds where few have access to English instruction. Some raise questions about whether assimilationist arguments for restricting immigration in particular ways are a means of masking prejudice.[33] A few studies have found evidence that many Americans are put off by hearing foreign language spoken or being exposed to it in written or online communications.[34] These results have been interpreted as evidence of "cultural threat" to national identity or ethnocentrism.

But there is good reason to think that results such as these have less to do with any widespread insistence on linguistic homogeneity as a matter of cultural preservation than they do with concerns that immigrants are not *also* learning English in addition to whatever language they use in their day-to-day affairs. Indeed, Americans are strikingly supportive of linguistic pluralism – as long as one of the plural languages spoken is English. One recent study[35] finds that the vast majority of Americans are not "bothered" by bilingualism or immigrants' use of their native language even as large majorities are bothered when the people they interact with "do not speak English well." A different study by the same authors[36] shows that opinions about bilingual education policy were much more heavily influenced by pragmatic arguments about the need to learn English to get a job and the value of fluency in a second language in a globalized economy than they were by cultural arguments about the need to preserve English as a unifying national language or the distinct heritage of linguistic minority groups.

Whatever other factors are at work, much of the public considers functional assimilation far more important than any other aspect of cultural assimilation.

Support for the two pillars of functional assimilation – learning English and getting ahead through hard work – also appears to be closely connected in people's minds and to be rooted in abstract beliefs in economic individualism. In a 2018 national survey conducted through Lucid Labs, which we discuss at more length in Chapter 3, we asked people to say how important it was to them that immigrants assimilate in a variety of ways. By far the most highly rated were "work to provide for themselves" (64% thought this was extremely important) and "learn English" (65%). Only "treat people equally regardless of their backgrounds," an egalitarian credo (more on this later), came close (56%). This was followed by various indicators related to civic republicanism, including "stand during the national anthem at a sporting event" (40%) – an issue that, of late, has become almost literally a political football[37] – "know basic facts of American history" (38%), and "know basic facts about American politics" (30%).

As a testament to the "thinning out" of assimilationist norms we mentioned previously, aspects of cultural assimilation related to the private sphere lagged far behind: "socialize with people who are outside their own group" (20%), "celebrate American holidays" (20%), "enjoy the same kinds of entertainment as other Americans" (18%), "root for American athletes in the Olympics" (12%) – notably close to Norman Tebbit's famous "cricket test"[38] – "dress like most other Americans" (11%), and "eat the same kinds of foods most Americans eat" (9%). Finally, only a small minority of the sample rated as of the utmost importance that immigrants discard their distinct customs, including "stop speaking their native language" (14%), and "stop celebrating holidays from their country of origin" (6%).

Views about the importance of learning English and working hard were also both more closely associated with one another (r = .51) than either was associated with support for any other assimilationist requirement. They were at least three times more powerfully associated with a measure of economic individualism (about which more is in Chapter 3) than all but one of the other items.[39]

Formal Assimilation

Even as the requirements of functional assimilation have become thinner in many respects, assimilation's *formal* component – by which we mean immigrants' acquisition of official status in the country – has become a more prominent feature of political debates. In an era of worldwide mass migration, all developed states set limits and priorities on admissions and access to social benefits and voting rights. In a bygone age, coming "without papers" was a widely tolerated reality of mass immigration. Even then admission was contingent on thorough inspection, and illegal entry was regarded as a form of smuggling that was largely treated with benign neglect. Citizenship status was for much of the nineteenth century only a partial impediment to official participation in the democratic process, and citizens and noncitizens alike had access to many of the same sources of semiprivate largesse. Now large swathes of the noncitizen population are barred from receiving most public benefits, a rule backed by elaborate electronic verification systems.[40] Formal restrictions on the franchise and political participation have become more rigid in the United States even as other countries have loosened them.[41]

Outside the ivory tower, Americans haven't gotten the news that national sovereignty is in decline and global citizenship ascendant.[42] They insist that those who wish to live here respect the country's laws and institutions by lining up and following the rules and procedures set forth in the country's immigration laws. And most believe that those who want full membership rights ought to become full members by naturalizing. In the 2014 GSS, as we noted in Chapter 1, only 37% of Americans supported giving *legal* immigrant noncitizens the same rights as US citizens, while 51% opposed this. If anything, this probably overstates support for equal rights regardless of citizenship status. More specific questions about whether legal immigrants should have to wait some period of time to receive public benefits and whether they should be allowed to vote in local elections, serve on school boards, and perform jury service, elicit stronger opposition.[43] Becoming formally American presupposes becoming functionally American. Naturalization requires immigrants to demonstrate that they can speak English, for example. But to most Americans, being American "in all ways but on paper" is still not enough. They believe that immigrants must obtain an official status commensurate with the rights and benefits they expect in return, and many insist above all that immigrants "play by the rules."

The resonance of formal assimilation is tied to the creedal commitment to the rule of law but runs deeper than this consensual precept might suggest. Rhetorical emphasis on adherence to law plays to a legalistic strain of American political culture that Tocqueville saw as a bulwark against some of the excesses of democracy. America had no aristocracy, Tocqueville remarked, but it did have a politically entrenched lawyer class that substituted for many of the manners and customs associated with the upper class. Lawyers were trained to revere precedent, to value rules and customs, and to disdain arbitrariness. They were suspicious of the passions of the moment that could easily overtake democratic man, and indeed many were secretly contemptuous of mass democracy itself. These tastes would be a force for stability and the preservation of rights against the tyranny of the majority.[44]

For Tocqueville, legalism in American political culture begins with its barristers but does not stop there. Seeing lawyers occupy positions of political power and prestige, listening to them argue the issues of the day, and being exposed directly to the legal system through jury service, ordinary Americans internalized some of the lawyer's spirit, style, and lexicon. All political debates in America eventually made their way to the court system. All discussions about politics inevitably turned to disagreements over each side's legal merits. Since then, observers from the continent have often remarked on this aspect of American

What Is Civic Fairness? 33

political culture with a mix of admiration and amusement. Bernard-Henri Lévy's description of driving down Interstate 94 to Chicago is an example:

And then this legalism, too, this extraordinary sense of the law and the rules, which shapes people's conduct in general and that of motorists in particular. No excessive speeding, for instance. No screaming matches from car to car, as we have in France. No way, either, even on the outskirts of Battle Creek, where the traffic is at a complete standstill, to persuade Tim, the young man who is driving, to try to make up a little time by using the breakdown lane.[45]

But what Tocqueville saw as a crucial counterweight to democratic excesses and Lévy as an endearing national trait, other observers have cast in a more negative light. More than a century and a half after Tocqueville, Judith Shklar expounded on the legalistic political culture of the American judiciary.[46] Like Tocqueville, she remarked on the diffusion of legalism to the public. Americans talked about political issues using bastardized legal terminology and resorted quickly to arguments about what the official rules called for or disallowed. Whatever its virtues, this reliance on legal language and norms could stifle broader moral inquiry. Complicated questions of right and wrong are reduced into narrow and unimaginative debates about procedure or formal statuses – what the law is rather than what it ought to be.

As a result, political debates and clashes of competing values are reduced to disagreements about what the rules *are* or which position adheres to them. Just as Louis Hartz found the individualist component of the liberal tradition narrow and capable of stifling imagination and consideration of alternative views, Tocqueville and others have found Americans' legalism somewhat limiting and reductionist. By focusing political disagreements on rival conceptions of adherence to formal procedures and rules, one divorces them from broader ethical questions and social context, critics say. Instead of asking what is right, Americans often resort to asking instead what is permitted or simply equate the two.[47]

Within the broader politics of immigration, legalism is particularly relevant to public discourse about illegal immigrants. This is readily apparent in recent presidential rhetoric on the subject. Consider President Bill Clinton's 1995 State of the Union Address. Following a pledge to give Americans a federal government that works better and costs less, eliminate "16,000 pages of unnecessary rules and regulations," and empower states and local communities, he turned at length to the subject of immigration policy:

But there are some areas that the Federal Government should not leave and should address and address strongly. One of these areas is the problem of illegal immigration. After years of neglect, this administration has taken a strong stand to stiffen the protection of our borders. We are increasing border controls by 50 percent. We are increasing inspections to prevent the hiring of illegal immigrants. And tonight, I announce, I will sign an executive order to deny federal contracts to businesses that hire illegal immigrants.

34 *Civic Fairness and Group-Centrism*

Let me be very clear about this: We are still a nation of immigrants; we should be proud of it. We should honor every legal immigrant here, working hard to be a good citizen, working hard to become a new citizen. But we are also a nation of laws.

It was not the first time that Clinton had taken a hard line on illegal immigration, decoupling it from legal immigration. To the cheers of legislators in his own party a year earlier, he had touted his administration's "aggressive" moves to

secure our borders by hiring a record number of new border guards, by deporting twice as many criminal aliens as ever before, by cracking down on illegal hiring, by barring welfare benefits to illegal aliens ... We are a nation of immigrants. But we are also a nation of laws. It is wrong and ultimately self-defeating for a nation of immigrants to permit the kind of abuse of our immigration laws we have seen in recent years, and we must do more to stop it.

Clinton surely never imagined that his rhetoric would be co-opted by conservative media outlets, and, ultimately, marshaled in defense of Donald Trump's tough talk about illegal immigration. Clinton might have been a lot less surprised to hear an echo of his rhetoric in President Barack Obama's address to the nation on the night that he announced his Deferred Action for Parents of Americans and Lawful Permanent Residents (DAPA) executive action. Less than a minute into the speech, the first elaboration that Obama offered on how America's immigration system was "broken" was that "[f]amilies who enter our country the right way and play by the rules watch others flout the rules." Immediately after laying out the three components of the action – beefing up security at the borders and streamlining deportation proceedings, augmenting allowances for skilled immigrants and foreign students to stay in the United States, and taking "steps to deal responsibly with the millions of undocumented immigrants who already live in our country" – he used a familiar refrain: "Even as we are a nation of immigrants, we are a nation of laws. Undocumented workers broke our immigration laws, and I believe that they must be held accountable – especially those who may be dangerous." Obama even framed his action as a way of remedying a situation that was already, effectively, amnesty: "[n]ow here's the thing: we expect people who live in this country to play by the rules. We expect that those who cut the line will not be unfairly rewarded." Immigrants who meet a variety of conditions could therefore "come out of the shadows and get right with the law," and it would be national "hypocrisy" to deny "workers who pick our fruit and make our beds ... a chance to get right with the law."

Of course, Trump has taken a quite different approach to illegal immigration from any of his recent predecessors, both substantively and rhetorically. Clinton and Obama never even rhetorically advocated mass deportation, made sweeping generalizations about Mexicans, or insinuated that most of them were bringing violent crime and drugs to the United States. And though, as president, Clinton never pressed for a path to citizenship for illegal immigrants – one had

What Is Civic Fairness?   35

been enacted only six years before his presidency began – Presidents Obama and George W. Bush both made this a centerpiece of their immigration reform initiatives.

Yet the similarities apparent in Clinton's triangulation, Obama's reframing, and Trump's demagoguery reflect a now long-standing pattern of rhetoric that reifies the divide between illegal and legal immigration. Even when political leaders advocating comprehensive immigration reform have sought to bridge that divide by appealing to Americans' self-image as a "nation of immigrants," they have felt the need to acknowledge and tread carefully around the issue of amnesty and have run up against opponents who cast their efforts as an assault on the rule of law, an undeserved "inside track," or "rewarding lawbreakers."

As our references to presidential rhetoric about illegal immigration would suggest, we expect legalistic values to have an especially pronounced impact on public opinion in this domain. The value people place on adherence to the law should be tied to opinions about illegal immigration policy in particular. However, given the legacy of "law and order" as a dog-whistle appeal to racist whites during and after the 1960s Civil Rights Era, scholars have understandably been reluctant to take legalism in American public opinion about immigration at face value.[48] Treatments by public intellectuals have been similarly skeptical.[49] Legalism is always of course at some level an endorsement of social control, and it has often been racialized. This is why one of our goals in Chapter 4 is to tease apart its role as a rhetorical cover for prejudice from a sincere reason that people hold the opinions they do, whatever the distal origins of its grip on the public imagination.

One also encounters formalistic framing of issues that concern whether to extend rights and benefits to noncitizens. Unlike in the case of illegal immigration, these arguments seldom link the issue to the integrity of the rule of law and the undesirability of "rewarding lawbreakers," except inasmuch as illegal immigrants themselves are among the potential beneficiaries of expansions of political rights and public benefits to noncitizens.[50] But some of the arguments about these issues do share the quality of reducing complex debates to legal formalities and official statuses. Vetoing a California bill that would have allowed noncitizens to serve on juries, Democratic Governor Jerry Brown stated, "Jury service, like voting, is quintessentially a prerogative and responsibility of citizenship."[51] This statement is not really correct in historical context, but it posits a sharp legalistic barrier between citizens and noncitizens. While a broader range of considerations related to individualist norms and sociotropic threats surely come into play when people consider eligibility of legal immigrant noncitizens for welfare benefits,[52] a 2016 poll of non-Hispanic whites that we conducted through Survey Sampling International (SSI) (see Online Appendix for details) suggests that many are susceptible to thinking about benefits eligibility in legalistic terms as well. More than 70% of the sample, including a majority of Democrats, agreed that "If immigrants want to be able to receive public benefits, they should become U.S. citizens first," only slightly lower than the percentage that said the same about voting in US elections.

We expect that these different aspects of legalism generate particularly rigid opinions in the areas of immigration policy where they come into play, ones that apply in an undifferentiated way to whole categories of immigrants identified by the nominal status in question. Those who view illegal immigration issues or the extension of benefits and rights to noncitizens primarily through the lens of the acceptability of process and nominal statuses will tend to hold "categorical" opinions about these policies. We elaborate on this concept in Chapters 4 and 6, but the upshot is that where legalistic considerations predominate, they will override more nuanced judgments about individual immigrants' personal qualities, including those that bear on functional assimilation, and lead to all-or-nothing judgments that putatively uphold the integrity of the legalistic principle at stake.

We can provide a general idea of the salience of legalism in Americans' conceptions of political community by comparing their endorsement of different definitions of "America" and "the United States." In a California Field Poll conducted in October 2016 (see Online Appendix for details), we asked voters which of two statements best completes the sentence "America is a ... "; 23% of respondents chose "country based on laws that outline government's obligations and citizens' rights" while 13% chose "nation with a common heritage, set of core values, and unique sense of who we are." The modal answer, selected by 44% of respondents, was to say that both completed the sentence equally well, while 20% said neither completed the sentence well.

These results were corroborated in an August 2016 survey of California registered voters fielded by SSI (see the Online Appendix for details). This time, people were asked about the more official-sounding "the United States of America" rather than just "America," and 40% of respondents chose the legalistic response ("country governed by laws that guarantee individual rights and say what the government must and must not do") while only 9% chose the nationalist response ("nation whose people are united by a common identity, heritage, and set of values"), with 26% choosing both equally and 25% rejecting both. Half the respondents in the poll were forced to choose instead of being allowed to say both or neither, and 73% chose the legalistic answer while 27% chose the nationalist. Taken together, these polls give some initial evidence that Americans think about their country in the abstract as much as an association bound by rules and laws as they do as a social community whose members are bound by common norms, values, and shared identity.

Egalitarian and Humanitarian Values

Inevitably, many immigrants do not fully meet the criteria of liberal assimilationism right away – or ever. Americans must therefore balance liberal assimilationist norms against competing values such as equality of opportunity and a universalistic commitment to humanitarian goals such as family unity and

What Is Civic Fairness? 37

helping the oppressed. Nowhere are such issues on clearer display than in debates over illegal immigration policy. A great many Americans who dislike the idea of illegal immigration still have some inclination to bring the undocumented into the fold somehow and bristle at the idea of permanent second-class status and the harshness of mass deportation.[53] The status of child refugees or those "dreamers" brought to the United States illegally by their parents who have lived their whole lives in America further accentuate these tensions. Trump's decision to end the Obama Administration's Deferred Action for Childhood Arrivals program provoked opposition across much of the political spectrum, most of it couched in terms of sympathy for the dreamers' undeserved plight.

Thus, many Americans will amend or even abrogate the assimilationist contract on the basis of competing values and humanitarian exigencies. Those most inclined to egalitarian values will oppose policies that seem to guarantee "second-class citizenship," viewing the preservation of equal opportunity as the premier value at stake in these cases. Those most committed to the moral obligation to alleviate suffering among the "huddled masses yearning to be free" tend to view humanitarian goals – giving refuge to the oppressed, keeping families together, and avoiding disruptions to immigrants' lives and livelihoods when possible – as primary obligations of the political community.

Egalitarian values are central to the American creed, famously traced to the country's distinctive lack of experience with a feudal period[54] and the relative absence of status hierarchy in Presbyterian religious institutions.[55] Crucially, the "equality" that Americans almost universally endorse in the abstract is *political* equality and equality of opportunity, not equality of outcome. Americans tend to view equality as a desirable economic end state[56] but also widely resist a range of government efforts to effectuate greater equality in incomes and wealth unless they also give due deference to the individualist credo of hard work.[57] With the growth of the welfare state, there is far less support for pure laissez-faire capitalism than there probably was before the Great Depression, but there is still a wide gap between the consensual valuation of equality of opportunity and far greater suspicion of efforts to equalize material conditions. Nowhere is this "principle-implementation gap" more visible than in matters related to racial inequality,[58] a puzzle that has spawned an ongoing scholarly controversy about why Americans support racial equality in the abstract but tend to oppose programs such as affirmative action that are ostensibly tailored to bring it about.

Equality of status should play an important role in debates over illegal immigration policy and in particular in those having to do with efforts to normalize the status of the estimated 11 million undocumented immigrants living in the country. Framing this issue around concerns about status equality may have increased in recent years, but it is not new. President Jimmy Carter's August 1977 message to Congress about "Undocumented Aliens" raised the issue of "Adjustment of Status," noting "I have concluded that an adjustment of status is necessary to avoid having a permanent 'underclass' of millions of persons."[59] This argument could be used to justify efforts to deter or remove illegal immigrants, but it is usually invoked in support of policies such as a path to citizenship for undocumented immigrants.

Moreover, the mass protests of millions of immigrants in 2006 marked the emergence of large-scale grassroots activism about the rights of illegal immigrants that, like preceding social movements that influenced it, draws heavily on egalitarian themes.[60] These protests, spurred by harsh legislation passed by the House of Representatives (but not the Senate) in 2005, marked the beginning of a social movement in favor of immigrant rights that focused heavily on undocumented immigrants. The "rights" framing of this movement, which continues to this day and is made up of a variety of organizations, some led by undocumented immigrants themselves, is likely to engage general egalitarian values and make considerations about equality more salient to people's opinions about illegal immigration.

Distinct from egalitarianism as such, humanitarian values transcend categories and boundaries and go beyond equality to reflect a general desire to help people who are struggling or suffering. They are humanitarian in that they reflect a cosmopolitan concern for humanity as a whole rather than more selective commitments to particular groups of people. In practice, they are usually measured by gauging people's support for helping others in the abstract versus looking out for oneself. This measurement strategy captures the universalistic core of humanitarian aspirations. But it is questionable because it pits humanitarianism directly against narrow selfishness rather than, for example, a concern for those who are already part of one's political community (or narrower community). But superior measures of such universal concern for others are scarce in recent public opinion surveys. In any case, the existing measures are powerful enough to produce clear and intuitive relationships with opinions about public policy, such as the domain of social welfare, that is aimed at helping people who are in need.[61]

Humanitarian goals are an explicit aim of American immigration policy. They are most directly tied to refugee policy. But frames concerning help for the oppressed are invoked far more widely and routinely applied to issues concerning the condition of undocumented immigrants and opposition to replacing family-based visas with skills-based visas. Many Americans say that helping those who are in need is a priority of immigration policy, though far more endorse this for immigrants who are oppressed politically or subject to violence in their homelands than for economic migrants. Accordingly, research finds that humanitarian values are strongly related to liberal immigration attitudes.[62] We expect they will play the most pronounced role when the potential suffering and hardship of immigrants is made salient.

Summary

For convenience, we summarize in Table 2.1 the collection of values we consider part of civic fairness, along with various attributes we associate with

What Is Civic Fairness?

TABLE 2.1 *Elements of civic fairness*

Civic Fairness Norm	Immigrant/Policy Attribute	Value Underpinnings
Functional assimilation	English language ability Education, skill, human capital Evidence of "work ethic"	Beliefs in economic individualism, self-reliance
Formal assimilation	Legal status (legal versus undocumented) Citizenship status (citizen versus resident alien) Evidence of respect for rule of law	Adherence to procedural/formal legalism
Egalitarianism	Policy reflects ethnic or status-based discrimination, "second class citizenship"	Beliefs in equality of opportunity, status
Humanitarianism	Refugee migrant/immigration Family-based migrant/immigration	Beliefs in obligation to help others, alleviate distress

each. The left-most column lists the civic fairness norm in question. The center column gives examples of the kind of policy- or immigrant-specific information that we think cues that value. The right-most column lists the individual-level values we think underpin them.

Civic Fairness in Public Discourse about Immigration

To what extent do civic fairness values suffuse the rhetorical environment – broadly understood to include media, political elites, etc. – average Americans encounter when confronted by the immigration policy controversies of the day? Some allege that this environment is saturated with group cues, in particular those referencing Latinos.[63] We do not disagree. But the question for us is how often the former kind of information appears in isolation of the latter.

We assume that, at a minimum, people have to weigh considerations of *both* ethnicity and civic fairness when rendering opinions about immigration policy. This is because the latter contextualize what exactly it is that the ethnic group is supposedly doing that is newsworthy in the first place. For example, early April 2018 saw extensive media coverage of, and presidential fixation on, a large "caravan" of Honduran immigrants heading north toward the United States.[64] One cannot escape the fact that the immigrants' ethnic makeup is nonwhite and Latino. Yet at the same time, less sympathetic coverage (and the president himself) loudly proclaimed that the asylum seekers were coming to the United States to immigrate illegally and threaten social order whereas more sympathetic portrayals almost always questioned these notions and painted the immigrants as victims of a humanitarian crisis. Either way, ethnicity is cued but so are a slew of civic fairness considerations as well.

To see whether this pattern holds more systematically, we collected every immigration-related article published in four major newspapers – *New York Times*, *Washington Post*, *New York Post*, and *USA Today* – between January 1, 2000 and December 31, 2016. Our generous search parameters[65] returned over 100,000 hits, obviously too many to code by hand. Instead, we sampled 1,000 articles at random, filtering for those specifically about the immigration debate: that is, news articles, in-depth investigative pieces, and official editorial content where the main subject is either US immigration as a subject or individuals characterized as US immigrants. This left us with 888 immigration-germane articles to work with. To begin, we coded each according to whether it contained an ethnic cue, broadly defined as mention of immigrants' country of origin, nationality, or race, any mention of an ethnic-sounding name, and references pan-ethnic group identifications (Asian, Hispanic, etc.) or references to "ethnic" or "racial" minorities.

We then looked for considerations germane to civic fairness. Mentions of immigrants' legal or citizenship status,[66] as well as other violations of law directly related to immigration (e.g., document forgery and the like), we classified as "legalism." Under "functional assimilation," we included any mentions of immigrants' English language ability, human capital, work ethic or political engagement in the United States. Under "egalitarianism," we coded all mentions of second-class status, ethnic bias, immigrants' civil or constitutional rights, and references to legal, political, or social inequalities between immigrants and natives. Under "humanitarianism," we coded any instance of immigrants being victimized by crime (either in the United States or their home country), mistreatment at the hands of immigration authorities, political persecution, immigrants' families being separated, or would-be immigrants suffering in transit.

Media stories are often quite complex, and any attempt to code "considerations" in this way is bound to be reductive. For one thing, we made no attempt to code the tone or valence of the considerations. Some aspects of civic fairness are one-sided; for example, "humanitarianism" is virtually pro-immigrant by definition, since it captures mentions of immigrants victimized by crime or human trafficking, families torn apart, and the like. But most others can go either way: considerations about legalism or functional assimilation can just as easily paint an alarming picture as a reassuring one, and mentions of "egalitarianism" could (and often did) arise as *either* a criticism of the fact that illegal immigrants lack legal protections that citizens have or an endorsement of it. Combine this with the fact that many if not most articles contain multiple points of view, as any newspaper reader will recognize, and this makes coding and somehow aggregating valance or tone out of all this an extremely difficult task. Fortunately for us, it is also unnecessary.

What Is Civic Fairness? 41

Another point to raise here is that it is difficult to discern underlying truth and source credibility. This happens frequently in stories about politicians on the campaign trail, not only with respect to what they themselves claim (i.e. candidate Trump's various claims about Mexicans and Muslims), but also how they characterize their opponents (e.g. "Democrats want Open Borders").[67] It also happens when expert sources on one side or the other of an issue – say, for example, the economic impact of illegal immigration – weigh in on what "the evidence" shows. Our position here is simple: we need not become hopelessly entangled in what is true and what isn't. Rather, all we want is to understand the mix of considerations presented for readers' consideration, regardless of verisimilitude.

Finally, much depends on where and how people get their information. Breitbart readers, for example, get a very different set of considerations than consumers of mainstream media like the newspapers we sampled. Yet it is important to remember that very few people obtain their news primarily from Breitbart – approximately 3% of Americans in a typical week, according to the Pew Research Center.[68] To the extent that the great majority of Americans are exposed to news and public debate about immigration at all, they will tend to receive it from outlets that regularly furnish a mix of group cues and appeals to civic fairness, whatever their slant.

These caveats aside, what can we say? The first thing that emerges is that a large majority of our 888 stories (661, or 74%) contained some kind of ethnic cue as we define it here. Even keeping in mind that we included *any* reference to *any* ethnic or nationality group and not just references to Latinos, this is certainly a large proportion and in keeping with the literature on the subject. Clearly, newspaper readers have no shortage of encouragement when it comes to linking their thoughts about immigration to ethnic groups.

What matters for us, however, is that civic fairness–derived considerations are even more prominent. Out of the total set, 838 articles (94%) contained at least one reference to a civic fairness consideration or argument. What is more, whereas very few stories presented an ethnic cue in the absence of a civic fairness argument (33 articles, or 4%), a far larger proportion (227 articles, or 26%) broached the latter without any reference to the former. Thus, while we readily acknowledge the availability of ethnic cues in media stories about immigration, it seems fair to say that readers are also confronted with arguments, considerations, and evidence tied to concerns about civic fairness.

All aspects of civic fairness are well represented in these stories. Perhaps unsurprisingly, the civic fairness consideration raised most often is legalism, which features in 74% of the total set of articles. Yet functional assimilation, egalitarianism, and humanitarianism all put in a strong showing, appearing in 38%, 26%, and 30% of all coded articles, respectively. There is also considerable breadth in how these various dimensions show up in a given story: while the modal article references one category of civic fairness, over 50% of all articles we coded raise *at least* two dimensions, and 17% reference three or more. All of this suggests that while immigrants' ethnicity is often part of the story, it is typically only in conjunction with civic fairness that stories about immigration become newsworthy. Americans, as a result, are habituated to associating immigration controversies with the elements of civic fairness that we highlight. Public discourse about these controversies provides ample cuing to form opinions with such considerations in mind.

THE PREVAILING VIEW: GROUPS AND GROUP CENTRISM

The argument we will advance in the coming chapters is that such considerations about civic fairness often predominate in American public opinion about immigration policy, over and above the group-centric influences most emphasized in existing research – those based on ethnic and national identities. In the remainder of this chapter, therefore, we take a closer look at the particular group-centrist perspectives advanced in the literature and consider what existing research can tell us about the relative influence of group-centrism and civic fairness. We also identify particular group-centrist theories that directly challenge the validity of the civic fairness–based account that we are advancing. We then turn the tables and consider whether civic fairness is capable explaining two empirical patterns that have usually been attributed to group-centrism alone.

Varieties of Group-Centrism

Group-centrist theories are typically premised on the drive to enhance group interest and status. People have a primordial favoritism for an "us" who are attached to one another emotionally by virtue of common group memberships, and, sometimes, hostility for a "them" who are outside our communities and identity groups and whose interests and status have therefore been identified as antithetical to our own. Ingroup love need not necessarily fuel out-group hate, but that animus emerges from some combination of individual-level predisposition and a "threatening" social context, where threats could be material, cultural, or ideational.[69]

The human proclivity to group-centrism – that is, the tendency to evaluate policy alternatives on the basis of how they assist or harm groups we like or dislike – is widely considered one of the most potent and pervasive influences on mass opinion. Common group referents can help bring coherence and constraint to attitudes about otherwise substantively distinct policies.[70] Attitudes toward racial and ethnic groups in particular are at times some of the most crystallized and central in mass opinion, and when public policies are cognitively linked to particular groups, attitudes toward these groups are frequently some of the strongest and most consistent predictors of support.[71]

As far as immigration is concerned, group identity has figured in Americans' attitudes at least as far back as Benjamin Franklin's philippic against the

The Prevailing View: Groups and Group Centrism   43

"Palatine Boors" invading Pennsylvania in the eighteenth century, and probably further. Scholars of public opinion have understood this relationship through two separate though largely complementary lenses: ethnic identity and national identity. We present each in turn, and then draw them together before turning to the more values-based considerations we consider under the banner of civic fairness.

Ethnic Identity and Immigration in Three Flavors

Research linking racial and ethnic identity to public opinion on immigration taps into three different lodes to varying degrees. One is the rich historical literature on American political culture, and in particular that literature's treatment of immigration policy developments as the product of contestation over competing racist and egalitarian traditions.[72] A second, more sociological, tradition investigates the individual and structural factors that either encourage or hinder immigrants' assimilation to American society.[73] Finally, there is the large social-psychological literature on prejudice and intergroup relations, which convincingly establishes the pervasiveness of racial and national group identification, suggests psychological mechanisms to account for it, and explores the ways in which group identities are prioritized and in which intergroup tensions can be exacerbated or reduced.[74]

The story that emerges when these strands are drawn together is both vivid and compelling: in the foreground we have an innate human tendency toward ethnic group identification. This is set against (and set off by) structural forces that encourage such identifications, politicize them, and make their consequences real.

Three examples illustrate these themes. In their landmark work *Us against Them* (2009), Donald Kinder and Cindy Kam trace a variety of political attitudes to a deep-seated ethnocentric tendency, viz "the predisposition to divide human society into ingroups and out-groups" (p. 30).[75] In this formulation, people identify *with* their own ethnic group, and *against* all other ethnic groups in a generalized way.[76] This latent predisposition translates to restrictive policy preferences under two conditions: first, an issue must be made salient, and second, it must be framed by opinion leaders in an ethnocentric way. With respect to immigration, Kinder and Kam illustrate this argument by demonstrating strong correlations between ethnocentrism, on the one hand, and a variety of immigration-related policy attitudes on the other (p. 132). Furthermore, these correlations appear to stem from both ingroup loyalty and generalized, rather than group-specific, outgroup hostility. Finally, while the correlation is never altogether absent, it does strengthen as the issue becomes more politically salient – evidence, Kinder and Kam claim, of how context triggers ethnocentrism's punitive side.

Moving beyond generalized prejudice, Natalie Masuoka and Jane Junn show that the politics of race and immigration are inextricably tied. In *The Politics of Belonging* (2013), they contend that each racial group in society is situated within a two-dimensional hierarchy, that the consequent "prismatic" racial order is well known and widely recognized, and that individuals' location within it shapes and constrains their view of the political world. As in Kinder and Kam, the issue must be ethnically politicized in order for this to matter: "[w]hile racial patterns in opinion are not present for all issues, for those with clear racial undertones such as immigration policy, position in the racial hierarchy is the key feature to explain differences in public opinion" (p. 5). The social-psychological notion of identity enters the picture both via identification with the national community (a topic to which we return later) and perceived "linked fate" with co-ethnics. At the core of Masuoka and Junn's 2013 Racial Prism of Group Identity Model is the premise that both kinds of identification moderate the relationship between objective racial group membership and opinion on immigration.

Finally, in *White Backlash* (2015), Marisa Abrajano and Zoltan Hajnal describe a "partisan transformation of white America" (p. 83) toward the Republican Party, galvanized by inter-ethnic conflict and threat. Though less explicitly psychological than either *Us against Them* or *The Politics of Belonging*, the key ingredient in the story seems to be whites' tendency toward ingroup favoritism, set against the backdrop of a historical tension between "traditions" of racial hierarchy and egalitarianism. This latent predisposition has been touched off, Abrajano and Hajnal[77] argue, by the sheer scale of Latino immigration to the United States over recent decades, and "an on-going and often-repeated threat narrative that links the United States' immigrant and Latino populations to a host of pernicious fiscal, social, and cultural consequences" (p. 5). According to the authors, this fosters anxiety among whites, as well as the desire for a new political home: "when the two major parties chart divergent courses on the question of immigration, with one often bemoaning the social, cultural, and economic costs associated with immigrants, and the other frequently acknowledging the benefits . . ., the political choice for Americans becomes sharp. For those who fear the changes wrought by immigration, the Republican Party becomes a natural home" (p. 27). Thus, we have yet another story of racial group identity, translated into immigration attitudes by the politicization of threat.

Ongoing Debates in the Literature

As these examples suggest, recent work on immigration attitudes has developed along multiple related but still distinct theoretical lines. An emerging debate in the literature concerns the relative influence of white identity and anti-minority prejudice – ingroup favoritism versus outgroup derogation. Some emphasize whiteness as a politicized racial identity with the potential to trigger protectiveness of the dominant group's status and social control over subordinate groups[78] while others focus more on early socialization as a source of prejudice that endures through the life cycle and still others link prejudice to sociostructural theories of racial hierarchy.[79] These debates, which took on new urgency after the 2016 presidential election, have reanimated long-standing disagreements in public opinion research about the underpinnings of white Americans' opposition to race-conscious policies designed to help blacks: do whites oppose affirmative action, busing, and other race-conscious policies out of a sense of collective threat to their dominant group position or negative affect toward blacks?[80] Attention to white racial identity also more closely parallels research on the role of politicized ethnic identity in shaping nonwhites' opinions about immigration, inspiring work that compares the role of identity and beliefs in linked fate across America's largest racial groups.[81]

Distinct from the debate about "ingroup love" versus "outgroup hate," others focus on the relative influence of generalized prejudice against racial and ethnic "others"[82] versus group-specific animosities. Most have focused on whites' hostility to Latinos.[83] But as the Trump administration's policy initiatives have brought increased focus to Muslim immigration, the nature and role of group-specific prejudice against Muslims will likely become more central to academic debates about the sources of opposition to immigration.[84]

Other work highlights *implicit* (versus explicit) prejudice as a cause of systematic differences in the way that members of America's largest racial groups think and feel about immigration.[85] In this view, white Americans widely harbor negative attitudes about Latinos that they are often not aware of or refuse to acknowledge to themselves. These attitudes involve both feelings and beliefs.[86] They are mental associations formed through conditioning, socialization and exposure to mass media. They are triggered early in the opinion formation process when people encounter the symbol "immigration" and then subvert and bias information processing. This leads people to generate values-laden rationales to justify positions on immigration issues that are consistent with their implicit group biases. Efrén Pérez argues that such biases are so profound that whites will often *not* discriminate against Latino immigrants relative to those of European origin in conventional survey experiments.[87] The very issue of immigration triggers unconscious bias that then operates equally on immigrants from any background because the implicit attitudes engaged by a question about immigration so bias information-processing that they lead people to disregard ethnic cues and other information altogether. Policy judgments take shape before people process these cues in a discriminatory way.

Still another perspective on anti-Latino prejudice borrows from the literature on symbolic racism against blacks.[88] Proponents of this view juxtaposed the decline of "old-fashioned racism" in public opinion since the middle of the twentieth century[89] against the rise of a new "symbolic" racism against blacks. Whites imbibed negativity against blacks at an early age and learned to couch it in socially acceptable rationales that drew on traditional American values such as individualism, self-restraint, and family.[90] As applied to immigration, the thesis is that deep-seated anti-Latino bias acquired during early socialization promotes restrictive policy preferences. However, since overt prejudice is no longer socially sanctioned, whites rationalize opposition to immigration on the basis of cherished values, including those we have associated with civic fairness. They will also only express these discriminatory tendencies when furnished a normatively acceptable rationale to do so. By implication, perceived violations of norms committed by Latino immigrants will be regarded more harshly than the same violation by a white immigrant.[91] The prediction that whites will in these circumstances discriminate against Latino immigrants departs from Pérez's hypothesis that unconscious prejudice will produce opposition to immigrants irrespective of their backgrounds. Disconcertingly, theories of implicit bias against Latinos and symbolic racism against Latinos see evidence of ethnic group-centrism both in nondiscrimination and discrimination.

Setting aside their many differences, perspectives on group-centrism based on ethno-racial identities share the assumption that racial attitudes are pervasive influences on public opinion about immigration, an assumption that casual observation clearly sustains. They are *group-centrist* in that they take the central idea element in mass belief systems connected to immigration and immigration policy to be people's loyalties to their own ethnic groups and animosities toward others. Policies are chosen on the basis of their presumed benefit for members of the ethnic ingroup or their derogation of disliked or threatening ethnic outgroups.

National Identity and Immigration

It is by now a truism that nations are the "imagined communities"[92] at the core of citizens' relationship to the modern state, and what commands their ultimate loyalty "when the chips are down."[93] National identity, inculcated through repeated exposure to national symbols and slogans,[94] serves as both adhesive and lubricant. It holds people together when the state faces threat, and furnishes a basis for trust of one's fellow citizens that helps routinize everyday social, political, and economic interactions.[95] It overrides more particularistic loyalties, reduces intra-national ethnic tensions of all kinds, and fosters support for redistribution.[96]

National identities emerge from common allegiance to some unifying object or image. In "Nationalism," for example, Isaiah Berlin argued that national identity could only exist where society "carr[ies] an image of itself as a nation, at least in embryo, in virtue of some general unifying factor or factors – language, ethnic origin, a common history (real or imaginary)."[97] The rational basis of such imagery might remain "articulate in the minds of the better educated and more socially and historically minded," but dissolve to little more than an emotional vestige in the "consciousness of the bulk of the population." Nonetheless, that vestige can be a powerful basis for collective action and individual political choice.

In their quest to shape people's conceptions of their nation and foster allegiance to it, nationalist movements forge national identities that have multiple interlocking dimensions. Normative dimensions of national identity include beliefs about the nation's origins and mission – notions of what Berlin calls "what we are" – and schematic ideas about its members' defining attributes – notions of Berlin's "who we are." These beliefs function as a benchmark for categorizing both people and also ideas, actions, norms, and symbols into "ours" and "theirs," American and foreign (or un-American). They give the nation meaning not only by delineating its human boundaries but also its ideational and symbolic ones. Affective dimensions of national identity include patriotism, pride, and loyalty to the nation and its "true" members.[98] These emotions go hand-in-hand with the cognitive dimensions of national identity: positive feelings are directed toward national symbols, values, and fellow ingroup members; negative feelings or indifference flow toward what is alien.

Broadly, the positive feelings that accompany national identity can be divided into two kinds of attachments. *Horizontal attachment* refers to allegiance to the nation's members – an impulse to favor those who are categorized as fellow members of the national ingroup over those outside the "Circle of We." The emotional bonds of solidarity and altruism are what tie co-nationals to one another. Political choices that stem from feelings of horizontal attachment are group-centric because they are premised on co-identification among group members and favoritism for "us" over "them." *Vertical attachment*, on the other hand, refers to allegiance to the nation's symbols, including love of the flag and the country in the abstract, as well as its institutions, values, and ideals. Political choices premised on vertical attachment are not group-centric, as we have defined the term. Attachments to norms, institutions, or symbols that are associated with the group need not engage or precipitate feelings of solidarity with, or favoritism for, fellow group members.

There is naturally a good deal of overlap between normative understandings of "us" and "ours." A nation that enshrines hard work as an American value, for example, is also likely to view hard work as a personal marker of a "true American." But there are at least three reasons not to assume, as a general matter, that identifying *as* American also entails strong identification *with* other Americans. First, the sources of horizontal and vertical attachments may differ or be given different weight. Learning that an immigrant celebrates American holidays and roots for the national team in the Olympics may foster a strong sense of horizontal attachment even if neither of these things is seen as a particularly important duty associated with being American. Learning that an immigrant votes regularly in elections may not do much, in and of itself, to foster communal solidarity even though it is widely seen as an important American civic duty. The degree of overlap between schemas of "true Americans" and American values and symbols is an empirical question, not something that can be assumed. Second, and relatedly, attachments to a set of symbols and ideals may be stronger than feelings of ingroup solidarity with the masses of faceless others in the national community who are presumed also to cherish and abide by them. Third, even if the same symbols do promote horizontal and vertical attachments similarly, the relevance of each type of attachment to a particular political choice may not be equal. One may be guided more powerfully in forming issue opinions by a commitment to "Americanism," understood as a set of beliefs and values, than by horizontal attachments to fellow members of the national community. To underline these points, vertical attachments to national ideals, norms, or symbols may well be seen as entailing the *evenhanded* application of values associated with American national identity – the *refusal* to bend the rules in order to favor fellow members of the national ingroup over those who do not evoke feelings of solidarity and fellowship.[99]

This distinction between political choices grounded in attachment to national symbols and ideals and those motivated by ingroup favoritism for fellow members of the national community closely parallels the distinction others have drawn between "constructive patriotism," or "critical patriotism," and chauvinism.[100] Patriotism means love of country, but, as the modifiers suggest, this kind of attachment can spur people to criticize their country when it acts in ways that are contrary to its own values. In the same way, vertical attachment to the nation may at times lead people to exclude those who are felt to be "our own" and include "the other" if this is what people understand American values to require. Chauvinism, by contrast, means "my country, right or wrong." In the same way, taken to an extreme, political choices that are motivated entirely by horizontal attachments to co-nationals would mean "my countrymen, right or wrong." A pure emphasis on vertical attachment, by contrast, could mean "my country's ideals, fellow or stranger."

In keeping with our emphasis on assessing the relative influence of civic fairness and group-centrism, we are mainly interested in national identity as horizontal attachment. The idea that – that a sense of national community based on emotional kinship helps determine both the tone and timbre of intergroup relations – is central to the American political tradition as far back (more or less) as the Federalist Papers.[101] This notion forms the backbone of communitarian political philosophy espoused in Michael Walzer's *Spheres of Justice* and Alisdair MacIntyre's *After Virtue*, among others.[102] It is also picked up in the literature on American political culture, starting with Tocqueville and winding its way through S. M. Lipset's *Political Man* and *The Politics of Unreason*, and Samuel Huntington's *Who Are We?* with many stops in between.[103]

Recourse to horizontal attachment also abounds in normative theory. Since the study of nationalism began in earnest, it has been widely accepted that its importance lies in the mutual obligation among co-nationals, and that its power comes "from an emotional identification with compatriots that can overcome the competing pull of self-interest."[104] The heart of this connection is almost uniformly assumed to be an emotional tie between ingroup members, and the absence of such a tie (or even hostility) directed outside. Sigmund Freud recognized this in pointing to the "growth of emotional ties between the members of a united group of people" as "the true source of its strength."[105] What constitutes a fair and sufficiently inclusive set of values, from a normative

The Prevailing View: Groups and Group Centrism 49

standpoint, is a matter of long-standing debate between proponents of liberal nationalist, liberal-multiculturalist, and constitutional-patriot schools of thought.[106] The common thread, however, is that shared values matter *because* they generate mutual identification. As such, we have much debate around optimal *bases* of such a tie without ever really questioning the need for it in the first place.[107] As philosopher David Miller puts it, "trust requires solidarity not merely within groups but across them, and this in turn depends upon a common identification of the kind that nationality alone can provide."[108]

Finally, social and political psychologists have followed suit and generally embraced the conception of national identity as a community by *and* of mutual identification. Deborah Schildkraut, for example, argues in a recent review essay that American national identity is usefully analyzed through the lens of Social Identity Theory (SIT).[109] Through this lens, some of the key forms and functions of national identity in shaping public opinion about immigration are fundamentally group-centric. One needn't even bring along all the baggage one might associate with the word "community." SIT's foundation in the "minimal group paradigm" points to mere categorization into groups – without any normative source of meaning, common origin, or other appendages – as a sufficient condition for ingroup favoritism and outgroup derogation. Good feelings flow toward those who match the image of co-national, and, under some circumstances, bad ones flow toward "outsiders." People derive self-esteem in part by enhancing the status of the nation. To be sure, nations define insiders and outsiders on the basis of deeply ingrained norms, but the invocation of SIT suggests that the central function of these norms, as they relate to political choice, is that they divide favored ingroup members from disfavored outgroup members. Virtually every scholarly treatment of national identity in public opinion published over the past two decades attributes at least part of its force to group-centrism and horizontal attachment.[110]

To be sure, the relationship between SIT (in its original formulation) and horizontal attachment depends on how one construes the ingroup favoritism that the original "minimal groups" experiments elicited. Yet those who have built on it have embraced the importance of horizontal attachment much more explicitly.[111] As Citrin and Sears put it in *American Identity and the Politics of Multiculturalism*, identities "have political relevance because they channel feelings of mutuality, obligation, and antagonism, delineating the contours of one's willingness to help others as well as the boundaries of support for policies allocating resources based on group membership."[112] Similarly, Cara Wong's *Boundaries of Obligation* is framed as being "explicitly focused on 'community,' defined as 'an image in the mind of an individual, of a group toward whose members she *feels a sense of similarity, belonging or fellowship*,'" and goes on to argue that "self-defined membership can lead to an interest in, and a commitment to, the well-being of all community members (and only community members), *regardless of one's own interests, values, and ideology*."[113] Another case in point is Elizabeth Theiss-Morse's *Who Counts as an American,* which emphasizes the importance of "feeling a sense of connection with and commitment to one's fellow nationals ... Even in a country such as the United States, people can feel attached to the American people and a sense of obligation to that group."[114] The emphasis varies by account. But most share a clear commitment to horizontal attachment *with* Americans and ingroup favoritism as a motive for policy choice, going well beyond the idea that Americans endorse a particular set of civic values because they believe it is their duty to do so *as* Americans.

From this point of view, to understand the mass public's immigration policy opinions, one should focus on popular conceptions of "who counts as an American" as a precursor to ingroup favoritism. These conceptions, which differ across and within nations, are multidimensional, involving multiple characteristics. They can include ascribed group memberships, backgrounds, and individual qualities – criteria that are clearly ethnic, racial, or otherwise nativist. Hence the overlap with group-centrist accounts that emphasize ethnicity. But most Americans at least claim to reject racial definitions of America that view whiteness as important to making someone a "true American," though large minorities also openly endorse Christianity or American nativity or ancestry as criteria. Far larger proportions of the public say that "attainable" criteria such as feeling American, believing in American values, participating in politics, working hard, speaking English[115], and respecting the country's laws and institutions are important to making someone part of the American national ingroup. These "attainable" criteria imply that people can join the nation by assimilating in various ways – including, though crucially not limited to, functional and formal assimilation. In the group-centrist view, assimilation matters in public opinion about immigration because it is the way in which immigrants bridge the gap between their initial outsider status and their gradual integration as members of the national community. By assimilating and becoming "one of us," immigrants can come to evoke feelings of horizontal attachment that promote support for expansionary policies that increase immigrant admissions or expand immigrant rights. Those who are perceived not to have assimilated enough to join the "Circle of We" do not evoke these feelings of shared identity and communal belonging. To the extent that they seem to threaten the status, interests, or integrity of the national "we," they inspire hostility and promote support for restrictive policies.

CIVIC FAIRNESS AND GROUP-CENTRISM: THREE QUESTIONS

Which Predominates?

To a considerable extent, group-centrism and civic fairness are not mutually exclusive and, as we pointed out in Chapter 1, are often intertwined. The first question that we will probe in the coming chapters is which type of influence usually predominates when Americans form opinions about immigration

Civic Fairness and Group-Centrism: Three Questions

policy? Another way of putting this is to ask to what extent group-centrism and civic fairness bound one another's influence on public opinion. How powerfully do group-centric influences anchor citizens' opinions about different facets of policy? How much do opinions about different types of policies respond to the values that are at stake, over and above the influence of group-centrism?

The existing literature has not grappled much with this question. There has been little sustained effort to examine the strength of group-centric bases of opinion *against* norms and values when the two create tension. Instead, the main theoretical tussle in the research literature is between sociopsychological theories and economic accounts that emphasize narrow self-interested concerns about job loss, wage depression, and fiscal burden. This may have been warranted when *homo economicus* constituted the prevailing view of how people thought about immigration, as was the case in the 1980s and 1990s. But if a recent review of the literature was correct in dubbing egocentrism a "zombie theory,"[116] continuing to argue for group-centrism *as a stronger force than self-interest* is beating an undead horse. Group-centrism now sits virtually unchallenged as the default explanation for all things immigration. So the time has come to reckon with the degree to which it really does constrain and taint opinions that are widely defended on the basis of appeals to values. We will approach this question by pitting these two perspectives against one another as competing, though not mutually exclusive, explanations for the attitudinal ambivalence we highlighted at length in Chapter 1.

In this regard, we aim to take the literature on public opinion about immigration in a direction that some other areas of public opinion research have already gone. For example, general principles have been a central and ongoing debate in research on public tolerance for free expression.[117] As the prior discussion would suggest, the domain of race-conscious policies such as affirmative action, busing, and government aid to blacks has also inspired a lively debate (and something of a bitter stalemate) between those who view racial prejudice as the dominant influence and those who assert that widespread opposition among whites to latter-day civil rights initiatives is attributable to a significant degree to "traditional" values, including those such as individualism and suspicion of large government that are part and parcel of the liberal tradition.[118] Our view is that these debates, even if unresolved, have been fruitful. They have revealed important aspects of public opinion about these topics that would not have been evident if research on values and group-centrism had proceeded on separate tracks.

Does Group-Centrism Subvert Civic Fairness?

In the limited cases where researchers have focused on the relative influence of values and ethnic group-centrism on public opinion about immigration, they have sometimes implied that citizens' pretensions to principled judgment are "suspect."[119] In these cases, the empirical evidence gathered to date is ambiguous and sometimes contradictory – convincingly establishing that group attitudes influence immigration policy opinions but not showing that these influences override or distort the way that citizens respond to cues related to assimilationist norms or egalitarian or humanitarian goals at stake in a policy choice.

Recent research adapting the symbolic racism model, itself originally developed to explain whites' opposition to race-targeted policies as a manifestation of deep-seated prejudice against blacks, is a case in point.[120] Todd Hartman and colleagues (2014) show that whites punish Latino immigrants more than white immigrants even when the infraction is the same. This may be evidence of an ethnic double standard but not one that necessarily rules out the sincere application of values to these opinions. For one thing, as the authors themselves point out, their experiments also reveal great antipathy toward European immigrants who violate norms of law-abidingness and English proficiency. But even beyond that, the authors' experiments cannot determine whether the information that immigrants have violated a given norm is applied inconsistently to immigrants from different ethnic backgrounds. This is because the authors do not measure the degree of support that immigrants from different ethnic backgrounds enjoy at baseline or when they are stipulated to have *complied* with these norms. Therefore, some whites may bring an ethnic bias to bear on their choices regardless of any norm violation, but the great majority may be putting a premium on norm compliance that is independent of immigrants' ethnic backgrounds. The experimental design cannot fully establish the contention that punitive reactions to violations of norms are being applied insincerely as a way of rationalizing discrimination against Latinos.

Similarly, Efrén Pérez makes a persuasive and novel case that implicit attitudes toward Latinos are strongly linked to whites' opinions about immigration.[121] But Pérez is on less firm footing in relegating values to the function of post hoc rationales rather than true influences on opinion formation. There is no evidence in Pérez's analyses that values people actually invoke to justify their positions are insincere or that their application to questions of immigration policy is subverted by implicit ethnic bias.

We will have much more to say about these studies and the interpretive issues they raise in Chapter 5. For now, the point is that otherwise strong research on the role of unacknowledged prejudice against Latinos makes some questionable claims about how often group-centrism distorts the sincere application of values to immigration policy choices.

Are All Group-Related Influences Indicative of Group-Centrism?

To up the ante a bit, some of the empirical patterns commonly invoked to support group-centrist theories of public opinion about immigration are more ambiguous than is usually appreciated. In such cases, it is clear that there is a relationship between attitudes about social groups and opinions about immigration policy. But this alone does not prove that the psychological mechanism assumed to be at work actually is, especially if a civic fairness-based interpretation is also plausible. We consider two examples: the role of bias against Latinos and the interpretation of the importance of assimilationist norms in opinions about immigration policy as a manifestation of group-centrism predicated on feelings of horizontal attachment toward immigrants who are perceived to be fellow members of the national community. The differences between the civic fairness and group-centrist accounts of these cases can be subtle, but they are empirically tractable and carry major theoretical and practical implications.

Anti-Latino Bias

Much recent research on the sources of Americans' immigration policy opinions uses survey experiments that randomly prime ethnicity or vary the ethnic background of a hypothetical immigrant, sometimes along with other attributes. People's negative reactions to cues about Latino ethnicity are often taken as prima facie evidence that immigration policy judgments emerge out of deep-seated animus toward Latinos as a group. But they may also reflect stereotypes functioning in a more heuristic, albeit still prejudicial, fashion, which is to say *not* anchored to such animus. Since Latino immigrants are stigmatized in mass media as less likely to conform to the standards of functional and formal assimilation, Americans will widely read these kinds of personal qualities into Latino ethnicity if they have no information to supersede or counteract the stereotype. If so, one could maintain that prejudice plays an important role in the formation of opinions about immigration policy without necessarily concluding that the root motivation at work is group-centric in the sense that those who apply prejudice against Latinos necessarily care about the relative status or interests of racial groups per se.

This is akin to the distinction economists have drawn between "taste-based" and "statistical" discrimination in labor markets.[122] Taste-based discrimination is an end in itself. The intent, conscious or not, is to discriminate on the basis of race (or some other characteristic). Statistical discrimination is a means to an end. Those who engage in it believe that race or some other basis of discrimination is predictive of other qualities that they really care about. For example, there are concerns that forbidding employers from soliciting information about a job applicant's criminal record could lead employers who would otherwise have no inclination to engage in biased hiring practices to discriminate on the basis of race because race is predictive of criminal record in the United States. Statistical discrimination is predicated on beliefs about the way that social base rates vary by group rather than a particular desire to enhance the status of one's own group or harm members of another.

Group-centrist accounts of immigration that focus on prejudice against particular groups as a source of public opinion about immigration usually allege that ethnic biases in the public's policy preferences stem from a "taste" for immigrants of one racial background and a distaste for others. The role of stereotyping within the civic fairness framework is more consistent with "statistical" discrimination, with the important caveat that people often carry quite distorted notions of the actual base rates at which immigrants from different groups conform to their conceptions of civic fairness. For example, Americans may widely believe that Latino immigrants are less likely to be employed than whites or Asians. As a result, absent any stipulation that counteracts this stereotype, Americans are likely to engage in "statistical discrimination" against Latino immigrants. The motivation in such cases would not necessarily be to preserve white supremacy or keep a disliked racial group out or down but to choose policies that conform to individualist values, albeit (perhaps unwittingly) by using what the psychologist Philip Tetlock and colleagues call a "forbidden base rate."[123] Both views agree that ethnic stereotypes play an important role as "intermediary" in opinion formation. Group-centrism sees these stereotypes as the link between deep-seated group animosities and immigration policy opinions. Civic fairness sees them as a link between values and these same opinions. The existence of ethnic biases in some circumstances cannot alone adjudicate between these two interpretations.

The group-centrist interpretation of anti-Latino bias is ill-equipped to reckon with an important empirical anomaly: the degree to which survey experiments find bias against Latino immigrants varies dramatically from study to study even when the method of administration and the sample of respondents are similar.[124] As we show in Chapter 5, the civic fairness framework provides a compelling explanation for why this is so. These studies vary in the amount of additional information they give about immigrants' functional and formal assimilation, in effect altering the heuristic worth of automatic stereotyping as a guide to whether a policy conforms to standards of civic fairness. This pattern has not been mentioned in previous research, but such variability is consistent with the civic fairness interpretation of ethnic biases and not well accounted for by group-centrism.

Horizontal Attachment and National Community

Those who study immigration from the standpoint of national identity have also identified empirical patterns potentially consistent with either civic fairness or group-centrism but interpreted them largely through a group-centrist lens. These accounts suggest that Americans' support for assimilation and reliance on other values associated with American identity is predicated on feelings of social solidarity directed at those of "them" who have joined the national "Circle of We," a powerful group identity for most Americans. Leading studies of multiculturalism in American public opinion, for example, focus on the relative influence of different types of group attachments – how citizens tend to prioritize and balance attachments to their ethnic groups and to the nation.[125] The question in these studies is which attachment predominates, rather than how citizens manage instances in which their values and attachments to social groups push in different directions.

What has not received much systematic attention is whether assimilationist conceptions of American national identity influence policy choice because they engender horizontal attachments (group-centrism) or because they are linked to values that are strongly rooted in American political culture (civic fairness). As we noted previously, there are many cases in which these perspectives lead to equivalent empirical expectations. But there are other important cases in which such equivalence cannot be assumed.

Group-centrist interpretations of support for assimilation and its relationship to public opinion about immigration cite as evidence the links between individual conceptions of what makes someone a "true American" and the attitudes that people express vis-à-vis immigrants who are perceived to meet these criteria or fail to meet them. Simply put, such conceptions are usually read as indicating the outer limits of the mutual fellow-feeling and obligation people associate with the national community. Yet as we show in Chapter 6, these conceptions may also simply indicate on what basis people would judge which immigration policy choices are fair, irrespective of any feelings of shared group identity with those who conform or animus toward those who do not "belong" within the national ingroup.

Summary

As Jens Hainmueller and Daniel Hopkins have pointed out, attitudes about social aggregates – especially race and nation – are unquestionably tied to opinions about immigration, but it is less clear what theoretical significance these relationships have.[126] Researchers have tended to assume that they indicate a strong bent toward group-centrism. But this is only one possible interpretation. Although ethnic biases in Americans' immigration policy opinions may stem from deep-seated prejudice against particular immigrant groups, they may also reflect the heuristic use of ethnicity as an (often incorrect) informational source. Links between civic conceptions of American national identity and immigration policy opinions may indicate that people are using values to categorize immigrants into a "favored us" and "disfavored them," or that people use civic values as procedural rules regardless of their feelings of shared identity with the immigrants who would be affected. Digging more deeply into these correlations is essential if we are to understand what is really driving them.

WHERE GROUP-CENTRISM AND CIVIC FAIRNESS COLLIDE:
SIX HYPOTHESES

To probe further, our approach throughout is to examine the choices that Americans make between policy alternatives in the common instances where civic fairness and group-centrism are in tension. These tensions arise in the informational cues embedded in the articulation of poll questions about immigration. In Chapter 1, we looked at the wide range of responses that different types of immigration policy questions elicit, arguing that these differences were predicated on the cues embedded in these questions. We can also vary these cues experimentally by altering the description, framing, or information provided along with a poll question. This allows us to isolate the cues that are influencing citizens' choices and to manufacture different types of direct collisions between group-centrism and civic fairness.

What kinds of group cues and civic fairness cues are we talking about specifically? At the most basic level, the mere mention of "immigration" or "immigrants" is a clear group cue that the policy issue in question will affect a foreign "them." People doubtless tend to make assumptions about the group identities of these foreigners. We can accentuate, focus, and – crucially – control this type of information by attaching explicit group cues pertaining to immigrants' ethnic background or national origin. We cue aspects of civic fairness using information that bears on the indicators of formal assimilation, functional assimilation, humanitarianism, and egalitarianism summarized in the middle column of Table 2.1. These may include references to functional assimilation with words such as "job" and "English" or formal assimilation with references to legal status or citizenship. Cues about formal assimilation imply distinctions in status that therefore provide information about the implications of a policy for egalitarian ideals. References to immigrants' well-being, their family unity, or their vulnerability to oppression or violence would be considered cues about humanitarian values.

If we are correct that Americans routinely apply values even to policies that clearly pertain to broad swaths of foreigners or nonwhites or that refer to or imply an impact on a particular ethnic group, cues about how policies relate to liberal assimilationist, egalitarian, and humanitarian goals should have pronounced effects on citizens' choices, over and above any responsiveness to the stipulated or presumed ethnic identity of the immigrants who would be affected by them. Therefore, our first hypothesis is that *cues about civic fairness will influence citizens' choices between immigration policy alternatives even when direct or indirect ethnic group cues are also present.* All else equal, information that indicates that a policy satisfies the norms of functional assimilationism or meets humanitarian or egalitarian goals should bolster public support. Information that indicates a policy is out of keeping with these goals or at odds with the requirements of formal assimilation will lower support. It would certainly be difficult to mount a case for the centrality of civic fairness versus group-centrism if cues tied to the former have little impact on policy opinions, or if this influence is greatly diminished when group cues are provided.

Moreover, the way that citizens respond to these cues should vary according to their predispositions to prioritize some values over others. Our second hypothesis is therefore that *measures of citizens' commitments to values that are linked to civic fairness should (a) predict differences in people's policy stances (i.e., identify the sorts of people who might wish to reduce legal intakes but still support a path to citizenship, or vice versa) and (b) moderate the effects of informational treatments that amplify the values at stake, such that those with high levels of abstract commitment to values associated with civic fairness are also most responsive to treatments that evoke them.* Once again, these effects should be present even if ethnic cues are either held constant or independently varied by design. And they should hold even when we control for people's racial attitudes and other factors that might be correlated both with their endorsement of particular abstract values and immigration policy opinions. Making some allowance for the imperfect way we measure values, the civic fairness framework is on thin ice if we find little correspondence between measures of abstract values and reliance on theoretically pertinent civic fairness cues.

A third hypothesis makes the stronger claim that *the effect of informational cues related to civic fairness is unmoderated by the presence of group cues.* A less technical way of putting this is that civic fairness judgments are not formed selectively depending on the ethnic background of the immigrants in question. This hypothesis is opposed to the claim advanced in some research on symbolic racism and implicit prejudice against Latinos that values are being applied insincerely so as to rationalize policy choices that were really crafted on the basis of favoritism for some groups and dislike of others. Finding that the weight people place on civic fairness cues varies a great deal depending on the availability of particular group cues would constitute evidence against this hypothesis.

These three hypotheses, taken together, constitute the basis on which the civic fairness framework resolves the puzzle that we began with in Chapter 1: If public opinion about immigration policy is supposed to be formed group-centrically, and the political world reinforces these tendencies, why are people's policy opinions so mixed? To illustrate this point, we tailor our studies to gauge the effects of cues about civic fairness that also mimic distinctions between the types of policy issues that we took as our point of departure in Chapter 1. Chapter 3 examines how public responsiveness to cues about functional assimilation and humanitarian exigencies explain why Americans tend to want to restrict immigration in the abstract but are "operationally" accepting or even supportive of particular policies that entail large-scale legal admissions. It shows that cues about functional assimilation matter most to those with strongly individualistic values and that cues about alleviating human hardship and suffering matter most to humanitarians. Chapter 4 illustrates that legalistic and egalitarian values often cause citizens' opinions about legal admissions and the legalization of illegal immigrants to diverge. It zeroes in on how these values shape the emphasis that people place on legal status per se, often leading to categorical opinion.

Civic Fairness and What We Thought We Knew

Ethnic Bias

We noted that in some cases, group-centrist perspectives of anti-Latino prejudice lay claim to empirical patterns that civic fairness may explain at least as plausibly. We gave the example of ethnic biases in Americans' immigration policy choices. These biases obviously amount to ethnic discrimination in the most basic sense of the word, and to the extent that prejudice is defined as making inferences about individuals' personal qualities based solely on the groups they belong to, such biases are clear evidence of the influence of prejudice on policy opinions. Moreover, these inferences often rest on myths and misperceptions about demographic base rates. On all of these points, the civic fairness and group-centrist perspectives agree.

To the group-centrist view, however, these biases reflect deep-seated racial animus against particular stigmatized groups or groups that are perceived to pose the greatest threat to the majority or dominant racial group. The civic fairness perspective, on the other hand, interprets this type of discrimination as a result of heuristic processing of ethnic cues on the basis of prevalent group stereotypes, specifically in cases where superseding information to guide perceptions of civic fairness is unavailable. This latter claim is the crux of our fourth hypothesis, which we explore in Chapter 5: *Ethnic bias in survey experiments that vary hypothetical immigrants' ethnic backgrounds should dissipate when unambiguous information about civic fairness becomes available.* If the ethnic biases found in some studies (but not others) reflect deep-rooted beliefs about racial stratification or blind loyalty to one's own racial ingroup, they should persist or even increase, via motivated reasoning, when information becomes available that reduces the heuristic utility of the group cues. This would be evidence against Hypothesis 4.

Horizontal Attachments to "True Americans"

As noted, civic fairness and group-centrism offer different accounts about why American public opinion about immigration is so strongly keyed to assimilation. In the group-centrist view, assimilation matters *because* it determines whether immigrants are categorized as favored members of the national "Circle of We" or disfavored outsiders. Civic fairness instead roots the importance of liberal assimilationist norms in underlying values. People respond to cues about formal and functional assimilation because it addresses concerns related to the values of individualism and legalism. These value criteria are applied irrespective of whether people "identify with" immigrants in a social sense.

These accounts make distinct predictions about how people will make immigration policy choices. The group-centrist account predicts that cues about assimilation that powerfully engender horizontal attachment will also strongly influence policy choices and that cues about assimilation that do not engender horizontal attachment will not strongly influence policy choices. The civic

Where Group-Centrism and Civic Fairness Collide

fairness account, on the other hand, anticipates that *cues about formal and functional assimilation will influence policy opinions even if they do not engender feelings of horizontal attachment; moreover, cues about other dimensions of assimilation that do not relate closely to individualistic and legalistic values will at most weakly influence policy opinions even if they do promote horizontal attachment.* This two-part expectation is our fifth hypothesis, which we test in Chapter 6.

The group-centrist and civic fairness perspectives also make different predictions about what kinds of people will be most predisposed to apply civic criteria to immigration policy opinions. If it is true that citizens apply values to immigration policy choices as a way of supporting subjectively defined members of the national ingroup, then these values should matter more to people who themselves most strongly identify with the nation. Categorizing an immigrant as "one of us" should more strongly engender feelings of horizontal attachment among people who also see this "us" as an important social identity. Thus, the group-centrist view anticipates that assimilationist norms of American identity will be more powerfully tied to immigration policy opinions among those who strongly identify with the American nation than among those who weakly identify with it. On the other hand, the civic fairness perspective sees formal and functional assimilation as distinctively important and maintains that their importance is tied to values and overrides feelings of horizontal attachment. Consequently, our sixth hypothesis is that *support for norms of functional and formal assimilation will be have a strong influence on immigration policy opinions regardless of an individual's attachment to the American*

TABLE 2.2 *Summary of hypotheses*

Hypothesis #	Empirical Expectation	Chapters
1	Civic fairness cues influence policy opinions (people respond to information about the values at stake)	3, 4, 5, 6
2	Values moderate effect of civic fairness cues (value prioritization as individual-level predisposition)	3, 4, 6
3	Presence of ethnic cues does not alter effect of civic fairness cues (even-handedness)	4, 5, 6
4	Civic fairness cues mitigate effects of ethnic cues (statistical, not taste based, discrimination)	5
5	Cues about functional and formal assimilation strongly influence policy opinions even if they only weakly affect horizontal attachment; cues about other dimensions of assimilation only weakly influence policy opinions even if they strongly affect horizontal attachment	6
6	Support for norms of formal and functional assimilation influence policy opinions irrespective of one's attachment to the nation	6

nation. As we elaborate in Chapter 6, some caution is in order here because we are hypothesizing the absence of a significant interaction between personal attachment to the nation and support for particular norms; the absence of evidence for such a relationship is certainly not evidence of absence.

In short, Chapters 3, 4, and 5 test how citizens navigate situations in which ethnic identities and values cross-pressure each other. Chapter 6 corroborates the general patterns discussed in Chapters 3 and 4 but also tests how citizens react when they identify *with* immigrants who do not meet the criteria of formal assimilation and when they do not feel a sense of shared community with those who do. Table 2.2 summarizes these six hypotheses. All six reflect the idea that the values that shape most citizens' conceptions of civic fairness tend to override the influence of group-centrism when the two come into direct conflict. In this sense, these values reflect the idea that the "American ethos," with its rationalistic appraisal of available information and its moralistic elevation of values over prejudices and group loyalties, guides most Americans' opinions about immigration policy.

We have covered a great deal of ground in this chapter. We started by establishing the main claims we make on behalf of the civic fairness model, and followed by discussing what particular values we placed under that banner and why. We then considered group-centrist accounts of immigration attitudes, and the relationship between these and civic fairness. We ended by deriving six hypotheses about what ought to happen when the two perspectives collide. Now it remains to test them.

3

Functional Assimilation, Humanitarianism, and Support for Legal Admissions

There is little doubt that, in the abstract, Americans are wary about the number of immigrants coming into the United States.[1] Gallup began asking in 1965 whether the level of immigration should be increased, decreased, or kept the same. For most of the last half century, support for increasing immigration hovered in the single digits or low teens. As of 2019, it has never exceeded 30%.[2] Wariness about rising levels of immigration is evident even when surveys clarify that they are asking about *legal* rather than illegal immigration, a distinction to which we return at length in Chapter 4. For example, a Fox News[3] poll conducted in April 2013 asked a national sample "Do you think the United States should increase or decrease the number of LEGAL immigrants allowed to move to this country?" The majority, 55%, said the number should be decreased, compared to 28% who said it should be increased, with 10% volunteering that the number should not be change and 7% unsure. These numbers were little changed from earlier polls conducted in 2007 and 2010, though other time series do show marked increases in support for preserving and even increasing legal admissions in the last several years.[4] Despite recent rises in public support for increasing immigration and drops in support for decreasing it, Peter Schuck's pithy phrase remains true of a broad cross-section of the public: "Americans do not oppose immigration in principle, in general, or unalterably, but they do want less of it (or at least no higher)."[5]

Yet this abstract wariness readily gives way once we start considering specific policies and eligibility criteria. Schuck notes that "even here, [Americans] are open to argument and evidence about what the levels and mix should be." For example, a Fox News[6] poll from December 2011 revealed that 63% of Americans favored increasing legal immigration "as long as they agree to work, pay taxes, and obey the law." An April 2013 Gallup Poll[7] found that 52% of Americans would support a law "creating a work visa

61

program that allows a specified number of immigrants into the United States each year to work at generally lesser-skilled jobs." And, finally, research by Irene Bloemraad and colleagues finds that appeals to family resonate strongly in public opinion about immigration, including among conservatives.[8]

The disjuncture between what we might call "abstract restrictivism" versus "operational openness" is the central puzzle of this chapter. Our explanation is that specific policy questions more readily prime Americans to think about civic fairness and reassure them that a given policy keeps these considerations front and center. Put another way, functional assimilation – expectations that immigrants learn English and hold a job – and humanitarian values turn out to be paramount in structuring public opinion about legal admissions policy. More to the point here, they help explain why Americans are relatively more open when it comes to policy particulars than they are about immigration in the abstract.

The evidence supports this argument even when group cues are available and survey respondents know that their support for particular policies will raise (or at any rate not reduce) overall immigration levels. We also examine whether segments of the population whose opinions prior research suggests ought to be constrained by group loyalties or animosities – prejudiced whites and racial minorities – respond to the informational treatments we present. Finally, we explore, using recent case studies of salient immigration policy controversies, whether the public reactions that surface when immigration controversies come to the fore tend to revert to blanket restrictionism or hew to civic fairness.

CIVIC FAIRNESS AND SUPPORT FOR INCREASING IMMIGRATION FROM MEXICO

As the first order of business, we want to see whether information about functional assimilation influences opinions about legal immigration policy and whether this is true even when it is obvious that a policy will accelerate racial change. We further assess whether a humanitarian appeal can counteract opinions that those who might not meet the criteria of functional assimilation, and could compete with American workers to boot, should be kept out. To this end, we had 2,100 respondents in a Lucid Labs national Internet survey conducted between April 30 and May 1, 2018, participate in a randomized experiment that solicited opinions about a policy proposal that would admit an additional 100,000 immigrants from Mexico each year.[9] By making the policy explicitly about Mexico, we fix the ethnic cue for all participants in the study, and eliminate the possibility that assumptions about which ethnic groups are more likely to meet civic fairness criteria are driving our results.

Experimental Design

Respondents in the experiment were randomly assigned to one of six versions of the question. Those in the *control* condition of the experiment were asked the following question:

A nonpartisan commission has recommended increasing the number of legal immigrants allowed to come to the United States from Mexico each year by 100,000. Would you support or oppose this proposal?

In keeping with prior polling on support for increasing immigration, we expected significant public division on this proposal. Recent national polls have found the public roughly evenly split over whether to keep the level of legal immigration the same, reduce it, or increase it, with pluralities supporting neither an increase nor a decrease.[10] Our allusion to a "nonpartisan commission" might boost support if people found the recommendation reputable. On the other hand, support for *increasing* legal immigration, let alone by a very large number, is, as we have noted, a minority position in most polls.

Respondents in the *functional assimilation (FA)* condition were given the same question but also told that "In order to be admitted, these immigrants would have to agree to work, support themselves financially, and learn English." Support for the policy should be higher here, because respondents are reassured that the policy takes functional assimilation seriously. A third set of respondents, assigned to the *FA+one-sided negative* condition, were given an explicit rationale to reject the policy – that "critics of the proposal say that these immigrants might take jobs from Americans or use welfare" – and no additional argument in favor. This argument provides two common points raised against increasing immigration, one of which directly challenges the idea that the additional immigrants would be economically self-supporting. We included this to test the strength of the *FA* cue in the face of a common counterargument. Perhaps reassurance about functional assimilation would bolster support for the policy but so weakly that such a counter would erase this effect. Or if supportive reactions to the *FA* condition primarily reflected social desirability pressures, the counterargument would allay these concerns by indicating that there is ostensibly reasoned opposition to the commission's proposal. Certainly, if people's opinions about whether to increase the level of immigration were firmly anchored in animus toward foreigners or dislike of Latino immigrants in particular, we would expect limited effects of the *FA* cue alone and that these effects would be overpowered by the opposing argument.

A fourth set of respondents in the *negative* condition were randomly assigned a version of the question that made no reassurances about functional assimilation – that is, no reference to the immigrants' agreeing to work, provide for themselves, and learn English – but did include the counterargument to the effect that the immigrants might take jobs from Americans or end up using welfare. Intuitively, we expected that this one-sided argument would reduce support for the policy proposal, unless the concerns articulated in the argument were already "baked in" to opposition in the *control* condition or respondents widely regarded these possible consequences as unlikely or relatively unimportant.

Including the *negative* condition also provided a benchmark against which to gauge the power of cues about another aspect of civic fairness, namely the humanitarian goals of alleviating human suffering or keeping families together. To do this, a fifth set of respondents, in the *refugee* condition, were told that:

A non-partisan expert commission has recommended increasing the number of legal immigrants allowed to come to the United States from Mexico each year by 100,000 to protect innocent people whose lives are threatened by violent drug cartels. In order to be admitted, these immigrants would have to demonstrate that their own safety or the safety of their families is in serious danger.

The respondents were then given opposing arguments. The negative argument was the same as that included in the *negative* and *FA+negative* conditions. The positive argument accentuated the humanitarian goals of the policy. It stated that "Supporters of the proposal say that Americans must not turn a blind eye when innocent people are tortured or killed through no fault of their own." We expected this humanitarian rationale would substantially boost support for the policy over the *negative* condition. This would bolster the idea that many Americans set aside reservations about large-scale immigration and potential abrogation of the assimilationist "contract" (e.g., that immigrants might become dependent on welfare) if they are encouraged to think about the policy along humanitarian lines. Those determined for group-centric reasons to oppose the policy, however, were given the kind of ammunition needed to do so without appearing racist.

Finally, a sixth group of respondents were assigned to the *family* condition, which was similar to the *refugee* condition except that it gave family reunification as the rationale for admitting an additional 100,000 immigrants from Mexico each year. The respondents were told that "in order to be admitted, these immigrants would have to be sponsored by a sibling, parent, or adult son or daughter who is a U.S. citizen," categories that currently account for hundreds of thousands of green cards issued each year but are subject to quotas that exempt minor children and spouses. Respondents in this condition were also given accurate background information about the long backlogs in processing family-based visas due to caps on the total number of immigrants accepted from each country:

U.S. citizens who legally sponsor their close relatives to immigrate to the U.S. often wait more than 10 years for them to receive a visa because of restrictions on annual immigration from each country ... Supporters of the proposal say that we should reduce the amount of time that U.S. citizens have to wait in order to be reunited with their families.

Proponents of cutting the level of such family-based immigration have often, and now controversially, referred to it as "chain migration."[11] We opted to refer

Civic Fairness and Support for Increasing Immigration

clearly to family ties and backlogs so as to be clear about the basis on which these immigrants are admitted and one of the most commonly invoked rationales for preserving or increasing family-based admissions – that those who avail themselves of the opportunity to sponsor relatives often endure a long wait.

Again, the point is to test whether bringing to mind families evokes humanitarian considerations that counteract other concerns about mass immigration, including those that pertain to economic costs and functional assimilation, which we make explicit. Were our respondents strongly invested in curtailing immigration – and perhaps especially immigration from Mexico – based on anxiety over racial change or dislike of Latinos, they could easily reject this proposal on the ostensible basis that it would increase immigration and potentially lead to job loss or fiscal drain and dependency. But if these group-centric motivations were relatively weak compared to sympathy for naturalized immigrants who take the legal opportunity to sponsor their families to immigrate to the United States, we would expect this policy, so framed, to be widely supported.

Table 3.1 summarizes the treatment conditions in this experiment. Since each treatment layers a civic fairness cue onto the control, the differences in

TABLE 3.1 *Summary of treatment conditions*

Condition	Treatment
Control	A nonpartisan commission has recommended increasing the number of legal immigrants allowed to come to the United States from Mexico each year by 100,000. Would you support or oppose this proposal?
Functional assimilation (FA)	[Control +] In order to be admitted, these immigrants would have to agree to work, support themselves financially, and learn English.
FA+Negative	[FA +] Critics of the proposal say that these immigrants might take jobs from Americans or use welfare.
Negative	[Control +] Critics of the proposal say that these immigrants might take jobs from Americans or use welfare.
Refugee	[Negative +] to protect innocent people whose lives are threatened by violent drug cartels. In order to be admitted, these immigrants would have to demonstrate that their own safety or the safety of their families is in serious danger.
Family	[Negative +] In order to be admitted, these immigrants would have to be sponsored by a sibling, parent, or adult son or daughter who is a U.S. citizen. U.S. citizens who legally sponsor their close relatives to immigrate to the United States often wait more than 10 years for them to receive a visa because of restrictions on annual immigration from each country ... Supporters of the proposal say that we should reduce the amount of time that U.S. citizens have to wait in order to be reunited with their families.

average support for the policy in each condition furnish a straightforward test of Hypothesis 1 – that civic fairness cues strongly influence policy support, including in the presence of group cues.

Measures of Values

If we are correct about how these treatments engage the individualist underpinnings of support for functional assimilation and the humanitarian underpinnings of support for refugee and family-based admissions, we should observe their strongest effects among respondents who are predisposed to value such considerations. This is Hypothesis 2: Measures of support for values moderate the impact of civic fairness cues on policy support. To test this, much later in the survey and after many questions that were unrelated to immigration, we measured support for individualism and humanitarianism using two batteries of agree/disagree questions. The *individualism* scale included six agree/disagree questions, some of which were borrowed from the Pew Research Center and others of which we devised to measure the abstract valuation of hard work as a core element of economic individualism in America:

- Success is pretty much determined by forces outside our control.
- It is very important to work hard to get ahead in life.
- People should take care of themselves and their families by their own efforts.
- Those who are born poor cannot be expected to advance without the help of others.
- Hard work is a mark of a strong personal character.
- People who work very hard often lose sight of what is really important in life.

These items encompass the view that hard work is a reliable source of economic success, a normative imperative, and a desirable personal quality. They formed an acceptably reliable scale (Cronbach's alpha = .63), though items worded in different directions tended to be weakly intercorrelated. We created an additive index of these items and rescored it to range from 0 (least individualistic) to 1 (most individualistic). The mean of the scale was .64, indicating a strong overall bent toward individualism, but with considerable variation (sd = .16).

The *humanitarianism* scale was borrowed from a battery often included in the American National Election Study. It consists of four agree/disagree items:

- One should always find ways to help those less fortunate than oneself.
- It is best not to get too involved in taking care of other people's needs.
- People tend to pay more attention to the well-being of others than they should.
- A person should always be concerned about the well-being of others.

Civic Fairness and Support for Increasing Immigration

These items also formed a scale with acceptable reliability (alpha = .66), with weaker correlations once again between items worded in opposite directions. We created an additive index of the four items and rescored it to run from 0 (least humanitarian) to 1 (most humanitarian). This index again shows a strong bent toward humanitarian values, with a mean of .65, and considerable variation (sd = .19). Since they are only trivially correlated in our sample (r_{xy} = .08), *humanitarianism* and *individualism* indices clearly measure distinct constructs.

Ethnocentrism and Ethnic Identity

We also wanted to see whether these treatments mattered less among segments of the public most predisposed to group-centrism. Intuitively, one such group is ethnocentric whites. To measure ethnocentrism, we included two measures of stereotypes toward the end of the survey. We asked respondents to rate whites, blacks, Asians, and Hispanics on successive seven-point scales. The first set of scales asked them to place these groups on a scale from hard working to lazy. The second set ranged from intelligent to unintelligent. These are identically worded to stereotype items in the American National Election Study. Work ethic and intelligence stereotypes for these groups were strongly correlated among whites (.72 for ratings of blacks, .58 for Hispanics, .67 for whites, and .65 for Asians). The ethnocentrism scale among white respondents was constructed by taking the mean of whites' ratings of whites and subtracting from it the mean of whites' ratings of the three other groups.[12] The mean of the scale, rescored to run from −1 (least ethnocentric) to 1 (most ethnocentric) was slightly above zero (.02), with one-third of whites displaying at least some favoritism for their own group and a 35% scoring precisely at the midpoint of zero.

We also asked respondents to rate the importance of their racial or ethnic group to their own identity, with the wording of these single items also coming from the 2012 American National Election Study (ANES). Response options were extremely, very, moderately, slightly, and not important at all. Twenty percent of whites rated their ethnic or racial identity extremely important, with another 19% saying it was very important. The same figures for blacks were 52% and 21%, respectively (N = 264) and for Latinos 38% and 22% (N = 335). If these respondents are as attuned to the racial implications of mass immigration policy as group-centrist accounts suggest, they should display little responsiveness to our treatments. If, on the other hand, they are also focused on whether a policy is consistent with prevalent norms of civic fairness, they should also respond to the treatments in our experiment.

Results

As displayed in Figure 3.1, which depicts mean policy support for each treatment condition (with 95% confidence intervals for each estimate), the results

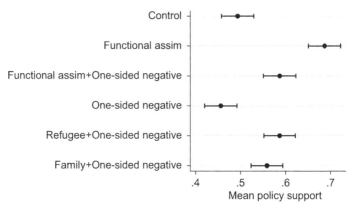

FIGURE 3.1 Mean support for policy to increase immigration from Mexico by 100,000 annually, by treatment condition
Note: The figure shows the estimated mean support, with 95% confidence intervals, for the policy proposal to expand immigration from Mexico by 100,000 annually in each treatment condition. The dependent variable is a five-point strongly support-strongly oppose measure, rescaled to run from 0 to 1 where 1 is most supportive. Full tabulations of the dependent variable in each treatment condition are provided in the Online Appendix.

handsomely align with all of our expectations. Policy support, the dependent variable, was measured on a five-point scale from strongly support to strongly oppose, which we rescored to run from strong opposition (0) to strong support (1). In the control condition, respondents were fairly evenly divided, with 41% in support and 38% opposed and a mean score of .49. The effect of adding a single phrase reassuring respondents that the large additional group of immigrants would be held to the standards of functional assimilation – self-sufficiency and learning English – is, in a word, enormous. With this proviso, respondents supported the bill overwhelmingly, 67% to 16%, with a mean of .69. Recall that this means that only one in six respondents even somewhat opposed a policy that would dramatically increase immigration from Mexico, down from nearly two in five in the control condition, as a result of the functional assimilation cue.

Nor did giving respondents an explicit reason for rejecting the proposal return the level of support to anywhere near baseline, let alone below it. Given the functional assimilation cue as well as the opposing argument, respondents still supported the proposal by 2–1, 56% to 28%, for a mean score of .59. Reminding people about some of the most common arguments for limiting immigration does significantly reduce support for the proposal, but the functional assimilation cue predominates just the same. Most respondents do not appear poised to latch on to arguments against a proposal to increase immigration that makes the sorts of stipulations about functional assimilation that our experiment offered. This is hardly the sort of reaction we would expect from a

Civic Fairness and Support for Increasing Immigration 69

public that weighs such proposals on the basis of xenophobia or racial threat. It is precisely the sort of reaction we would expect if, as we have argued, the predominant question in people's minds is whether a policy satisfies prevailing understandings of civic fairness, and functional assimilation in particular.

As expected, the negative argument by itself reduced support for the policy to 37% (and boosted opposition to 44%), though not significantly lower than baseline. This may mean that the negative considerations this argument makes explicit were already on many people's minds anyway, that those who were willing to support such a large increase at baseline either tend to find the argument not credible or believable but not so worrisome.

It is unambiguous that a great many Americans view the humanitarian goals that are central to refugee admissions and family-based admissions as sufficient reason to override whatever other considerations give them pause about large-scale immigrant admissions. Support for the policy in the *refugee* and *family* conditions, which include the negative argument and no reassurance about functional assimilation, rises a great deal over the *negative* condition, which provides this negative argument alone. The *refugee* policy garners 49% support to 27% opposition (mean = .59). The *family* policy is about equally popular, with 50% support and 29% opposition (mean = .56). Both of these are significantly higher than support for the policy in the *control* and *negative* conditions and comparable to the level of support among respondents who received the *FA* cue along with the counterargument. What this appears to illustrate is the power of humanitarian considerations that are part of many Americans' conceptions of civic fairness to override other concerns about large-scale immigration, including even when immigrants' functional assimilation is called into question (*negative*) or left to the imagination (*control*).

Moderation by Values Predispositions

We hypothesized that the effect of the *FA* cue would be larger among respondents with strong individualistic values. To test whether this was the case, we estimated an ordinary least squares regression on respondents assigned to the first four treatment conditions (i.e., not the *refugee* and *family*) in which the dependent variable was policy support and the independent variable was a dummy variable identifying the two treatment conditions in which the *FA* cue was provided (*FA* and *FA+negative*) – as opposed to the two in which it was not provided (*control* and *negative*) – interacted with the indices of humanitarianism and individualism.[13] The results are summarized in Figure 3.2. As a robustness check, we verified that the results did not change substantially in a saturated model where we also included controls for age, gender, education, race, Latino identity, and political party identification, liberal-conservative self-identification, and the average of the intelligence and laziness stereotype measures for each of the four racial groups we asked about, as well as the interaction of all of these with the treatment dummy. A full tabulation of both the sparser

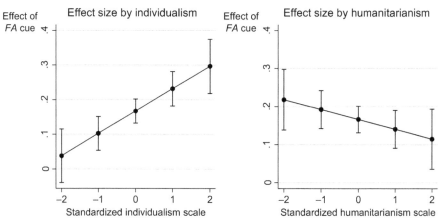

FIGURE 3.2 Effect of functional assimilation cue by individualism and humanitarianism
Note: The figure displays the estimated effect of the *functional assimilation* cue, pooling across the *FA* and *FA+negative* conditions as well as the pure *control* and *negative* conditions, for z-scores on the *individualism* and *humanitarianism* scales ranging from −2 to +2. The estimates are drawn from an OLS regression model in which the dependent variable is the measure of policy support and the regressors are the pooled treatment conditions interacted with both the *individualism* and *humanitarianism* scales. Full tabulated results from this regression analysis are provided in the Online Appendix.

model used to create the following figures and the more saturated model used as a robustness check is provided in the Online Appendix.

As hypothesized, more individualistic respondents were significantly more responsive to the *FA* cue, with a positive coefficient on the interaction term significant at p < .001. By contrast, more humanitarian respondents were, if anything, less swayed by the *FA* cue, though the interaction between humanitarian values and the *FA* dummy was not statistically significant. Figure 3.2 juxtaposes these patterns by plotting the estimated effect of the *FA* cue against a standardized measure of each value. Looking at the left-hand panel, one sees that respondents with little commitment to individualism were barely swayed by the stipulation that the immigrants would have to agree to learn English and provide for themselves. But among the most individualistic respondents, the effect of the *FA* cue was to boost support for the policy by nearly a third of the entire scale of the dependent variable.

We also expected that respondents with stronger humanitarian values would be more responsive to the *family* and *refugee* treatments relative to their baseline, the *negative* condition. We did not have any expectation that individualism would moderate responses to these treatments. As shown in the right-hand panel of Figure 3.3, respondents who score higher on the *humanitarianism* scale are indeed more swayed by these rationales for accepting a great

Civic Fairness and Support for Increasing Immigration

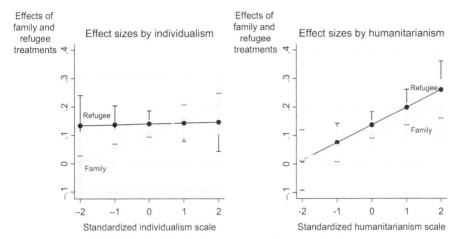

FIGURE 3.3 Effect of family and refugee treatments by individualism and humanitarianism
Note: The figure displays the estimated effect of the *refugee* and *family* cues, relative to the *negative* condition, for z-scores on the *individualism* and *humanitarianism* scales ranging from −2 to +2. The estimates are drawn from an OLS regression model in which the dependent variable is the measure of policy support and the regressors are a dummy variable indicating each of the treatment conditions (*family* and *refugee*) interacted with both the *individualism* and *humanitarianism* scales. Full tabulation of this regression analysis is provided in the Online Appendix.

deal more immigration than are respondents who score lower on the scale. The interaction between this measure and the *refugee* treatment effect relative to the *negative* condition is significant at p < .05, and the interaction between the *family* treatment effect relative to the *negative* condition is marginally significant at p = .06. The estimated effects of the *refugee* and family treatments on respondents who score 1 standard deviation below the mean on *humanitarianism* are both less than one-half the estimated effect on those who score 1 standard deviation above the mean on this scale.

By contrast, *individualism* does not moderate the effect of the *refugee* treatment at all, as shown by the black line in the left-hand panel of Figure 3.3. The most highly individualistic respondents are no more swayed by the humanitarian appeal than are the least individualistic. Interestingly, individualistic values *do* significantly moderate the effect of the *family* treatment. At first, this appears puzzling: why should individualists be especially responsive to such an appeal for an increase in immigration, especially against the backdrop of the *negative* argument that raises the specter that the immigrants might use welfare? On further inspection, the reason appears to be that individualism is correlated with conservative self-identification, and conservative self-identification heightens sensitivity to family-based appeals about immigration.[14] In a model that accounts for the distinctly supportive reactions of conservatives to such appeals, the moderation effect of individualism displayed in Figure 3.3 is more than cut in half and is no longer significant.[15]

In keeping with the first two hypotheses advanced in Chapter 2, it is clear that public support for a large-scale increase in legal admissions – even when a clear ethnic cue is provided – is highly responsive to civic fairness cues (Hypothesis 1). These cues communicate whether an immigration policy alternative is consistent with the liberal assimilationist contract that Americans widely endorse and whether it furthers humanitarian values as well as others we have given less consideration, such as family unity. As a result, we see the greatest effects of these informational cues among respondents who are most predisposed to value the individualistic underpinnings of liberal assimilationism in its thin, modern incarnation – which insists on self-sufficiency through hard work as a condition that immigrants are expected to meet – and the humanitarian rationales behind refugee policy (Hypothesis 2).

What about Those Predisposed to Group-Centrism?

Our survey allows us to test whether the treatment effects displayed in Figure 3.1 are smaller among prejudiced whites and among whites, blacks, and Latinos who rate their racial or ethnic identity especially important. To the extent that such people are motivated by group-centric considerations, our civic fairness cues should matter less for them. After all, every treatment condition solicits opinions about a massive *increase* in immigration from Mexico.

In fact, we find quite the opposite. Unsurprisingly, the 479 whites who scored above zero on the *prejudice scale* were a great deal more opposed to the idea of admitting an additional 100,000 immigrants from Mexico in the *control* condition (mean policy support = .27) than whites who did not (mean policy support = .53). There, the ethnic cue and the promise of many, many more foreigners admitted each year is about all that respondents had to go on in making their choice. But the effect of the FA cue on prejudiced whites (.26, $p < .000$) was at least as large as its effect on unprejudiced whites (.20, $p < .000$). Moreover, the *negative* cue reduced policy support by more among *unprejudiced* whites (-.07, $p < .01$) than among prejudiced ones (-.02, $p = .58$). Perhaps more surprisingly, even the *refugee* and *family* treatments boosted support by more among prejudiced whites (.19, $p < .000$ and .13, $p < .05$, respectively) than among unprejudiced whites (.10, $p < .01$ and .09, $p < .05$, respectively).

What about white ingroup identity? Whites' assessment of the importance of their own racial identity is only weakly correlated ($r = .27$) with *ethnocentrism*. But when we turn from outgroup animus to ingroup identification, the upshot remains much the same. At baseline, these respondents were much more opposed to the policy (mean policy support = .37) than were those who rated their racial identity at most somewhat important (.48). But they were again significantly more responsive to the FA cue (.26 versus .11, difference in effects

The Green Card Experiment

73

significant at p <.05) and about equally responsive to the *negative, family, and refugee* cues.

Nonwhites (N = 709) were more supportive than whites of the policy proposal at baseline by .16. Nonwhites' support for the policy was boosted by the *FA* cue by almost as much as that of whites, with an insignificant difference in the treatment effect of .05, and, if anything, more sharply reduced by the *negative* cue than whites' (difference in treatment effect = .07, p < .1). A strong sense of racial identity is associated with stronger policy support in the *control* condition, among nonwhites but there are no statistically significant differences in the effects of the treatments among nonwhites with high ethnic consciousness and low ethnic consciousness. Although policy support was high at baseline among the 204 minority group respondents who said that their ethnic identity was "extremely important" to them, the treatments nevertheless significantly influenced policy support in all of the ways that the civic fairness perspective would predict: the *FA* cue raised policy support by .12 (p < .01), the *negative* cue diminished it by .14 (p < .01), and the *refugee* and *family* treatments increased support over the *negative* baseline by .23 (p <. 01) and .17 (p < .05), respectively.

Our survey, conducted only in English, surely does not fully represent the US Latino public as a whole, and therefore does not permit definitive inferences about that group. But the picture does not change when we confine the analysis to Latinos in our sample (N = 291). The effect of the *FA* cue is positive and significant (.11, p <.05), of the *negative* cue negative and insignificant (–.05, p = .36), and of the *refugee* and *family* treatments both positive but only one marginally significant (.07, p = .30 and .12, p < .1, respectively). There is no evidence that the strength of Latinos' ethnic identity moderates any of these effects, though particular caution is in order due to small samples and correspondingly imprecise estimates.

With the many caveats we have issued in mind, what we can say is that the scope conditions of the civic fairness model appear quite wide as it pertains to the disjuncture between abstract restrictionism and operational expansionism. The two elements of mass perceptions of civic fairness that we have emphasized, functional assimilation and humanitarianism, go a long way to explaining why so many Americans who would like to see the number of immigrants reduced nonetheless support policies that would sustain or even increase the level of immigration. Strikingly, this is true not only of the public as a whole but of segments of the public that group-centrist theories of public opinion about immigration would expect to be most attentive to the ethnic cue that is held constant throughout the experiment or most reliant on their general attitudes about foreigners.

THE GREEN CARD EXPERIMENT

One possible criticism of the previous experiment is that the information and cues are artificial. Moreover, while the 100,000 figure is large, respondents may not fully appreciate the scale of the policy they are endorsing. In response to these concerns, we ask whether functional assimilation and humanitarianism operate similarly in a less contrived, and, some would say, heavy-handed environment. Put simply, we will strip away all explicit mention of ethnicity, civic fairness requirements, and counterarguments, leaving only questions about the bases on which people can legally immigrate to the United States. But we make it clear to people that they are weighing in on the very policies that produce the current admissions status quo.

Most "green cards" are allocated on the basis of three ostensible objectives of America's immigration policy established by the 1965 Hart-Celler Act, all of which are closely related to values associated with civic fairness: keeping families together, filling labor shortages, and giving the oppressed refuge from persecution. In recent years, more than two-thirds of the roughly 1 million visas issued per year go to those who have close relatives who are US citizens or legal permanent residents. Slightly under 15% go to immigrants who have skills that are supposedly in short supply in the US labor market. The number of refugees has fluctuated with presidential edict and international circumstances,[16] although to give an idea, approximately 15% of green cards in 2015 were awarded to provide a haven for those experiencing violence and political persecution in their home countries.

We ask whether simply making the official basis on which legal immigrants are admitted to the country more obvious to people dampens whatever restrictionist tendency they hold in the abstract. The idea is simply that most Americans, asked without any context, will consider only whether they "like" or "dislike" the idea of immigration in some general way. But if they are gently reminded about *why* we admit immigrants in the first place, this may encourage them to reconsider their opinion.

To investigate this, we assigned approximately 1,000 respondents on a national Internet survey fielded by Survey Sampling International (SSI) in the summer of 2013 either to receive the standard, general question about the level of immigration or to weigh in on more specific questions about whether the level of family, skilled, and refugee immigration should be increased, decreased, or kept the same.[17] This is about as subtle a way to prime civic fairness as we could conceive: unlike the previous study, there is no artificial policy to consider, nor is there any argumentation or mention of likely consequences. Rather, we are simply asking people about the different preference categories under a policy that currently exists, in order to assess whether this slight difference alone can help engage alternative sets of considerations about what immigration is for.

The results of the experiment are consistent with a theory that sees group-centrism as a source of constraint but not a firm anchor in the face of cues that relate a policy to considerations about functional assimilationism and humanitarianism. Figure 3.4 illustrates the share favoring an increase, decrease, or no change in response to each question, without information about the status quo.

The Green Card Experiment

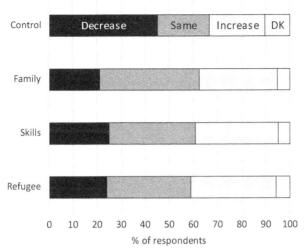

FIGURE 3.4 Response to the "Green Card Experiment"
Note: The figure displays the percentage of respondents in the 2013 SSI national survey Green Card Experiment who wanted to increase (a lot or a little), decrease (a lot or a little), or keep the same the level of immigration in each category. Respondents were randomly assigned to be asked the standard level of immigration question or all three of the more specific questions in random order. Full tabulations of these results can be found in Levy, Wright, and Citrin 2016.

The topmost bar corroborates the standard polling result about the overall level of immigration: in general, more Americans prefer reductions over increases. Yet public opinion also responds sharply to information about the basis on which immigrants would in fact be admitted. In each case, considerably more Americans favor increasing family, skilled, and refugee immigration than decreasing them. Again, this shift in opinion is produced merely by hinting at the actual economic and humanitarian aims of immigration policy, without making *any argument whatsoever* on one side or the other. In short, providing a clear civic or humanitarian rationale for immigration policy – precisely the rationales that justify the various visa categories in the first place – inverts a public of seeming restrictionists to one that is at least accepting of the (expansionary) status quo.

A random subset of our respondents received some background information about visa allocations and the proportion of visas allocated under each category in 2012. As it happens, informing people that they were weighing in on the three streams that account for approximately 95% of all legal immigration did not greatly weaken the impact of these cues. Those so informed still showed far less preference for decreasing immigration in each category than they did for decreasing immigration in the abstract. Instead, learning that family reunification is the dominant preference category appears to have

76   *FA, Humanitarianism, and Support for Legal Admissions*

prompted a large number of people to support rebalancing admissions. Support for family immigration goes down, but those decreases are fully offset by still higher support for increasing, rather than decreasing, the number of immigrants allowed in on the basis of their employment skills or humanitarian needs.

As a follow-up in a module fielded with the 2015 Cooperative Congressional Election Study (CCES), we sought to load the deck in favor of rigidity and restriction even more strongly than we did in the original experiment (for details about this survey, see the Online Appendix). Right after asking respondents their preferred level of *legal* immigration on the standard item (rectifying the potential confound with illegal immigration in the SSI study), we informed them not only of the distribution of annual green cards but the overall number issued each year, a figure that we expected to draw respondents' attention to the large number of prospective immigrants they would be admitting if they endorsed the status quo or supported even more expansionary policy.

As you may know, approximately one million immigrants each year who have applied to enter the United States LEGALLY are given a Green Card, which allows them to live in the country permanently.

Among these **legal** immigrants,

- about 70 out of every 100 (700,000) are admitted to join family members who are U.S. citizens or legal permanent resident of the U.S.
- about 15 out of every 100 (150,000) have skills U.S. employers say are needed
- about 15 out of every 100 (150,000) claim to be fleeing the threat of violence or oppression in their home countries

Should the number of immigrants in each of these categories be increased, decreased, or kept about the same?

To provide an expansionist answer to the three specific questions, therefore, many respondents would have to in effect change their minds on the spot and override their previous judgment that the number of legal immigrants should be reduced. This contrasts with our previous iteration, in which respondents were randomly assigned *either* to weigh in on the total level of legal immigration *or* to choose whether to increase, decrease or leave unchanged the volume of immigration in the three major preference categories.

The CCES respondents would also have to face the fact that their answer would sustain an already large volume of legal immigration or even add to it. In a similar vein, knowing the approximate absolute number of immigrants admitted because of family ties would presumably make it even easier for respondents to advocate reducing that contingent *without* making offsetting changes to the volume of skilled and refugee admissions. Prior research illustrates that correcting Americans' by and large inflated perceptions about the

The Green Card Experiment

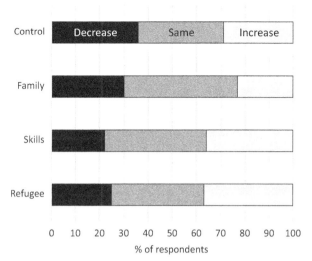

FIGURE 3.5 The Green Card Experiment, version 2.0
Note: The figure displays the percentage of respondents in the 2015 CCES Green Card Experiment who wanted to increase (a lot or a little), decrease (a lot or a little), or keep the same the level of immigration in each category. All respondents answered the standard level of immigration question (control) first and then encountered the questions about family, skills, and refugee admissions in random order. Full tabulations of these results are shown in the Online Appendix.

size of the immigrant stock does not make them more inclined to increase immigration overall.[18] However, if they are strongly motivated to support reductions to legal immigration but deterred by the seeming meanness or irrationality of cutting the three status quo categories, the "sticker shock" of making salient the total number of immigrants admitted each year should give them a clear impetus not to deviate from their abstract preference for greater restriction.

Despite all of these forces promoting restrictive choices, the pattern of responses (summarized in Figure 3.5) resembles the results of the SSI survey among those who were informed about the distribution of visas across preference categories. A substantial number of Americans who had just a moment earlier expressed a preference for reducing immigration opt not to follow through by making the cuts necessary to do so. Support for *expanding* family immigration is more muted than in the SSI results, as might be expected given the information respondents received that it accounts for the bulk of legal immigration. But support for cuts is nevertheless significantly lower than in the control condition. Restrictionist preferences in the other two categories decrease markedly. Averaging across the responses to the specific questions about whether to increase family, refugee, and skilled immigration, 28% wanted a net reduction in legal immigration (and only 62% of those who had only a moment ago said the level of legal immigration generally should be reduced), 28% answered in ways that suggested no change to the level of legal immigration (either by saying that the level of immigration in all three categories should be kept the same or offsetting desired decreases in one category with increases in others), and fully 44% wanted a net increase in the level of immigration across the three categories (39% of those who had wanted legal immigration overall kept the same and 19% of those who wanted it *reduced*).

Of course, these results should not be taken as evidence that Americans are enthusiastic about immigration. Although the more specific questions tend to elicit more support for increasing than reducing legal admissions, the modal preference remains to keep things the same as they are now. Whatever, exactly, that response means, it is clearly far softer an expression of restrictionism than saying that immigration should be reduced, often the modal preference when people's preferred level of immigration is solicited without articulating the basis on which people would be admitted.

How Do Those Especially Prone to Group-Centrism React?

Once again, we are interested in whether those with intense group animosities and affinities hold more firmly to their general views about whether immigration should be increased or decreased, notwithstanding the basis for their admission. As in the previous experiment, we examine differences between whites and racial minorities, between prejudiced and unprejudiced whites, and between whites and minorities who are strongly racially identified and those who are not. And again, while fully acknowledging the limitations of minority samples that are small and surely unrepresentative of the larger population, we see no evidence that the treatment effects among nonwhites are smaller than those among whites. Nonwhites begin with modestly more "pro-immigrant" attitudes about the level of immigration, but they respond to each of the treatments to a degree that is statistically and substantively indistinguishable from whites.

We can compare prejudiced and unprejudiced whites with confidence, using the same feeling thermometer measure of prejudice or ethnocentrism that is conventionally used in the literature[19] and in our overview of the 2016 ANES from Chapter 1. Again, we find no evidence that prejudice promotes resistance to the treatments. To be sure, prejudiced Americans are considerably more likely to agree in the abstract that immigration should be reduced. Fully 58% of racially prejudiced white respondents in the SSI survey wanted to reduce the level of immigration at baseline, compared to only 34% of the unprejudiced. But prejudiced whites are no less responsive to the cues about family, humanitarian goals, and recruitment of skilled workers than are other whites, and perhaps more so. Only 30% of prejudiced whites wanted to reduce family-based immigration, 32% skill-based immigration, and 32% refugee-based immigration – still much higher than the 13%, 18%, and 12%, respectively,

Case Studies: Latent Opinion and External Validity　　　79

of unprejudiced whites who supported reducing immigration in these categories but also much lower than the baseline appetite for cutting immigration. This basic pattern holds true whether we consider generalized ethnocentrism, affect toward Latinos in particular, or the difference between ingroup affect for whites and affect for Latinos.

This result should not get lost in the shuffle: even among Americans *who openly acknowledge prejudice against racial minorities*, less than one-third wishes to cut the level of immigration in each of the three preference categories that make up the expansionist admissions status quo. Nor does providing information about the dominance of family immigration or the overall volume of immigration seem to furnish prejudiced whites the "excuse" they need to resist the family, refugee, and skills cues. In the SSI survey, prejudiced respondents who received this information about the status quo distribution of green cards across the three categories made *smaller* adjustments on average than did the unprejudiced. And in the CCES-based Version 2.0 of this experiment, where respondents were also told the overall annual number of green cards issued to immigrants from each of these preference categories, prejudiced whites were no less responsive to the treatments than were unprejudiced whites.

In all cases, the effects of switching from abstract to concrete policy preferences are more pronounced among prejudiced whites than unprejudiced whites. Preferences for less immigration are malleable for Americans in general and also, strikingly, among those who score high on standard measures of racial prejudice. These findings are inconsistent with the idea that group animus or affinity dominates the opinion formation process, overwhelming information or diverting it selectively to support whatever position respondents' group-centric reactions predisposed them toward in the first place. Naturally, prejudiced Americans want less immigration in any way, shape, or form than do the unprejudiced. But even many prejudiced Americans take sufficient stock of the cues we provided – cues that are drawn from the very pillars of a more than half-century-old US legal admissions regime – to override their more general preference for less immigration.

CASE STUDIES: LATENT OPINION AND EXTERNAL VALIDITY

It is often difficult to know, from the snapshot provided by a given survey, which of the attitudes elicited reflects the "latent" opinions that would come to the fore during a public debate about the issue.[20] We have argued that people's concrete policy attitudes are both less hostile than, and not especially constrained by, their desire to reduce immigration in the abstract. Perhaps, a skeptic would say, abstract measures represent likely public response better than concrete questions do. Confronted directly and in a vacuum about the particular cuts required to reduce immigration, citizens might shy away from endorsing greater restriction. But, in the actual event, they might more readily give in to their underlying impulse to slam the gates. The evidence from

80   *FA, Humanitarianism, and Support for Legal Admissions*

available commercial polling strongly suggests otherwise. Two recent examples help establish this point.

I. LEGAL IMMIGRATION REFORM: GANG OF EIGHT BILL AND THE RAISE ACT. "Comprehensive immigration reform" is often associated with its most intensely controversial component – a path to legal status for at least some of the estimated 11 million illegal immigrants living in the United States. But each of the last several proposals to founder in Congress has also included measures that would reform *legal* immigration as well. The 2013 Gang of Eight Bill, which passed a Republican-controlled Senate with 68 votes but never came up for debate in the House, sought to increase the number of visas awarded to highly skilled workers. To offset these increases, the bill proposed cutting family-based legal immigration by eliminating the "fourth preference" visa category that reserves tens of thousands of green cards for US citizens to sponsor their foreign siblings. These proposals largely got lost amid overwhelming attention in mass media – and highly critical right-wing talk radio shows – to the "amnesty" that would have given illegal immigrants a chance to get legal status – and naturalize after about thirteen years – if they paid a fine, enrolled in English classes (or knew English), and passed a criminal background check.

As a result, there was a great deal more polling on this aspect of the policy, some of which we return to in the next chapter, than on its proposed changes to legal immigration. But the limited polling that exists on proposed changes to legal immigration closely matches the concrete policy preferences our experiments elicited. A January 30–31, 2013, Gallup Poll[21] asked Americans whether they would vote for or against several provisions linked to comprehensive immigration reform proposals then in circulation. One of these was "Increase the number of visas for legal immigrants who have advanced skills in technology and science." An overwhelmingly majority, 71%, said they would vote for this, compared to 27% against. An ABC News/Washington Post[22] poll taken three months later, on March 27–30, 2013, asked, "Overall, do you support or oppose allowing more highly skilled non-Americans to live and work in the United States?" This was supported by a similar margin, 72% to 27%. The level of support was even higher, 78–19, for a policy polled by Gallup[23] in June 15–16, 2013, that would "allow engineers and scientists from other countries who earn graduate degrees in the U.S. to remain in the U.S. to work."

Even when it comes to aspects of the bill that would have augmented low-skilled immigration, the abstract restrictive bent in US public opinion appears to have a limited grip on opinion formation. The idea of *increasing* immigration among those who come to work consistently garnered more support than opposition. An April 9–10, 2013, Gallup Poll[24] found a majority of Americans in support of "a law creating a work visa program that allows a specified number of immigrants into the U.S. to work at generally lesser-skilled jobs,"

Case Studies: Latent Opinion and External Validity   81

though by a tighter margin of 52–44. An ABC News/Washington Post[25] poll conducted during this period, from April 11–14, 2013, corroborates these results. By 60–37, Americans supported "More visas for highly skilled workers from other countries." By 56–40, they supported "A guest worker program for low-skilled workers from other countries." And when it came to the possibility of "reducing the number of visas for family members of legal immigrants," they opposed this measure 53–41, even though the bill called for such reductions to offset the other increases. These polls strongly suggest that when Americans are confronted with live policy proposals, they prove quite open to expanding the level of immigration, *provided that, consistent with what we showed in the Green Card Experiment, there are cues about employment or family ties.*

Still, one could argue that these proposed changes were not the most salient aspects of the Gang of Eight Bill, and thus failed to penetrate most Americans' awareness and bring them back into line with their abstract leanings in favor of cutting immigration. This argument would be more difficult to press when it comes to the RAISE Act, co-sponsored in 2017 by Senators Tom Cotton of Arkansas and David Perdue of Georgia. This bill would move the United States to a language- and skills-based "points system" akin to those used by Canada and Australia and cut the level of legal immigration dramatically, by about 50% in the next ten years and 40% almost right away. The Trump administration, and the president himself, gave this bill a full-throated endorsement via an address before a joint session of Congress, multiple press conferences, and, of course, in multiple tweets. If abstract restrictionism were to win the day, we might at least expect that poll questions asking about whether to cut legal immigration without referencing the preference categories that many Americans seem to like would generate plurality or even majority support. To the contrary, an August 3–6, 2017, CBS News[26] poll found that only 30% of respondents supported reducing legal immigration, while 43% wanted to maintain its current level, and 23% wanted it increased, similar to previous results for this question since 2010. An NBC News/Wall Street Journal[27] poll also found that 45% of Americans rejected the Cotton–Perdue legislation when described as a switch to a skills- and English-based points system with reductions in family visas and a 50 percent reduction in legal immigration overall while only 27% supported it.

2. TRAVEL AND REFUGEE BAN. For further evidence about whether Americans' reactions to specific policies being debated hew to abstract restrictionist leanings, we turn to an issue that received intense media coverage for weeks. The Trump administration's executive order, Protecting the Nation from Foreign Terrorist Entry into the United States (henceforth "executive order") would seem to be precisely the sort of issue where the support for refugee admissions we find in our experiments would be a less accurate reflection of the way reactions to the policy itself would take shape. It was framed loudly and

clearly as an anti-terrorism measure, and it more or less obliquely took aim at the admission of a group, Muslims, that a substantial minority of Americans express frankly bigoted attitudes about in public opinion surveys. Indeed, the executive order's many critics saw it as an effort to deliver a legally permissible approximation to the indefinite ban on all Muslim immigration that Trump had proposed during the Republican primary. Some wondered whether it would be the first step to a more comprehensive or enduring ban on immigration from the Muslim world.

Signed on January 27, 2017, just a week into Trump's presidency, the executive order had three main components – a 90-day ban on all travel of foreign nationals from seven majority Muslim countries to the United States, a 120-day moratorium on the intake of all refugees, and an indefinite suspension of refugee intakes from Syria. The administration's messaging was subverted by overwhelmingly negative media coverage that focused on the chaos it had sown – people stranded at airports, families separated, Iraqi translators who had worked for the US military denied entry days before their anticipated and previously authorized immigration, and green card holders in limbo. Protests against the executive order mounted at airports across the country, notably with only scant countermobilization by supporters of Trump's order.

Awareness of the executive order spread rapidly. In a Pew Research Center poll[28] conducted ten days after it was signed, from February 7–12, 2017, 78% of Americans reported having heard a lot about it, another 18% a little, and only 4% nothing at all. If the bulk of the public was strongly committed to reducing immigration and only casually interested in the plight of refugees, surely concern about terrorism would have furnished a sufficient rationale to support the executive order. Many, overwhelmingly Trump's core supporters, in fact did. But more almost certainly did not. The Pew poll found 38% approving of the order as a whole and 59% disapproving. Most other polls reached similar conclusions, though the degree of opposition varied by firm. The order fared poorly enough in public polling to elicit a classic Trump tweet: "Any negative polls are just fake news, just like the CNN, ABC, and NBC polls in the election. Sorry, people want border security and extreme vetting."

More telling than the overall assessments of the executive order, which were undoubtedly pegged to the growing unpopularity of Trump himself, were the differences in support for its various components. A Gallup Poll[29] taken a few days after the order was signed, from January 30 to 31, found 42% of Americans supporting "Ordering a temporary ban on entry into the United States for most people from seven predominantly Muslim countries" with 55% opposed. But the prospect of "Indefinitely suspending the United States' Syrian refugee program" polled even worse, with only 36% support and 58% opposed. A Quinnipiac poll[30] from several days later, February 2–6, found slightly more support for the travel ban, 46–51. However, it found considerably less support (37%, compared to 60% opposed) for a 120-day suspension of refugee

Case Studies: Latent Opinion and External Validity 83

admissions. Even this paled in comparison to the 70% who opposed "suspending all immigration of Syrian refugees to the U.S. indefinitely." Only 26% of the public supported this proposal. Thus, weak support for the executive order as a whole nevertheless vastly overstated the public's eagerness for major or potentially lasting cuts to refugee intakes. It seems unlikely that these differences are driven by social desirability bias since the travel ban itself was so widely maligned that anyone concerned about appearing anti-Muslim or favorable to Trump would have claimed to support or declined to opine on the travel ban itself too.

The pattern of results was unchanged in a Quinnipiac poll[31] taken ten days later. It held also in response to Trump's issue of a revised executive order in early March, three weeks after the initial one was blocked by the courts. It explicitly exempted green card holders and removed a provision that had accorded precedence to refugees from "religious minority" groups, which in effect was taken to mean Christians over Muslims. Before that order, too, was legally enjoined, a Quinnipiac Poll[32] found support for the travel ban at 43% to 55% opposed and for a temporary ban on all refugee intakes at 35%, compared to 61% opposed.

If opposition to cutbacks remained firm, it did not begin that way. We can see this by looking at the trajectory of public opinion about Syrian refugees in particular. The strong opposition to suspending intakes indefinitely is a startling reversal from a spate of polls about the intake of 10,000 Syrian refugees that were fielded in 2015. A Quinnipiac Poll[33] in December 2015 found 42% support for "accepting Syrian refugees into the U.S." and 52% opposed. Bloomberg[34] found similar levels of opposition. What accounts for these changes? Most of the early polls on Syrian refugees were taken shortly after the major terrorist attacks in Paris, and a CBS/New York Times[35] poll from the same period indicates that addressing concerns about security would ratchet up support for taking in refugees. It found the public evenly divided over whether to allow refugees from Syria into the United States "as long as they go through a security clearance process" versus not allowing any refugees from Syria into the United States "at this time." Still, polls going back further showed similar levels of opposition to taking in Syrian refugees.[36]

An additional factor may have been the Syrian refugee program's close association with a then fairly unpopular President Barack Obama, whose own approval rating hovered for much of his second term in the low 40s. Once hostility to Syrian refugees became associated with an even less popular Trump and the shock of the Paris and San Bernardino terrorist attacks waned, some Americans may have changed their attitudes accordingly.

Shortly before President Trump's inauguration, in January 2017, a Quinnipiac poll[37] explicitly pitted the specter of terrorism against the prospect of "turning away refugees": "Do you support or oppose suspending immigration from 'terror prone' regions, even if it means turning away refugees from those regions?" A public committed to reducing refugee intakes should latch onto the terrorism frame as a rationalization for doing so. And indeed,

48% supported suspending immigration from terror-prone regions while 42% opposed it, virtually unchanged from a month earlier. By March, 55% of the public was opposed with only 42% in support.[38] It is impossible to know on the basis of these data whether the change occurred because citizens were exposed to the humanitarian consequences of slamming the gates, information suggesting that with the current vetting regime refugees were in fact not so dangerous after all, or simply that Trump was the major sponsor of this policy so that his declining popularity meant less support for cutting refugee intakes too. These are worthwhile questions but tangential to the main point here, which is that restrictive attitudes grounded in fears of "the other," a marginalized group associated with violence and hostility to American society, nevertheless yielded on a large scale when confronted with the standard suite of information and sponsorship cues discussed in much research on public opinion. If immigration were such an easy issue because of its group-centric foundations, opinions about refugee intakes should have been more resistant to these influences.

Even as the "travel ban" has come under legal scrutiny, polling continues to reveal considerable flux in Americans' opinions. A Morning Consult poll[39] found that 57% of Americans supported multiple circuit courts' decision to block the ban from taking effect. The next month, however, 60% of Americans[40] also approved of the rather confusingly worded "new guidelines which say visa applicants from six predominantly Muslim countries must prove a close family relationship with a U.S. resident in order to enter the country," with even Democrats about evenly split. The key words appear to be "family relationship." More than two-thirds of Americans also believed that not only people with a spouse or parent in America but also with a sibling or grandparent should be allowed to enter the United States. Clearly, attempts to gauge *the* level of public support for the travel ban miss the larger picture. Most Americans' attitudes even about this area of policy are highly differentiated and apparently quite flexible as well in the face of additional considerations that relate to priorities they care about.[41]

Summary

Survey experiments seek to mimic the kinds of cues and arguments that citizens would be exposed to in the real world when confronted with immigration policy controversies, and indeed the kind we found in our content analysis of newspaper articles described in Chapter 2. However, there is always the risk that these manipulations are processed artificially and do not tell us about the choices that people would make in the context of a real political debate. These two case studies provide reassurance that, in the context of intense public debate, the public responds strongly to cues about functional assimilation and humanitarian concerns in weighing legal immigration and refugee policy.

TAKING STOCK

We saw in Chapter 1 that most Americans' generalized attitudes about the level of immigration lean toward increased limits, but that these are not altogether stable and that whatever restrictive attitudes people have in the abstract often give way to openness when it comes to policy particulars. Here, we zeroed in on the ability of information that taps into public conceptions of civic fairness to shape distinct – and generally more expansionist – opinions about specific policies that would increase legal admissions. This is emphatically not to suggest that the American public is fundamentally "pro-immigrant." It is to call attention to the values criteria that Americans appear to apply when confronted with many specific proposals that would increase legal admissions. We have focused here on functional assimilation, along with its underpinning in economic individualism, and humanitarianism, though there are probably others at play. Even when group cues are made salient or people are forced to reckon with the fact that their preferences sustain or even increase status quo immigration levels, information that engages these values dramatically influences public opinion. In keeping with Myrdal's conception of the American ethos, when push comes to shove, these values to a large degree override ethnocentrism in public opinion about legal admissions.

4

Civic Fairness and the Legal–Illegal Divide

Chapter 1 showed that much of the American public differentiates sharply between its views on the appropriate level of legal immigration and its views about how to address the status of the estimated 11 million illegal immigrants living in the United States. Americans certainly like legal immigration more than illegal immigration, and enforcement measures to stem the flow of illegal immigration or prompt some illegal immigrants to return to their countries of origin tend to be very popular as long as they do not involve heavy-handed or sweeping attempts at mass deportation.[1] And illegal immigrants themselves are unfailingly viewed more "coldly" than immigrants generally. On the other hand, as we documented in Chapter 1, the most salient policy proposal for dealing with illegal immigrants already in the country – furnishing some sort of earned legal status or a "path to citizenship" for some or all in this group – receives overwhelming support in many polls.

Much of the political conflict over immigration reform has been specifically keyed to *illegality*. Most commentary has focused on conservative Republicans' efforts to decouple legal and illegal immigration rhetorically, much as California Governor Pete Wilson and others capitalized on the slogan "immigration yes, welfare no" in promoting sharp cuts to social benefits for legal and illegal immigrants twenty-five years ago.[2] "Amnesty" has been the "third rail" of efforts at comprehensive immigration reform and the source of their repeated demise.[3]

We contend that a great many Americans are particularly vexed by illegal immigration because they view it as a violation of the legalistic norms widely seen as part and parcel of civic fairness. But, no less strikingly, another aspect of civic fairness – egalitarianism – leads at least as many of them to support giving illegal immigrants, a widely disliked group, a way to stay permanently and eventually gain citizenship. In Chapter 2, we defined *legalism* as belief in the importance of rigid adherence to rules and laws, and, as far as civic fairness is

Civic Fairness and the Legal–Illegal Divide

concerned, as an integral piece of formal assimilation. We defined *egalitarianism* as an aversion to differentials in status and opportunity within a political collective. We contend that these two aspects of civic fairness – legalism and egalitarianism – are substantially more relevant to citizens' opinions about illegal immigration than about most legal admissions controversies. Elite framing of a path to citizenship for illegal immigrants as an amnesty that "rewards lawbreakers" appeals especially to those with stronger legalistic orientations and urges them to take a harder line on illegal than legal immigration. Egalitarians, on the other hand, view the persistence of an illegal "underclass" lacking basic rights and privileges of membership in society as an affront to equal opportunity.

In short, the distinction that Americans draw between legal and illegal immigration policy is a testing ground for the first three hypotheses we elaborated in Chapter 2. We expect that civic fairness cues that are distinctive to questions about illegal immigration policy will exert an independent influence on policy opinions, over and above ethnic group attitudes, even when ethnic group cues are available (Hypothesis 1). We further expect that the influence of these civic fairness cues will be correlated with the priority that individuals accord to the values they evoke (Hypothesis 2). And we anticipate that the influence of group cues will be unmoderated by the presence of ethnic cues – that is, civic fairness values will be applied evenhandedly to immigrants from different ethnic groups (Hypothesis 3).

The primary group-centrist alternative to this argument is that the public differentiates between legal and illegal immigration because it more closely associates illegal immigration with Latinos. This alternative tends to focus on opposition to legalization programs. In this view, rhetoric about "illegality" resonates with many Americans because it evokes racial predispositions. Recourse to the "rule of law," in this view, is a façade that perpetuates the post-Civil Rights use of racial appeals that masquerade as concerns about "law and order" and gives racial bigots a socially acceptable rationale for endorsing policies that deny equal status to minorities. Indeed, the very term "illegal" has become controversial (even verboten in politically correct circles), in part because of its allegedly dehumanizing and racial overtones,[4] a theme that rich scholarship on immigration politics and discourse has developed.[5] Research suggests that the effort to change immigration attitudes by changing terminology may be futile.[6] These efforts can surely reach a point of absurdity. Chicago Mayor Rahm Emanuel recently referred to this class of immigrants as "those who may not have all their papers in order."[7] But evolving terminology is an indication of the sensitivity around the widespread allegation that making sharp, ostensibly legalistic distinctions between legal and illegal immigration masks xenophobia, racism, and the derogation of immigrants and Latinos.

While some who harp on "illegality" no doubt aim at racial demagoguery and find a receptive audience, we show that legalism is by no means simply a stand-in for prejudice. Americans with varying commitments to egalitarianism and legalism tend to differentiate between legal and illegal immigration policy in the ways our theory would predict. Distinctions between legal and illegal immigration, and their association with measures of legalism and egalitarianism, persist when immigrants' ethnic backgrounds are held constant and over and above statistical controls for survey respondents' attitudes toward Latinos and other ethnic groups. And the premium that Americans place on legal status, as well as the exception that many of them make for "Dreamers" brought to the country as children and therefore less accountable for breaking the law, applies as much to Europeans and Asians as to Latinos immigrants.

OBSERVATIONAL EVIDENCE FOR CIVIC FAIRNESS AND GROUP-CENTRISM

We begin by considering whether the relationships between opinions about immigration policy and measures of values and group attitudes line up well with the predictions of the civic fairness and group-centrist perspectives. Our interest in both cases is to examine whether these measures are independently associated to different degrees with opinions about legal immigration and illegal immigration policy.

Opinions about Legal and Illegal Immigration Policies Are Linked to Different Values

If one wishes to identify the types of citizens who draw the sharpest distinction between legal and illegal immigration policy, our framework suggests that we need to look for survey measures of legalism and egalitarianism. We begin by showing this to be true in publicly available survey data and then turn to one of our own surveys, which was designed to investigate precisely those relationships.

With respect to legalism, we know of only one publicly available major national survey that allows a rudimentary first cut: the 2004 General Social Survey, which asked the standard level of immigration question as well as the question about whether the government should increase efforts to exclude illegal immigrants. The latter is less than ideal for our purposes because it strikes us more as a "border security" item than one concerned about what policies should be applied to those living in the country without permission. This is the controversy that has been framed in the most legalistic terms, as an unacceptable "amnesty." But it is the best we can do with these data. Both of the immigration items are scaled to run from 0 to 1, where 1 is the most "pro-immigrant" response. We also analyze the difference between the illegal immigration and level of immigration items, as a rough measure of how much *more* respondents oppose illegal immigration than immigration generally. For our main independent variable, a rudimentary measure of *legalism*, we draw on two questions that the General Social Survey (GSS) also asked, tapping

Observational Evidence for Civic Fairness and Group-Centrism 89

into, respectively, the idea that a "good citizen" should never to try to evade taxes and always obey laws.[8] Our "legalism" scale is simply the mean of these two items, rescaled to run from 0 (least legalistic) to 1 (most legalistic).[9]

We regressed the two immigration items, and their differential, on the legalism item along with controls for age, education, race, sex, and party identification. The GSS data are limited in that they lack the ethnic group thermometers that are often used in this sort of research. The closest we can come is an indirect measure of attitudes toward blacks: whether the federal government should spend more, less, or the same to aid blacks. With these caveats noted, the results do show a link between legalistic attitudes and differentiation between illegal and legal immigration. The coefficient on the legalism scale is large and marginally significant for the illegal immigration item $(-.09; p < .1)$, meaning that those who express more legalistic attitudes tend to take a harder line on illegal immigration. When it comes to the level of immigration, however, the relationship is *positive* and statistically insignificant $(.08, p = .14)$, meaning that those who score high on this scale are, if anything, a little more supportive of large-scale legal admissions. The legalism measure predicts a substantial and highly significant degree of differentiation between opinions about legal and illegal immigration. Those at the high extreme on the legalism item are on average 17 points $(p < .01)$ more supportive of legal immigration than illegal immigration. Since these measures are on different scales, standardizing each dependent variable can give a sense of the magnitude of these effects. Moving across the full span of the legalism scale boosts support for excluding illegal immigrants by about one-third of a standard deviation but *increases* support for legal admissions by a little over one-quarter of a standard deviation, which is statistically insignificant.

These relationships do not appear to be confined to whites. The sample is too small to say much with certainty, but among the 73 Hispanic respondents available for analysis, the estimated effect of legalism on the difference measure $(.19)$, though statistically insignificant due to the small sample size, is on par with that found among non-Hispanic whites $(.23, p < .001)$. They may not obtain among African Americans, however. Among the 130 black respondents available for analysis, the same estimate is close to zero and even slightly negative $(-.06, p = .75)$, though the difference in effects by race (comparing whites and blacks) is not quite statistically significant $(p = .11)$. Black respondents' interpreting and applying the legalism items differently would be in keeping with other research that shows that the political relevance of authoritarianism is distinctive among African Americans relative to whites.[10] It is also consistent with research by Natalie Masuoka and Jane Junn indicating that blacks differentiate between the threats posed by legal and illegal immigration less than whites do, possibly because the standard "law and order" mantra has often been used as a pretext for repression and discrimination against their group.[11]

We have more to go on in publicly available data when it comes to assessing the role of egalitarianism. The American National Election Study

(ANES) has regularly asked a battery of questions aimed at measuring egalitarian values:

- Our society should do whatever is necessary to make sure that everyone has an equal opportunity to succeed.
- We have gone too far pushing equal rights.
- One of the big problems in this country is that we don't give everyone an equal chance.
- This country would be better off if we worried less about how equal people are.
- It is not really that big a problem if some people have more of a chance than others.
- If people were treated equally in this country we would have many fewer problems.

We take the average of the egalitarian measures and rescale them to run from 0 to 1, where 1 indicates the highest level of commitment to the value of equality. We focus here on the 2008, 2012, and 2016 surveys, all of which have the standard level of immigration question as well as several questions pertaining to offering legal status to illegal immigrants. Figure 4.1 summarizes

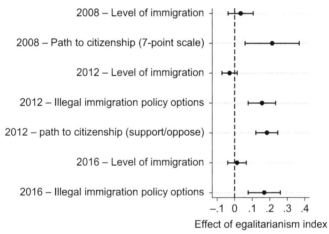

FIGURE 4.1 Effect of egalitarianism on opinions about level of legal immigration versus legalization for illegal immigrants (ANES 2008, 2012, and 2016)
Note: The figure displays the point estimates and 95% confidence intervals from ordinary least squares (OLS) regressions in which the dependent variable is the item labeled on the y-axis. Both the egalitarianism index and all dependent variables are rescaled to run from 0 to 1 where 1 = most egalitarian and 1 = most supportive of increasing immigration or providing legal status to illegal immigrants. Control variables include age, education, sex, race, party ID, liberal-conservative identification, authoritarianism, feeling thermometers for whites, blacks, Asians, and Latinos, and the four-item racial resentment index (see Online Appendix for details of all these measures).

Observational Evidence for Civic Fairness and Group-Centrism 91

the effect of egalitarianism on each of these questions, all rescaled from 0 to 1 where 1 indicates the most "pro-immigrant" response, as estimated in an ordinary least squares regression model. The ANES furnishes a much richer set of statistical controls than was available in the GSS analysis of legalism. In addition to standard demographics and party identification, we include controls for liberal-conservative self-identification, authoritarianism (as measured by a standard four-item battery that asks about child-rearing priorities), feeling thermometers for whites, blacks, Asians, and Latinos, and the four-item racial resentment index. The last variable is included to isolate as best as possible the effect of egalitarianism in the abstract from attitudes about race.

As expected, egalitarianism matters much more with respect to illegal immigration than to opinions about the level of immigrant admissions. The question of whether to give legal status to illegal immigrants clearly puts special pressure on the opinions of those who are most committed to equal rights and opportunities and hence would be most receptive to the argument that withholding a chance to achieve political equality and equal status is at odds with their values. Spanning the measure of egalitarian values increases favorability toward the idea of a path to citizenship substantially – by between .15 and .23 across these measures – and significantly (all $p < .01$). However, all else being equal, egalitarianism does not promote support for preserving or increasing the level of immigration. These effects are null, with estimates near zero, in all three years of available data.

Again, some caution is in order given that opinions about legal and illegal immigration are not being measured on a common scale but by different survey indicators. Standardizing both dependent variables allows us to measure how much more supportive egalitarianism makes people of legalization or expansive admissions *relative to others in the sample*. In all cases, when we do this, the differences remain large. In 2008, for example, moving from the minimum to the maximum of the egalitarianism scale boosts support for legalization by .56 of a standard deviation but of legal immigration by only .12. The results in 2012 and 2016 are similar. That is, high levels of egalitarianism predict dramatically higher support than average for a path to citizenship but only slightly greater than average support for legal admissions.

The ANES in those years also has had a large enough sample to permit comparisons of these effects between whites, blacks, and Latinos, including oversamples in 2008 and 2012. Pooling across all three surveys, Latinos and blacks follow the same pattern as non-Hispanic whites, displaying considerably stronger positive relationships between egalitarian values and support for legalization than between egalitarianism and preferences about the level of legal admissions. The effect of egalitarian values in decoupling opinions about legal from illegal immigration policy holds strongly across these three groups. Thus, if legalism has a distinctively weak effect on blacks' views about illegal immigration policy, egalitarian values seem to come into play as strongly among blacks as among whites and Latinos.

Our own SSI survey from 2013 offers a chance to analyze the effects of legalism and egalitarianism on differentiation between legal and illegal immigration simultaneously and with a superior measure of legalism. The dependent variable concerning illegal immigration policy is a seven-point support–oppose item soliciting respondents' views about a path to citizenship for illegal immigrants. As a measure of views concerning legal admissions, we average responses to the three specific policy items asking about whether to increase, decrease, or keep the same the number of legal immigrants who have family in the United States, are escaping persecution, and have skills that employers say are needed (for more detail, see Chapter 3).

The legalism measure consists of a battery of five questions borrowed from the "trust in justice" module of the European Social Survey[12] about how seriously people regard several types of infringements on the law – cheating on taxes, running a red light or stop sign, making a false claim on an insurance document, and avoiding paying a fare on public transportation. Response options are "not at all wrong," "a bit wrong," "wrong," and "seriously wrong." All items skew toward the "wrong" and "seriously wrong" responses (scale mean = .7), but there is considerable variation on the index scores, and the skew is far less serious than on the two-item GSS legalism index we used earlier. Egalitarianism is measured with the same items as in the 2016 ANES.

We regressed using ordinary least squares (OLS) both our illegal and legal immigration policy measures legalism and egalitarianism, along with a suite of standard demographic and attitudinal statistical controls similar to those used in the ANES analysis earlier. Figure 4.2 displays the coefficients on the measures of the values that we hypothesized would have different effects on support for legal immigration and opinions about whether to normalize the status of illegal immigrants.

The results, displayed in Figure 4.2, affirm the role that these competing values play in decoupling opinions about legal admissions from opinions about normalizing the status of illegal immigration. Those who score highest on legalism are predicted to be more than eleven points less supportive of a path to citizenship than those who score lowest on legalism. By contrast, spanning the legalism scale marginally and insignificantly increases support on the legal admissions measure by five points. Egalitarianism plays a seemingly even larger role in the opposite direction. All else being equal, those who score highest on egalitarian values are thirty-three points, or fully one-third of the scale, more supportive of a path to citizenship. But they are just under ten points more supportive of legal admissions. The "all else being equal" provision is especially important here because of the concern that legalism and tepid support for egalitarianism are merely racism in polite disguise. Including the standard measures of group affect in the model helps guard against this possibility.

Standardizing the dependent variables again helps compare the magnitudes of these effects, which is otherwise difficult since they are measured on different scales. Moving from the minimum to the maximum score for legalism lowers

Observational Evidence for Civic Fairness and Group-Centrism 93

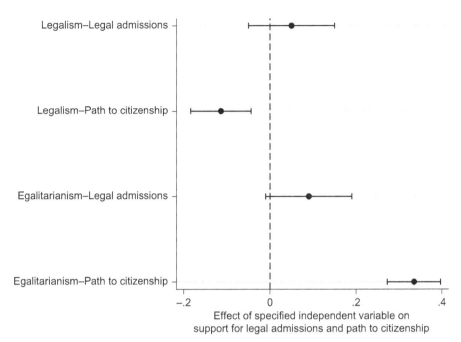

FIGURE 4.2 Legalism and egalitarianism across the legal–illegal divide (Survey Sampling International, 2013)
Note: The figure displays the point estimates and 95% confidence intervals from an OLS regression in which the dependent variable is the legal or illegal immigration support measure, as specified before each dash on the y-axis labels, and the independent variable is specified after each dash on the y-axis labels. All variables are coded to run from 0 to 1 where 1 = more legalistic and more egalitarian and where 1 = more supportive of increasing legal immigration and more supportive of a path to citizenship. Control variables are age, education, sex, race, party ID, liberal–conservative identification, authoritarianism, humanitarian values (see Online Appendix), and feeling thermometer evaluations of whites, blacks, Asians, and Latinos.

support for a path to citizenship by .37 of a standard deviation but increases support for legal admission by about .20 of a standard deviation. Moving from the lowest to the highest score on the egalitarianism scale boosts support for a path to citizenship by almost a full standard deviation (.97) but for legal admissions by less than one-half that, .42 of a standard deviation. Thus, measures of legalism and egalitarianism help us identify people who differ quite a bit from their fellow citizens in support for legalization but only modestly, if at all, in support for expansive legal admissions.

Are these patterns unique to whites? In a word, no. Fully 23% of our sample in the SSI survey was nonwhite (19% of the US-born respondents), including 202 African Americans, 115 self-identified Latinos, and 142 Asians (188, 102, and 75, respectively, among those born in the United States). We make no claim

94 *Civic Fairness and the Legal–Illegal Divide*

that these subsamples are representative of their respective populations in the United States – especially the Latino and Asian subsamples since all interviews were conducted in English. But we can still test whether the patterns we have reported are *confined* to whites. That they are present as well among the nonwhites in our sample is an indication that very large numbers of nonwhites are drawing on the values we have highlighted in making choices about legal and illegal immigration policy. These results described so far obtain across all subsamples of whites, blacks, Hispanics, and Asians – again, with one exception: as in the GSS, legalism did not predict opposition to a path to citizenship among blacks and therefore also did not differentiate opinions about legal and illegal immigration. This strikes us as further corroboration that blacks widely view the "law and order" framing of illegal immigration with particular suspicion given its connection to anti-Civil Rights politics and racial repression.[13] With this one important exception in mind, however, we can say that the distinctive effects of legalism and egalitarianism on opinions about legal and illegal immigration do not appear to be confined to non-Hispanic whites. Our best guess is that these values' impact is similar among whites and a broad swath of the nonwhite population, including among large numbers of Latinos and Asians.

Murkier Evidence for a Distinctive Relationship between Anti-Latino Attitudes and Illegal Immigration Policy

We noted earlier that a group-centrist explanation for the distinctions people draw between illegal and legal immigration policy is that each domain may evoke feelings toward different ethnic groups. Researchers have known for some time that attitudes toward Latinos and Asians are robustly correlated with opinions about immigration policy,[14] a pattern that has strengthened of late.[15] But the question here is whether these kinds of group favorability ratings, ubiquitous in the literature on race and ethnic politics, give us any purchase on why people see legal and illegal immigration differently. Put another way, are attitudes toward Latinos more distinctly tied to opinions about illegal than legal immigration policy?

The ANES is useful here because it has regularly asked questions about legal and illegal immigration as well as feeling thermometer measures about whites, blacks, Asians, and Latinos. We also analyze our own SSI data, again comparing the correlates of the legal admissions index to the correlates of the path to citizenship item. In Table 4.1, each row shows the coefficients on the feeling thermometer ratings for Latinos, Asians, whites, and blacks, drawn from the same OLS regression models that were used to generate Figures 4.1 and 4.2. If the group-centrism argument is correct, we would expect peoples' feelings about Latinos to be tied to illegal immigration attitudes especially strongly. For ease of interpretation, all of the feeling thermometer measures have been reverse coded and rescaled to run from 0 (most *negativity* toward the group) to

Observational Evidence for Civic Fairness and Group-Centrism 95

TABLE 4.1 *Ethnic group affect and policy opinions in the American National Election Studies*

	Hispanics	Asians	Whites	Blacks	N
2008 ANES					
Path to citizenship	.33**	.02	−.10	.00	730
Level of immigration	.24***	.23***	−.25***	.00	1,459
2012 ANES					
Illegal immigration policy options	.30***	.12*	−.19***	−.03	4,763
Path to citizenship	.19***	.09*	−.03	−.04	4,766
Level of immigration	.22***	.11***	−.22***	−.03	4,713
2016 ANES					
Illegal immigration policy options	.37***	−.05	−.113*	.03	2,684
Level of immigration	.25***	.08*	−.19***	−.02	2,686
2013 SSI					
Path to citizenship	.35***	.00	−.10**	−.04	2,405
Legal admissions index	.27***	.05	−.12***	.04	1,134

Note: The table displays coefficients on the feeling thermometers from OLS regressions on the ANES and SSI data in the specified years. The models include all the covariates from the models described in the notes to Figures 4.1 and 4.2. * $p < .05$, **$p < .01$, ***$p < .001$.

1 (the most *positivity*). The measures of immigration attitudes have also been rescaled and recoded to run from 0 (most restrictivist) to 1 (most expansionist). We focus on the 2008, 2012, and 2016 ANES as well as our own 2013 SSI survey for comparability with the earlier results.

As Table 4.1 shows, attitudes toward Hispanics are the dominant group attitude when it comes to predicting attitudes about both legal admissions and legal status for illegal immigrants. Attitudes about Asians, America's fastest-growing immigrant group for several years now but a relatively small portion of the illegal immigrant population, are more weakly tied to opinions about either type of policy. As partial support for the group-centrist story offered earlier, the coefficients for attitudes toward Latinos are a shade stronger for measures of opinions about illegal immigration than legal immigration. However, a closer look suggests that at least part of this apparent difference is an artifact of scaling. We can see this by standardizing all of the dependent variables and reestimating all the equations. In the 2008 ANES, for example, the apparent difference in coefficients translates into a miniscule difference in how much the Latino feeling thermometer boosts either standardized measure. The most pro-Latino Americans are .88 of a standard deviation more pro-immigrant than the most anti-Latino Americans when it comes to the level of legal admissions. Strikingly, the most pro-Latino Americans are also precisely

.88 of a standard deviation more pro-immigrant than the most anti-Latino Americans when it comes to their opinions about a path to citizenship. The 2012 and 2016 ANES give limited opportunity to compare since our legalization dependent variables all have only two or three categories. But our SSI data corroborate the result from the 2008 ANES. The most pro-Latino Americans are 1.0 standard deviation more supportive of a path to citizenship and a slightly higher 1.1 standard deviation more supportive of legal admissions than the most anti-Latino Americans.

Unsurprisingly, ethnocentrism promotes negative attitudes toward immigration. What is more, alongside others,[16] we can see here that these ethnocentric tendencies have increasingly focused on Latinos. Attitudes toward Asians, whites, and blacks are also frequently, though inconsistently, tied to opinions about both types of policies, in keeping with a role for generalized ethnocentrism in promoting opposition to all kinds of immigration. But attitudes toward Latinos stand out for their close relationships with opinions about immigration policy. Still, the measures of attitudes about Latinos are not much help in explaining the differently valenced opinions about legal and illegal immigration policy that so many Americans hold. Anti-Latino sentiment predicts both types of opinions quite strongly – correlations that, we will see, are harder to interpret than it might initially seem – but for now the point is that they do not predict support for one type of policy all that much more strongly than they predict support for the other.

Summary of Results from Observational Studies

Provisionally, then, we see empirical relationships that are consistent with an important role for civic fairness in promoting attitudinal distinctions between legal and illegal immigration. Measures of legalistic and egalitarian values predict citizens' propensity to have different opinions about legal and illegal immigration in ways that support our theoretical predictions. The group-centrist explanation for these policy distinctions is not clearly corroborated.

EXPERIMENTAL EVIDENCE

In the preceding analysis, much is riding on the statistical controls – too much, perhaps. Take the examples that are supportive of civic fairness. If there is unmeasured animus against Latinos lurking in the background,[17] perhaps some that our respondents are not even aware of, this "all else being equal" assumption may not hold. Some of the apparent influence of legalism or egalitarianism might therefore still be capturing attitudes about Latinos, or generalized prejudice, and we may be ascribing differentiation to civic fairness that is in fact group-centric.

The observational approach also does not permit us to isolate illegal status per se as the as the catalyst for legalistic and egalitarian reactions to the issue of

Experimental Evidence

a path to citizenship. Since people may imagine that legal and illegal immigrants tend to differ on many dimensions (not only race), we cannot say with much assurance on the basis of the what we've shown so far that official status is the reason that egalitarianism and legalism come more strongly into play in citizens' assessments of illegal immigration policy. If, for example, people imagine illegal immigrants to be economically worse off than legal immigrants, egalitarianism might promote greater support for helping them because of aversion to economic (rather than political) inequality. Or if people assume that illegal immigrants are more likely to commit crimes, those with staunch legalistic values might be particularly inclined to reject giving them the right to stay in the United States legally. These types of thinking could still be construed as civic fairness, but they involve a different set of considerations that are not tied specifically to *formal assimilation*, which is what we want to argue here.

As in Chapter 3, experiments can help us isolate the key ingredients in the formation of immigration policy opinions with greater precision than the observational evidence. By controlling for the ethnic background of hypothetical immigrants as well as other salient characteristics, we are also subtly changing the question we are asking. Earlier, we compared people whose feelings toward Latinos as a group (and other groups) are the same. We asked whether their commitments to egalitarianism and legalism affected their propensity to hold differing opinions about legal and illegal immigration policy. In the experimental setting, by contrast, we ask whether citizens draw distinctions between legal and illegal immigration, *all else being equal*.

Here is how we went about this: We put respondents to our 2013 SSI survey in the position of a policy maker assigned to evaluate five pairs of immigrants in terms of whether one of the pair, neither, or both should get a green card. Each hypothetical immigrant in our experiment was defined by six features: national origin (Mexican, German, Chinese, Pakistani, and Nigerian), recent employment status (has been mostly employed, has been mostly unemployed), English proficiency (speaks fluent English, speaks broken English, does not speak English), educational attainment (high school degree or less, some college, college degree), age (30–70), and religion (Christian, Muslim, or not religious).

Every piece of information – both within and across these hypothetical immigrants' profiles – was generated entirely at random. This method, called "conjoint choice analysis," allows us to observe which of these attributes people take into account when making choices. If we varied one attribute at a time – say, English proficiency – we would learn how big an advantage English-fluent immigrants have in the public's estimation over those who do not speak English. But we would not be in a position to say whether a preference for English-fluent immigrants emerges *because* people care about language fluency per se or because they tend to assume that immigrants who speak English are more educated and employed, or less likely to be members of ethnic groups they dislike. Explicitly providing information about employment and national origin (a stand-in for ethnicity) helps rule out these alternative explanations for an

98   *Civic Fairness and the Legal–Illegal Divide*

aggregate preference for English-fluent over non-English speaking immigrants.[18]

To assess the effect of legal status per se and how that effect differs by the emphasis that Americans place on legalism and egalitarianism, we randomly assign people to one of three different versions of the experiment. In the *Legal* condition, the prompt was:

There are different opinions about what sorts of people from other countries should be given official permission to come to the United States **legally** and live here permanently. We'd like to know your opinion. For each pair of people you see, please indicate which of the two you would prefer be given official permission to come to the United States **legally** and live here permanently, or whether you would prefer that neither or both be given permission.

In the *Illegal* condition, it was:

There are different opinions about what sorts of people from other countries who are living in the United States **illegally** should be given official permission to live here permanently. We'd like to know your opinion. For each pair of people you see, both of whom are living in the United States **illegally**, please indicate which of the two you would prefer be given official permission to live here permanently, or whether you would prefer that neither or both be given permission.

Finally, in the *Dreamer* condition, it was:

There are different opinions about what sorts of people from other countries who were **brought here as children** and are living in the United States **illegally** should be given official permission to live here permanently. We'd like to know your opinion. For each pair of people you see, all of whom were **brought here as children** and are living in the United States **illegally**, please indicate which of the two you would prefer be given official permission to live here permanently, or whether you would prefer that neither or both be given permission.

These conditions were designed to be as comparable as possible to isolate the effect of legal status per se. They do conflate the issue of already being in the United States versus coming from outside, which is something to bear in mind but essentially unavoidable if any realism is to be preserved.

In the study, a grid appeared with Immigrant 1 and Immigrant 2 as columns, and a set of attributes as rows. Below the grid, respondents were asked: "Which of these two individuals, both of whom are [illegal immigrants/legal immigrants/illegal immigrants brought to the United States as children], do you think should be granted legal status in the United States with an opportunity eventually to become a citizen?" They could answer Immigrant 1, Immigrant 2, Neither, Both, or Don't Know.[19]

If legalistic concerns about "playing by the rules" matter to a sizeable portion of the public, we would observe correspondingly more support for applicants for legal admission than for applicants present illegally who are seeking legal status. Assuming that Dreamers evoke greater sympathy than do

Experimental Evidence

illegal immigrants generally and are seen as less responsible for breaking a rule, they would be expected to receive more support. On the other hand, people with a strong legalistic orientation might view giving Dreamers a break as a recipe for moral hazard or unfairly rewarding parents for their infractions. Dreamers may also evoke the most intense support from egalitarians since their status deprives them from childhood of equal rights and opportunities in American society.

If civic fairness is indeed at work, it should influence *how* people think about immigration as much as it influences *what* they think about it. Arguments about illegal immigration tend to be made categorically, by which we mean that policy prescriptions are applied to *all* illegal immigrants as a class.[20] As a result, we expect that respondents in the *Illegal* condition will be especially prone to making decisions in *categorical* terms. They should, in other words, be more likely to reject (or accept) all "applicants" across the board when in the *Illegal* condition than those deciding about legal admissions. Moreover, we expect that categorical support for normalizing the status of illegal immigrants and especially Dreamers will be higher among those who espouse egalitarian norms and that categorical opposition to these programs will be higher among those who hold legalistic values.

The real advantage of the conjoint in this context is that, since all profile creation is done randomly, the only average difference between the immigrant profiles presented in the *Legal, Illegal*, and *Dreamers* conditions is legal status and, in the case of the *Dreamers,* how it came about. As a result, we can be more confident that whatever differences emerge across them are not simply a by-product of assumptions people tend to make about these types of immigrants' ethno-religious backgrounds, cultural and economic assimilation, and labor market skill level, because specific information on all of these fronts is provided in the profiles.

Formal Assimilation, Egalitarianism, and Humanitarianism

Put in the position of armchair immigration policy maker, how do our respondents behave? First, consider the rate at which respondents accepted immigrants in each category.[21] Remember that differences in the acceptance rate across the three conditions cannot be accounted for by respondents' filling in the blanks about immigrants' ethnicity, educational attainment, English proficiency, employment track record, religiosity, or age since we have explicitly told them this in every profile and it is on average exactly the same across them.

Consistent with public negativity toward the idea of illegality per se, legal immigrants are accepted at a substantially higher rate (45%) than illegal immigrants are (33%), a difference that is both substantively large and statistically significant. But, as expected, appending Dreamer status to illegal immigrants restores most of this lost support. Either because people feel sympathetic toward Dreamers, view them as not personally responsible for breaking the

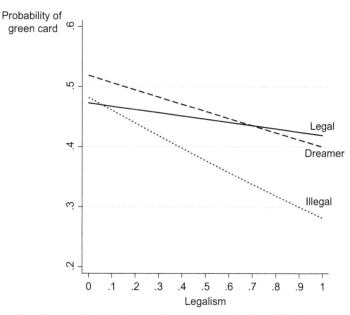

FIGURE 4.3 Legalism and admissions preference across the legal–illegal divide (2013 SSI)
Note: The lines in the figure are the model-estimated probabilities of accepting an immigrant in the conjoint experiment in each experimental condition, at each value of the legalism scale with all other covariates in the model held at their sample means. The model, a logistic regression in which the outcome is whether an immigrant was accepted and standard errors are clustered by respondent, includes interactions between all of the control variables described in Figure 4.2 and dummy indicator variables for treatment status (*Illegal* and *Dreamer* conditions). The interaction between the illegal treatment dummy and legalism is statistically significant at $p < .1$. The other two slopes do not differ significantly from one another. Full tabulations are in the Online Appendix.

law, or regard leaving the Dreamers' status unchanged as an unacceptable breach of egalitarian principles, illegal immigrants brought to the United States as children are admitted at a rate of 43%, almost as high as legal immigrants. Thus, we know two things: (1) people are less willing to accept illegal immigrants than legal ones, which we already knew anyway and (2) that this is *not* a straightforward by-product of group-centric reasoning based on a tendency to reject Latino immigrants and accept others.

As further evidence for our story, Figures 4.3 and 4.4 illustrate what happens when we divide our respondents according to how "legalistic" and "egalitarian" they appear to be based on our survey measures. The figures plot predicted probabilities derived from a logistic regression that modeled each immigrant's likelihood of acceptance based on the experimentally varied attributes as well as an array of respondents' demographic and attitudinal characteristics similar

Experimental Evidence

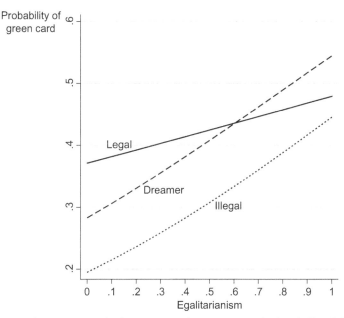

FIGURE 4.4 Egalitarianism and admissions preference across the legal–illegal divide (2013 SSI)
Note: The lines in the figure are the model-estimated probabilities of accepting an immigrant in the conjoint experiment in each experimental condition, at each value of the egalitarianism scale with all other covariates in the model held at their sample means. The model, a logistic regression in which the outcome is whether an immigrant was accepted and standard errors are clustered by respondent, includes interactions between all of the control variables described in Figure 4.2 and dummy indicator variables for treatment status (*Illegal* and *Dreamer* conditions). The interaction between the *Illegal* and *Dreamer* treatment dummy variables and egalitarianism are both statistically significant at $p < .05$.

to those we deployed earlier in this chapter. For clarity, we have left confidence intervals out of the charts and instead refer to the statistical significance of relevant differences in text and footnotes.[22] We are particularly interested in differences between the slopes of the relationships between measures of these values and respondents' choices in each of the three experimental conditions (*Legal*, *Illegal*, and *Dreamer*). All of the respondent-level characteristics are interacted with the randomly assigned status of the immigrants they assessed – legal, illegal, or Dreamer – although the substantive results are not dependent on this particular specification.

Legalistic values are very weakly (and insignificantly) associated with people's acceptance rates for legal immigrants. They are, by contrast, very sharply and significantly associated with choices about whether to grant legal status to illegal immigrants.[23] Respondents who scored at the low level of legalism accepted applicants for legal admission and for legalization at approximately the same rate. But the rate of accepting illegal immigrants into a hypothetical legalization program drops by over twenty percentage points as one moves to the maximum of the legalism scale. The association of legalism with choices about Dreamers falls right in between, showing a statistically significant and negative relationship with the rate of acceptance but one that is a good deal weaker than that observed for illegal immigrants generally and not significantly different from the association observed in evaluations of legal immigrants. This is consistent with the conjecture that many respondents with strong legalistic inclinations nevertheless see the Dreamers' background as absolving them of any personal responsibility for breaking the law. Others may nonetheless feel that "bending the rules" for these immigrants contravenes their rigid conception of what the rule of law requires.

Egalitarianism also has a much more pronounced effect on assessments of illegal than legal immigrants.[24] Moving from the most inegalitarian to the most egalitarian score on this scale does boost the average rate of accepting legal immigrants for a green card by a statistically significant seven percentage points. But the association with choices in the illegal and Dreamer tasks is more than three times as large. There is no evidence, however, that egalitarian values are more powerfully engaged for those who assessed Dreamers versus illegal immigrants. In both, moving from the minimum to the maximum of the scale boosts acceptance rates by approximately twenty-five percentage points.

On further inspection, what really seems to differentiate reactions to illegal immigrants and Dreamers is the degree to which these categories evoke humanitarian sympathy. Figure 4.5 shows how support for immigrants in each task varies with humanitarian values. Illegal immigration generally seems to tap into impulses to help those in need far less than does the question of Dreamers' status in particular, perhaps because the unique plight of someone brought to a country as a child and with no country to return to one strikes Americans as particularly poignant. Prospective legal immigrants also fare significantly ($p < .05$) better among respondents who express humanitarian inclinations. The difference in the associations between humanitarian values and choices in the *Legal* and *Dreamer* conditions is statistically insignificant, however.

As noted earlier, all of these patterns are derived from a model in which we control for ethnocentrism. We show the distribution in the Online Appendix but it is worth noting that the feeling thermometer measure registers more ethnocentrism (about 65% of whites) than the stereotype-based measure we used in Chapter 3. Most of these preferences are not extreme, but the willingness of so many respondents to acknowledge some racial bias outright should somewhat allay concerns about social desirability bias. Using this measure, we can also examine the independent relationship between ethnocentrism and choices in each frame, based on the same statistical model. Figure 4.6 displays how the predicted probability that an immigrant in each of the three frames is

Experimental Evidence

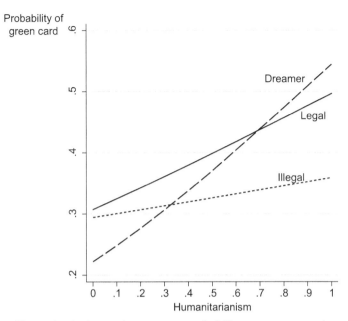

FIGURE 4.5 Humanitarianism and acceptance probability across statuses (2013 SSI)
Note: The lines in the figure are the model-estimated probabilities of accepting an immigrant in the conjoint experiment in each experimental condition, at each value of the humanitarianism scale with all other covariates in the model held at their sample means. The model, a logistic regression in which the outcome is whether an immigrant was accepted and standard errors are clustered by respondent, includes interactions between all of the control variables described in Figure 4.2 and dummy indicator variables for treatment status (*Illegal* and *Dreamer* conditions). The interaction between the *Dreamer* treatment dummy variable and humanitarianism is statistically significant at p < .05. The other two slopes do not differ significantly from one another.

granted a green card varies with respondent ethnocentrism. Moving from the extreme left, where respondents rate Hispanics, Asians, and blacks all with the highest (warmest) score, a 100, on the feeling thermometer measures and whites with the lowest (coldest) score, a flat zero, to the extreme right, where whites were rated 100 and all three outgroups zero, reduces the probability of accepting legal immigrants and Dreamers by approximately 45 percentage points and illegal immigrants by a smaller but still quite substantial 25 percentage points.

Unsurprisingly, prejudiced Americans are considerably more opposed to immigration than are unprejudiced Americans and vastly more opposed than are those who express a preference for nonwhites over whites. However, *at least with immigrants' ethnicity held constant by design*, ethnocentrism has no stronger relationship with assessments of illegal immigrants than prospective legal immigrants. In fact, it has a significantly (p < .05) weaker association

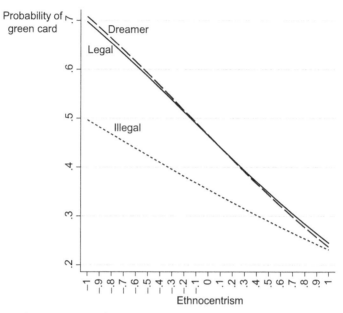

FIGURE 4.6 Ethnocentrism and acceptance probability across statuses (2013 SSI)
Note: The lines in the figure are the model-estimated probabilities of accepting an immigrant in the conjoint experiment in each experimental condition, at each value of the ethnocentrism measure with all other covariates in the model held at their sample means. The model, a logistic regression in which the outcome is whether an immigrant was accepted and standard errors are clustered by respondent, includes interactions between all of the control variables described in Figure 4.2 and dummy indicator variables for treatment status (*Illegal* and *Dreamer* conditions). The interaction between the illegal treatment dummy variable and ethnocentrism indicates statistically weaker (less negative) slope in the *Illegal* condition, meaning that ethnocentrism is more weakly correlated with opposition to immigrants in the *Illegal* than the *Legal* condition. The other two slopes do not differ significantly.

with assessments of illegal immigrants generally. Highly prejudiced individuals are reluctant to admit immigrants in *any* category, though about one-quarter of immigrants in all three conditions nevertheless wind up getting their nod. Americans who are unprejudiced are highly supportive of legal immigrants and Dreamers, with the very least ethnocentric granting a green card to about 75% of the immigrants in these categories. But many also demur when it comes to illegal immigration in general. Respondents who express the *most* favoritism for nonwhites over whites nonetheless see fit to reject one-half of the illegal immigrant profiles they encounter.

Another way to put this is that distinctions in legal status matter *less* to very highly ethnocentric people, consistent with the intuitive scope conditions to the civic fairness framework. For this minority of Americans, some form of group

Experimental Evidence 105

centrism – in this case generalized prejudice – dampens the propensity to distinguish between these types of policy choices. The great majority who are *not* so highly ethnocentric draw sharper distinctions between legal and illegal immigration on the basis of legality per se, over and above the attributes controlled in the experiment. They also sharply distinguish between illegal immigrants in general and Dreamers. But at very high levels of ethnocentrism, those differences vanish. Among those who bluntly acknowledge a strong preference for whites over various groups of nonwhites, immigration policy choices are consistent with a central and predominant aversion to admitting or giving legal status to foreigners generally, and very few of the immigrant profiles in any of our tasks hold a status or set of personal attributes that pass muster. The other side of this, however, is that the far greater number of individuals who express low levels of animus toward the ethnic groups that most of the immigrants (and most of the profiles in our experiment) hail from draw sharp distinctions between legal and illegal immigration even with immigrants' ethnic backgrounds and other attributes held constant. Not surprisingly, given that the sample is heavily white, all of these relationships are unchanged when we confine the analysis to non-Hispanic white respondents.

The multiple treatments in the experiment and the small numbers of non-whites in any group make it difficult to examine differences between white and nonwhite groups' choices. However, at least some of the patterns we have identified appear to hold among nonwhites as a whole. For example, nonwhites admitted 50% of the legal immigrants they evaluated but only 44% of illegal immigrants and 51% of Dreamers, paralleling the patterns observed for whites. Latinos did not show any less inclination to differentiate legal from illegal immigration: they accepted 61% of legal immigrants, 45% of illegal immigrants, and 54% of Dreamers. Among Asians and blacks, the differences between treatment conditions were quite muted. Further research would be needed to determine whether these results indicate something different about the way these groups make such choices or are simply a result of small and unrepresentative samples. Relationships between legalism and egalitarianism and choices across treatment conditions appeared to be less sharp among nonwhites than among whites, but once again, data limitations may be at work. A standard statistical test does not reject the null hypothesis that these relationships were the same among whites and nonwhites.[25]

In Chapter 2, we noted our expectation that judgments about illegal immigration would be more "categorical" due to their underpinnings in legalistic values that promote all-or-nothing judgments on the basis of immigrants' status. Figure 4.7 confirms this in spades. Only 12% of respondents rejected all ten legal immigrants they encountered. This rate nearly triples, to 33%, among those assigned to evaluate illegal immigrants. Keep in mind that to reach this bar, respondents had to look at ten illegal immigrants of all different origins, in five successive choice screens, and socioeconomic statuses, *and say "no" to every single one of them.*[26] It is hard to square any of this with

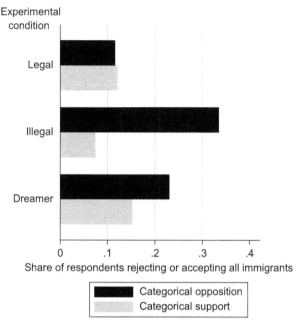

FIGURE 4.7 Categorical judgments (positive and negative) across statuses (2013 SSI)
Note: The bars show the percentage of respondents assigned to each experimental condition in the SSI conjoint who rejected all (categorical opposition) or accepted all (categorical support) of the ten immigrant profiles they were shown.

group-centrism because, for one thing, our hypothetical immigrants are racially balanced across each condition, and, for another, to qualify as "categorical," respondents need, virtually by definition, to reject not only illegal immigrants that they imagine to be Hispanic but also many Europeans and Asians.

Interestingly, categorical rejection drops significantly, to 23%, among those who evaluated Dreamers. This may be because being brought to the United States as children makes these immigrants seem blameless for the legal infraction that other illegal immigrants are categorically held to account for. Still, it is clear that there is a sizeable pocket of blanket resistance to the idea of legalizing even these unauthorized immigrants.

There are lower levels of categorical support (versus rejection) for immigrants among both illegal immigrants and Dreamers. Contrary to what might have been expected from the morally freighted arguments in favor of blanket amnesty, we see marginally (and insignificantly) less blanket support for illegal immigrants than for prospective legal ones. There is better evidence that Dreamers evoke some categorical support relative to other illegal immigrants. Twice as many (16%) of those evaluating Dreamers voted to give them all legal status than did so for illegal immigrants generally.

Experimental Evidence

Differences in the level of categorical opposition across conditions are not significantly different among whites and nonwhites. Among nonwhites, categorical opposition rises from 10% among evaluations of *Legal* immigrants, to 23% in evaluations of *Illegal* immigrants, and back down to 16% in evaluations of Dreamers. The respective levels of categorical support among nonwhites also follow similar patterns to whites: 16% among legal immigrants, 13% among illegal immigrants and 22% among Dreamers. Among Latino respondents, the figures for categorical opposition are 6% among legal immigrants, 21% among illegal immigrants, and 12% among Dreamers. Categorical support among Latinos also varies in similar ways to whites across treatment conditions: 19% for evaluations of legal immigrants, 12% for illegal immigrants, and 24% for Dreamers. In general, nonwhites are more supportive of immigration across all three conditions than are whites, but all three groups draw similar types of distinctions when it comes to their propensity to treat immigrants from these different groups on the basis of their legal status alone, disregarding other personal attributes. Once again, small samples prevent firm conclusions about any differences in the way that whites and nonwhites apply legalistic and egalitarian values to these distinctions. At the same time, however, the data furnish no indication that sharp differences exist. Formal tests of the statistical significance of racial differences in the relationships between these values and categorical opinion across frames do not reject the null of no difference.

In sum, these results again indicate that Americans do widely distinguish legal from illegal immigration on the basis of illegality per se, in keeping with civic fairness, and not simply because these classes of immigrants are associated with different ethnic imagery. The large differences in support overall and especially in the rate of categorical opinion to illegal and legal immigrants obtain over and above explicit national origin cues as well as a range of other attributes that signal assimilation and likely economic self-sufficiency. And they track in theoretically sensible ways with values that we expected the dominant public frames of these issues would engage.

Functional Assimilation and the Relative Weakness of Ethnic Cues in People's Decisions

Categorically minded respondents are unique in that, apart from legal status, they ignore everything else in the profiles of our hypothetical immigrants. Most people do pay attention, however, even when they are evaluating illegal immigrants. What sorts of things do they value? The civic fairness model highlights functional assimilation: learning English and otherwise taking steps to provide for oneself in America. Sociotropic models of opinion about immigration tend to emphasize educational attainment and professional skill, on the assumption that citizens prefer immigrants who are poised to contribute to the national economic well-being and that they perceive such immigrants as best equipped

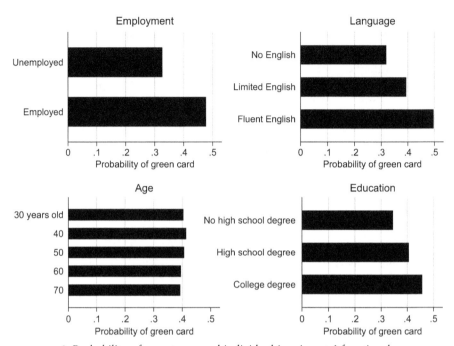

FIGURE 4.8 Probability of acceptance and individual immigrants' functional assimilation and human capital (2013 SSI)
Note: The bars display the share of all immigrants accepted from among those in the specified category, pooling across all three conditions (*Legal, Illegal, Dreamer*). The difference in means across categories of employment, language, and education but not age are statistically significant at p < .05. Full tabulation of the OLS models from which these estimates and significance tests are derived, including by experimental condition, is provided in the Online Appendix.

to do so.[27] And, as noted throughout, group-centric accounts emphasize a variety of channels through which ethnic cues play on peoples' loyalty to race and nation. Here we consider these various influences.

Figure 4.8 displays the probability that an immigrant with each of these attributes is accepted, pooling results over all three legal statuses.[28] The results point to a strong influence of attributes marking functional assimilation, with a split decision for the indicators of sociotropic motivations. Immigrants who have been steadily employed are more than fifteen points more likely to gain acceptance than those who have been unemployed. English-fluent immigrants have a nearly twenty-point advantage over those who do not speak English. This corroborates decades of research on the importance of linguistic and economic assimilation to attitudes about immigration.[29] Education matters (albeit somewhat less), with college-educated immigrants getting about a ten-point boost over those without a high school degree, and a college degree in and

Experimental Evidence 109

of itself conferring a less than five-point advantage over high school graduates. Contrary to our expectation, there is no evidence that immigrants in their working prime are preferred to those near or at the likely end of their ability to participate in the labor market. Americans, then, seem to think immigrants should take the steps necessary to provide for themselves and reward the ones they assume will be better able to do so.

The impact of these attributes does not vary by much in evaluations of legal immigrants, illegal immigrants, and Dreamers. Crucially, this does not mean that norms of functional assimilation are irrelevant to the distinctions that people draw between illegal and legal immigration. If people prefer immigrants who are employed, speak English, and have more education, and *if* they believe that legal and illegal immigrants tend to differ a great deal on these dimensions, these beliefs may also translate into different opinions about legalization policies and legal admissions. Our experiment is not equipped to assess these beliefs directly, but other research has documented that the stereotypes citizens hold about legal and illegal immigrants are indeed different in just these sorts of ways.[30]

Ascriptive Attributes and Group-Centrism

What about attributes that should cue group-based thinking? As Figure 4.9 demonstrates, religion does seem to matter a great deal, with respondents notably less willing to accept Muslims than Christians or nonreligious people.[31] Being Muslim, rather than Christian, costs an immigrant more than one-half as much support as speaking no English versus English fluency and two-thirds the penalty imposed for being chronically unemployed rather than steadily employed. In Chapter 7, we note the importance of considering how and why the applicability of civic fairness and group-centrism as theoretical lenses might vary across immigrant groups. In particular, we return to the possibility that "Muslim exceptionalism" constitutes a distinctively virulent strand of old-fashioned nativism in contemporary politics, one that highlights a particularly tense struggle between evolving ascriptive traditions in American political culture and the liberal tradition. But for present purposes, we think it unlikely that Muslim exceptionalism contributes much to explaining the distinctions that so many Americans draw between legal and illegal immigration policy. Some people may be convinced that hordes of militant jihadis are slipping into the United States from Mexico undetected. More seriously, some of the 9/11 hijackers were illegal immigrants who had entered legally but overstayed their visas. But we assume that few Americans oppose a path to citizenship for illegal immigrants because they dislike Muslims in particular.

Instead, our focus is on the effects of national origin, a proxy for ethnicity. We see some evidence of discrimination by national origin, but it is quite limited. On the whole, German immigrants are selected two percentage points more often than Mexicans (p < .05) and one percentage point more often than Chinese (n.s.). They are also four percentage points more likely to be chosen

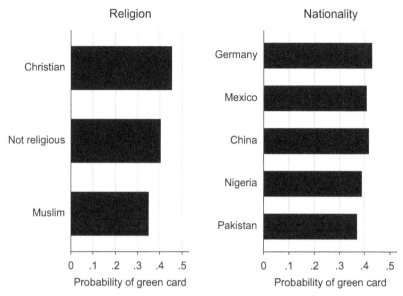

FIGURE 4.9 Probability of acceptance and ethnoreligious traits
Note: The bars display the share of all immigrants accepted from among those in the specified category, pooling across all three conditions (*Legal, Illegal, Dreamer*). The difference in means across categories of religion are statistically significant at p < .05. Significance tests for national origin categories are described in the text. Full tabulation of the OLS models from which these estimates and significance tests are derived, including by experimental condition, is provided in the Online Appendix.

than Nigerians (p < .001) and six percentage points more than Pakistanis (p < .001) even though religion is explicitly varied in the task. Perhaps Nigeria's lower standing reflects some mix of unfamiliarity or prejudice through association with blacks and African immigration. Pakistan, frequently in the news for associations with terrorism, might evoke fears of violent extremism or be another cue of Islam.[32] But the main conclusion is that the ethnic cues have fairly muted effects. Analyzing only white respondents made surprisingly little difference. The effects of ethnicity, with national origin as proxy, remain miniscule compared to the effects of the other attributes varied in the experiment.

Symbolic Racism

Nor is there evidence of symbolic racism against Latinos among white respondents in our sample. Recall from Chapter 2 that, according to that argument, whites only feel free to express ethnic bias against Latinos when furnished with a normatively acceptable rationale for doing so.[33] As Figure 4.10 illustrates, there is no evidence that whites apply harsher penalties for violating civic norms to Latino immigrants than to immigrants from other ethnic groups. The ethnic

Experimental Evidence

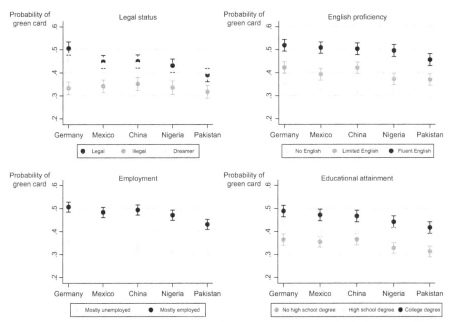

FIGURE 4.10 Penalties for norm violation by immigrants' national origin (2013 SSI)
Note: The figures display the model-estimated probabilities that an immigrant from each national origin category is accepted in the SSI conjoint, along with 95% confidence intervals, for immigrants in each of the indicated categories of language, employment, education, and legal status. These probabilities are estimated from logistic regressions in which the dependent variable is whether an immigrant is accepted and the regressors are indicators for the immigrant's national origin interacted with indicators for each of the other attributes. Full tabulations are available in the Online Appendix, including for the full sample (shown here) and restricting the sample to non-Hispanic whites.

biases are mostly small and are no larger among immigrants who violate the norm than those who did not. For example, Mexicans and Germans receive the same penalty regardless of what civic fairness norm they are violating (illegality, poor English ability, lack of gainful employment, and low education) relative to those who adhere to these norms (by applying legally to enter, speaking fluent English, working, and having completed a high degree of education).

All of this is consistent with our third hypothesis: people are responding to civic fairness cues in a more or less evenhanded way. The effects of these cues are almost identical regardless of the ethnic background of the immigrants in question. There is no support here for the symbolic racism theory that white people feel at greater liberty to unleash their prejudice under the cover of norm-violation.

These results in Figure 4.10 also help rule out another group-centrist explanation for the muted effects of national origin that has been proposed in the literature. People who dislike Latinos but are unwilling to acknowledge this to a survey researcher (or to themselves) might be tempted to support only those individual immigrants from the disliked group that they believe are rare. If such people tend to assume that Latino immigrants have little education, do not speak English, are illegally present, or tend not to be steadily employed, they might cover their tracks, so to speak, by going out of their way to support Latino immigrants who are college educated, English fluent, applying to immigrate legally, or have been consistently employed. This would allow them to demonstrate a willingness to accept the sorts of Latino immigrants that they believe to be unusual while still in effect expressing a preference for reducing less immigration. Some research[34] argues that this dynamic helps account for the "skills premium" that is touted as evidence for sociotropic motivations for immigration attitudes.[35] It demonstrates that people who express "cold" feelings toward Latinos award a *greater* premium to Latino immigrants whose occupation requires a high degree of education and skill than they do when it comes to European immigrants. However, it is not clear why respondents who had already expressed outright cold feelings toward Latinos as a group would then go to such lengths to avoid appearing prejudiced.[36] At any rate, the results in Figure 4.10 fail to corroborate this dynamic in our results, among the more than 20,000 choices that our respondents in this experiment made. This remains true when we confine the sample to whites, to prejudiced whites, and to whites who report colder feelings toward Latinos than toward their own racial group.

So Does Ethnicity Matter?

To be clear, these results do not mean that no segment of the population cares deeply about immigrants' ethnic background per se in making these kinds of choices. We already showed that generalized ethnocentrism strongly predicts opposition to legal and illegal immigrants alike, just as the feeling thermometer measures of group affect predicted opinions about legal and illegal immigration policy earlier in the chapter. Moreover, the treatment effects of the ethnic cues in our experiment speak to the *average* discrimination against Latino immigrants and those from other backgrounds. There is no inherent contradiction between the idea that the average citizen discriminates little against Latino immigrants in the context of our conjoint experiment and the idea that some Americans who are prejudiced against Latinos do discriminate substantially while most do not and some others (including some whites) even favor Latinos.[37]

Intuitively, Americans who unabashedly express relatively "colder" feelings toward Latinos than toward whites, Asians, and blacks would be expected to discriminate more than average against hypothetical Latino immigrants in our experiment. Indeed, this is what we find. Figure 4.11 plots the model-predicted probability of accepting a German, Chinese, or Mexican immigrant, pooling across all three legal status conditions, against Latino feeling thermometer ratings, with feeling thermometer ratings for the other three groups and their

Experimental Evidence

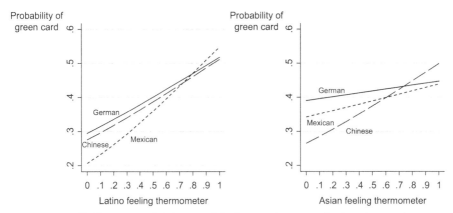

FIGURE 4.11 Feelings toward Asians and Latinos and support for immigrants from Germany, China, and Mexico (2013 SSI)
Note: The figures display the model-estimated probability that an immigrant is accepted at each score of the indicated group feeling thermometers, in each case with the other three feeling thermometers held at their sample means. The model is a logistic regression in which the dependent variable is whether an immigrant as accepted and an indicator variable for each randomly assigned immigrant national origin is interacted with each of the four feeling thermometer scores. Full tabulations are shown in the Online Appendix.

interaction with the national origin cues in the experiment all held constant.[38] For purposes of comparison, Figure 4.11 also plots these model probabilities against the Asian feeling thermometer ratings.

Respondents who express the coldest feelings toward Latinos show a pronounced tendency to discriminate on the basis of ethnicity: Mexican immigrants are disfavored by just under ten points relative to Germans and Chinese. However, this bias shrinks as feelings toward Latinos improve. Less than one-quarter of the sample expresses feelings toward Latinos that are "cold," in absolute terms (below the 0.5 midpoint of the scale), and those at the bottom end of the scale, who are most prone to discrimination, are fewer still. Thus, the small effect of Mexican national origin reflects the fact that the great majority of the sample gives little average weight to this cue of Latino ethnicity. A similar pattern obtains for anti-Asian sentiment: pronounced discrimination is evident among those who rate Asians very "cold" relative to other groups, but anti-Asian bias dissipates and even reverses among those with distinctively positive feelings toward Asians.

In both cases, there is little evidence that people who express neutral or lukewarm attitudes toward Latinos or Asians are concealing any powerful impetus to discriminate against immigrants from these backgrounds that they then reveal in their choices in the experiment. What you see is about what you get: most Americans discriminate little in these policy choices, and most of the ones who do discriminate have no compunction about stating bluntly on a survey that they have relatively cold feelings toward these groups. If the others do harbor unacknowledged prejudice, they are apparently able to suppress it in making these types of choices. Again, allaying concerns about social desirability bias, these patterns are no different when we examine only the first choices that respondents make in the conjoint task.

Figure 4.11 also reveals some counterintuitive patterns. Feelings about Latinos have the strongest effect on support for Mexican immigrants in the experiment, but they also clearly have strong effects on support for Chinese and German immigrants. Moreover, this pattern is much more weakly evident for attitudes toward Asians: they are only modestly correlated with respondents' propensity to give a green card to Mexican and German immigrants.

What explains this? At first glance, these patterns could seem to reflect generalized ethnocentrism, but recall that we have already isolated the effects of generalized prejudice by controlling for all four feeling thermometers in the regression model and interacting each of them with all the national origin cues. The relationships are therefore distinctive to attitudes about these specific groups.[39]

We conjecture that the strong correlation between anti-Latino sentiment and support for non-Latino immigrants arises because of something the literature has long acknowledged: the categories "immigrant" and "Latino" are highly conflated in many Americans' minds. When we canvas public attitudes towards "Latinos" as a group, the responses we get may thus in part be expressions of opposition to immigration in general rather than hostility toward Latinos or Latino immigrants in particular. Conflation is a two-way street. Researchers have focused on the likelihood that references to "immigration" will automatically bring to mind Latinos because media coverage and public discourse so often cover the two in tandem: immigrants are overwhelmingly portrayed as Latino, despite the fact that new cohorts of immigrants include more Asians than Latin Americans, *and* media references to Latinos as a force in American politics are overwhelmingly focused on immigration, despite the fact that more than two-thirds of Latinos are US-born. As a result, in measuring attitudes toward Latinos as a group, we wind up capturing more general antipathy to immigration. This general antipathy to immigration then predicts opposition to immigrants from other backgrounds.

Why, then, are attitudes about Asians more weakly correlated with support for non-Asian immigrants than are attitudes about Hispanics with non-Hispanic immigrants? We suspect that the answer is that Asians are widely regarded as "exceptional" immigrants, in keeping with the "model minority myth." As a result, people will frequently express feelings about Asians as a group that are distinct from their abstract attitudes about immigration. Measures of attitudes toward Asians are therefore less likely to reflect generalized opposition to immigration and predict support for immigrants who are not Asian in the experiment. Concretely, for example, people might express attitudes toward Latinos that reflect their feelings toward legal as well as illegal

Experimental Evidence 115

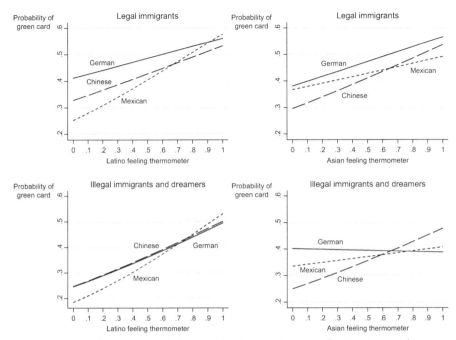

FIGURE 4.12 Feelings toward Asians and Latinos and support for immigrants from Germany, China, and Mexico by legal status (2013 SSI)
Note: The figures display the model-estimated probability that an immigrant is accepted at each score of the indicated group feeling thermometers, in each case with the other three feeling thermometers held at their sample means. The model is a logistic regression in which the dependent variable in each treatment condition (*Legal, Illegal, and Dreamer*) is whether an immigrant is accepted and an indicator variable for each randomly assigned immigrant national origin is interacted with each of the four feeling thermometer scores. Full tabulations are shown in the Online Appendix. The Online Appendix also shows full tabulations for these analyses when the sample is restricted to non-Hispanic whites.

immigrants but express attitudes toward Asians that exclusively reflect their feelings toward legal immigrants. If this is true, we would expect the Latino feeling thermometer to predict support for non-Latino immigrants who are applying to come legally as well as those who are illegally present in the country. But we would expect the Asian feeling thermometer only to predict support for non-Asian immigrants who are applying to come legally.

Figure 4.12 strongly supports this idea. It breaks down the results in Figure 4.11 by respondents who evaluated prospective legal immigrants (top panels) and those who evaluated illegal immigrants and Dreamers (bottom panels).[40] The Latino and Asian feeling thermometers perform similarly in predicting choices about legal immigrants. Both have a sizeable relationship with choices about Germans, Mexicans, and Chinese immigrants alike and a noticeably larger relationship with choices about immigrants who are supposedly from the ethnic group they solicit feelings toward. However, they perform in markedly different ways in assessments of illegal immigrants, which are two-thirds of the profiles in the pooled results from the previous figure. In the bottom left panel, the Latino feeling thermometer is very strongly predictive of choices about immigrants from all three national origin groups. Moving across its range boosts acceptances of Chinese and Germans by about twenty-five percentage points each and of Mexicans by thirty-three. However, in the right-hand bottom panel, moving across the entire range of the Asian feeling thermometer only boosts acceptance of Chinese immigrants in any large measure (about twenty-three percentage points) while raising approval of Mexican immigrants by only five and of Germans not at all. These patterns are just what we would expect if assessments of Latinos as a group draw heavily on attitudes about *legal and illegal* immigration while attitudes toward Asians only tap into attitudes about *legal* immigration.

If this conjecture is true – and, to be sure, it requires further corroboration in other studies that use different experimental designs, some of which we are able to provide in subsequent chapters – it complicates the conventional assumption in research on public opinion that, where group attitudes and policy opinions are associated, the former is "mover" and the latter "moved."[41] To be clear, we are not arguing that opinions about immigration *policy* are necessarily causally prior to attitudes about the ethnic groups associated with immigration. But we are suggesting that beliefs or attitudes about immigrants as a group or about the consequences of immigration – generalized attitudes about immigration, that is – may be "baked in" to the attitudes that people express about the ethnic groups most widely associated with immigration. Asked their feelings about Latinos, many respondents may have little else to go on than their general attitudes about immigration, and many surely overlook the fact that two-thirds of US Latinos were born in this country. Naturally, these general attitudes toward immigration as a demographic, social, and partisan phenomenon will be strongly predictive of opinions about immigration policy. This is true also of attitudes toward Asians, but the association is weaker and apparently confined to legal immigration. The measures of ethnic group attitudes that to a degree subsume them will be strongly predictive of immigration policy opinions.

By implication, well-documented statistical associations between attitudes toward ethnic groups and opinions about immigration policy may inflate the role of ethnic group-centrism in the formation of these policy opinions. These associations capture not only the effect of group attitudes about Latinos on immigration policy opinions but also the degree to which attitudes about Latinos tap into generalized attitudes about immigration in the first place. In technical parlance, this is an issue of discriminant validity with measures of group affect: they are likely to make respondents think of precisely the sorts of attitudes about immigration they are then shown to predict.[42] Less technically, we are dealing with a tautology, correlating a measure that reflects attitudes

Experimental Evidence 117

toward immigration with ... attitudes toward immigration. Some of this generalized opposition to immigration is surely rooted in ethnic animus. But people who are opposed to immigration for reasons other than animus against Latinos may also express distinctively cold feelings toward Latinos, a group that they conflate with the category immigrants.

Notably, this issue of discriminant validity may arise not only in explicit measures of prejudice, such as the ones we have used here, but also implicit measures of anti-Latino sentiment. If people strongly associate symbols of Latino ethnicity with immigration, those who dislike immigration for just about any reason might well be prone to associating those symbols with negative objects. This would be true even if their opposition to immigration were not distinctively focused on Latinos or grounded in racial categorization. Instead, their measured implicit bias against Latinos could reflect general negativity toward immigration that originates in some other source and spills over to Latinos as a group because people imagine Latinos to be immigrants.

In fact, Efrén Pérez, working from the standpoint of implicit racism, reports results that mirror the patterns in Figures 4.11 and 4.12.[43] His experiment varied the ethnic background of hypothetical immigrants (Mexican versus Irish, which is notable because Irish are not only likely to be thought of as white but even more divided from Americans than the English by a common language). He finds no significant difference in respondents' overall reactions to these two immigrants. More notably for purposes of the present discussion, he finds that an implicit measure of anti-Latino prejudice predicted support for both the Irish and the Mexican immigrants about equally. Pérez attributes this to the primal grip that implicit attitudes have on the formation of opinions about immigration. Specifically, implicit prejudice blunts and biases information processing in ways that respondents do not perceive: they genuinely think they are making an immigration policy choice based on nonracial considerations, but their snap reaction to anything immigration related is so heavily and immediately conditioned by their negativity toward Latinos that they will often simply disregard information – *even the immigrants' own ethnic background*.

We cannot definitively rule out that this dynamic contributes to the patterns shown, and perhaps such dynamics come into play more when it comes to implicit than explicit attitudes since the former are presumed to catch and motivate people unawares. But virtually all of the rest of the results in the conjoint suggest that people *are* quite sensitive to individuating information about immigrants as well as categorical information about their legal status. Respondents who are very high in anti-Latino prejudice (Latino feeling thermometer minus white feeing thermometer) simply (and intuitively) seem to respond to different types of information from those who are not prejudiced against Latinos: those who are high in anti-Latino prejudice rely more heavily on national origin cues, discriminate more based on religion, and value English fluency at least as much as and perhaps modestly more that the unprejudiced but care less, all else being equal, about employment status, educational attainment, and legal status.[44] We speculate that what Pérez has instead identified is a similar dynamic to the one we describe here: implicit or explicit measures of anti-Latino sentiment may be tainted by the accessibility of negative feelings about immigration (rather than ethnic animus per se). As a result, those measures predict opposition to non-Latino immigrants, not just to Latino immigrants.

Put differently, we might observe strong correlations between either type of measure of anti-Latino sentiment and immigration policy opinions even if all opposition to immigration emerged from sources other than ethnic animus. We are of course not asserting that this is the reality, but it is a useful thought experiment, and it leads to a caveat about the usual interpretation of correlations such as these (i.e., that they are simply indicative of a group-centric basis for opinion formation). Earlier in the chapter, we argued that anti-Latino sentiment was strongly predictive of opinions about both legal immigration and illegal immigration policy but provided limited leverage in explaining why people often had different opinions about the two. If it is true that the correlations between people's attitudes toward Latinos and opinions about immigration policy is inflated in the way that we have argued, then we cannot be certain about how much group-specific racial animus against Latinos is contributing to either of these issue opinions.

Some readers may by now understandably have thought to themselves that we have gone from bad to worse, normatively speaking. We have called into question what an important component of the evidence for group-centrism can really establish about whether people form opinions about immigration policy on the basis of their attitudes toward Latinos as a group. However, the alternative mechanism we have described suggests that opposition to immigration, originating for whatever reason, may be spilling over to negative attitudes toward Latinos as a group. That the immigration debate may be attaching a stigma to entire ethnic groups should provide no general moral reassurance that all is well in the domain of race and public opinion. But it is distinct from the idea that group-centrism predominates in the formation of policy opinions.

Is There Madness in Our Method?

We have repeatedly addressed concerns about how experiments like this one might artificially tamp down ethnic biases. It is worth contending with just a few more possibilities. Perhaps forcing people to make a sequence of choices about immigrants from different places might cue respondents that they should actively try to appear unbiased. This kind of social desirability is, we believe, unlikely to be a major concern in conjoint experiments for somewhat technical reasons,[45] but one simple indication is that the results do not change much when we examine only the first choices that respondents make. Alternatively, perhaps the experiment found little evidence of anti-Latino bias because it asks

Experimental Evidence

respondents to make choices about an unrepresentative sample of immigrant profiles. Finally, it may be the case that information about hypothetical immigrants' race is buried in a sea of other profile images, and as such does not matter as much as it would using approaches (such as vignettes) that make this plain. As we and others have argued at length elsewhere,[46] and as evidence based on other research designs described in later chapters will show, these methodological concerns are unlikely to be driving the small ethnic differences we observe in the experiment. One recent study, for example, found that discrimination against Latino candidates relative to whites was no more pronounced in a design that conveyed ethnicity through labels than in a setting that communicated ethnicity through names and pictures.[47] Moreover, the results in the next two chapters use different experimental designs that come closer to the vignette approach, and neither suggests so much as a hint of disagreement with the results described here.

A second concern, related to the external validity of results from experiments like these, is whether the choices that people make about counter-stereotypic immigrant profiles really have anything to do with the way they form judgments about the more abstract policy questions they are usually called on to answer. For example, do people's choices about whether to accept German or Chinese illegal immigrants really tell us much about their opinions about illegal immigration policy? Or are their policy opinions about, say, a path to citizenship for illegal immigrants in general related only to the way that they make choices about Mexican illegal immigrants? This question is similar to one raised by Martin Gilens in his investigation of racial attitudes and opinions about welfare policy.[48] Gilens found that white respondents in a survey experiment did not discriminate (on average) between a hypothetical black and white welfare recipient. However, only their attitudes toward the black welfare recipient were strongly related to their opinions about welfare spending in general while their attitudes toward the white welfare recipient were much more weakly related to this general opinion. The idea is that it is the black welfare recipient who occupies an outsized presence in people's minds when they make general choices about welfare policy.

Similarly, perhaps for all the even-handedness across ethnic groups that we find on average in this experiment, it would turn out that only opinions about Latino illegal immigrants in the experiment are strongly predictive of opinions about a path to citizenship for illegal immigrants. This worry turns out to be unfounded here: the choices that respondents made about whether to give illegal immigrants from each national origin group a green card are equally predictive of their opinions about a path to citizenship, as displayed in Figure 4.13. This remains true when we confine the analysis to the first choice that respondents make in the experiment and when we control for all four group feeling thermometers. Opposition to a path to citizenship is about equally tied to opposition to individual illegal immigrants from all national origin backgrounds.

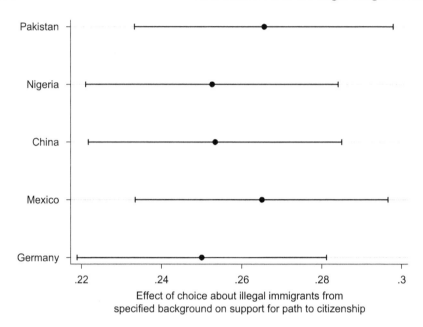

FIGURE 4.13 Support for illegal immigrants versus support for illegal immigration policy by national origin (2013 SSI)
Note: Displays the estimated effect of accepting an immigrant in the illegal condition of the conjoint on general support for a path to citizenship, with 95% confidence intervals. These estimates are derived from an OLS regression in which the *path* item is the dependent variable and regressors are the randomly assigned immigrant national origin categories, each interacted with whether an immigrant was accepted. In other words, the estimates reflect the model-estimated correlation between acceptance of illegal immigrants from each national origin and general support for a path to citizenship. There are no statistically significant differences across national origin categories. Acceptance rates of immigrants from all five countries are about equally predictive of a respondent's general support for a path to citizenship. Full tabulations are available in the Online Appendix.

Summary of Experimental Results

In the main, our experiment demonstrated three things. First, ceteris paribus, Americans judge illegal immigrants more harshly (and rigidly) than legal ones, and the distinctions that they draw are tied heavily to values that inform popular conceptions of civic fairness – procedural legalism, egalitarianism, and in the case of policies directed at Dreamers, humanitarianism. Second, ethnocentric Americans are more likely to reject *all* classes of immigrants, but they do not hold any special dislike of illegal immigrants versus legal ones. Third, by and large, when assessing hypothetical immigrants, Americans do not make the kinds of sharp distinctions based on national origin that a

Conclusion

group-centric model would suggest. The experimental results are not consistent with the idea that the greater tie-in between illegal immigration and Latino ethnicity than between legal immigration and Latino ethnicity is a major reason that so many Americans hold different opinions about these two areas of policy. The results also suggest that most Americans do not make choices about immigration policy primarily based on the ethnic background of the immigrant beneficiaries *when the sort of additional information that the conjoint framework provided is available* – a proviso we consider at length in the next chapter.

CONCLUSION

Throughout this chapter, we have had one main question in mind: what accounts for the distinctions that much of the public draws between legal and illegal immigration policy, including distinctive negativity toward illegal immigrants but also surprisingly high support for the idea of a path to citizenship for the undocumented? By contrasting people's attitudes about illegal immigration policy with their attitudes about legal admissions, we found some evidence of group-centric thinking. But on balance, people are harder on illegal immigrants (and accordingly less favorable to policies that would help them) because "illegality" engages their considerations of civic fairness in a way that legal immigration does not. These considerations – among them legalism, egalitarianism, and humanitarianism – move into overdrive when people are asked to consider what ought to be done about illegal immigration, and they do so independently of covert (symbolic) racism, ethnocentrism, and group-specific bias. The upshot is that people engaged in prejudiced thinking will line up against immigrants of all kinds. But, at the same time, the *additional* hostility we find directed against illegal immigrants comes into play as people reckon with the fact that those immigrants have violated norms of civic fairness. Thus, in a proximate sense, the evidence here makes a strong case that at least one aspect of the substantial nuance depicted in Chapter 1 – namely, taking stock of the values associated with public conceptions of civic fairness – is indispensable to explaining the distinctions that people make between legal and illegal immigration.

Our findings also help explain another puzzle in the politics of immigration reform. For almost a decade, commercial poll after commercial poll has found anywhere from a majority to an overwhelming majority of Americans support a path to citizenship for illegal immigrants *in the abstract*. Large majorities of whites and even pluralities or majorities of Republicans are usually in support of this. These polls, touted by a sympathetic media to bolster the legitimacy of bipartisan efforts to pass comprehensive immigration reform legislation, are difficult to square with a widespread and rigid ethnocentric base of opposition to immigration. Nor have they gone unnoticed in the research literature. Pérez, for example, expresses skepticism about whether these polling results should be taken at face value.[49]

We share Pérez's skepticism that these polls, *in isolation*, are genuine reflections of American public opinion about illegal immigration policy. Efforts to reform illegal immigration policy by giving illegal immigrants a path to citizenship have run into serious obstacles in the court of public opinion. The Senate version of George W. Bush's attempt at comprehensive immigration reform, for example, polled in the 30s in 2007.[50] In short, the overwhelmingly positive polling about a path to citizenship in the abstract does not anticipate the divisions in public opinion that emerge when the rubber meets the road.

Our inquiry in this chapter can, we think, shed some light on the reasons for this departure. There is no question that some Americans are hostile to Latinos on the basis of their ethnicity per se, perhaps threatened by the waning of the white majority or convinced that large-scale Latino immigration poses an existential threat to traditional American culture. But any model of immigration policy opinion that focuses on prejudice to the exclusion of civic values fares poorly as an explanation of the public fissures that tend to emerge when such proposals come to the fore. If there is one thing that Americans do not need to "discover" about illegal immigrants, it is that most of them are Hispanic. Citizens' second thoughts must be due to some other information that comes through in these debates.

An explanation better supported by the patterns documented here, we think, is in the way that public framing engages the conceptions of civic fairness that underpin Americans' differentiation between legal and illegal immigration. Some of these conceptions are nearly consensual. Americans overwhelmingly insist that immigrants assimilate functionally, at a minimum learning English and holding a job, and many of them harbor negative stereotypes about Latino immigrants in these regards that undoubtedly bolster public opposition to legalization programs. Americans disagree over what civic fairness requires in fealty to the letter of the law and the elimination of official barriers to status equality among those who have made their home in America, and differences in receptivity to these conflicting value frames promote differences in views about the acceptability – or imperative – of an amnesty.

Debates over the issue accentuate frames that speak directly to these concerns. Policies that refer to meeting conditions, fines, and English requirements tend to gain overwhelming support. Even Americans who support legalization tend to support these requirements. But, on the other hand, when policies delve into specifics that suggest anything resembling an "inside track" for illegal immigrants, support quickly breaks down. Prior to asking respondents about whether a vote for the Gang of Eight bill would make them more or less likely to vote for their congressman, a June 2013 United Technologies poll asked whether, *if the bill were passed*, immigrants who qualified should become eligible for government benefits such as Social Security, food stamps, and Medicaid ("welfare" was not mentioned) before they become citizens. Fully 77% said they should not be, and 20% said they should. Asked the same question about eligibility for assistance under the Affordable Care Act, 69%

Conclusion

were opposed and 27% in support. A Pew Research Center/USA Today poll conducted in the same month and year found that 76% of respondents said undocumented immigrants should have to "show they can speak and understand English before gaining legal status," compared to 23% who said they should not – substantially higher than the 55% who supported a ten-year waiting period for becoming a permanent resident and the 56% who said they should have to pay a fine. By a margin of 77–20, respondents agreed that this legislation should "include increased border security measures," though only 43% insisted that immigrants should have to wait until "after effective control of US borders has been established" before applying for legal status compared to 49% who said they should be able to apply "while improvements to border security are being made."

A poll conducted in deep blue California in 2013 arrived at similar conclusions.[51] While a whopping 68% of registered voters supported a path to citizenship for illegal immigrants, 80% said they should have to pass an English test to qualify and 67% said the Department of Homeland Security must certify that the border is secure before the program could go forward. More strikingly, almost one-half of Californians said that illegal immigrants should have to return to their home countries and apply through the same channel as legal immigrants in order to gain legal status, a provision that essentially nullifies the idea of a program that offers anything to illegal immigrants that is not available to aspiring legal entrants. Fifty-five percent said illegal immigrants who qualify for legalization should not be able to be hired to jobs that American citizens have also applied for. And 58% rejected the idea of making legalized immigrants eligible for public benefits. All of these specific questions query preferences about illegal immigrants, so the ethnic group imagery is unlikely to change much. Instead, cleavages emerge around questions of civic fairness that the specific questions amplify. These are the sorts of value conflicts that we would expect to rise to the top of political debates and deliberation in a public that by and large elevates values over base prejudices when the two come into direct conflict – what we would expect, that is to say, from a public with a strong moralistic and rationalistic ethos that guides its choices even in a domain such as immigration that by its nature evokes group-centric concerns.

As we have emphasized, however, the power of civic fairness does not refute the idea that prejudice is widespread and that it plays a role in public opinion about immigration. In this chapter, we demonstrated that values play a larger role than anti-Latino sentiment in explaining the distinctions that citizens draw between legal and illegal immigration policy. And we called into question what the correlational evidence tying attitudes toward Latinos to opinions about both these policy domains could really tell us about the extent to which immigration policy opinions are formed group-centrically, on the basis of a desire to withhold a benefit from a disliked ethnic group. However, the conjoint experiment mitigates by design another way that negative stereotypes about Latinos may contribute powerfully to the formation of opinions about immigration policy. When people are called on to make judgments without very much information that can be used to relate a policy question to civic values, or with ambiguous information on this score, they may instead rely on ethnic cues and automatic stereotyping as a heuristic source of information about civic fairness. It is to this type of influence of group-specific prejudice on immigration policy opinion, and what civic fairness and group-centrism can tell us about it, that we turn in the next chapter.

5

Civic Fairness and Ethnic Stereotypes

Civic fairness and group-centrism both expect significant ethnic biases in White's immigration policy opinions in everyday politics. What they differ on is *why*. Group-centric models tied to racial identities and prejudices argue that negative stereotypes flow out of defensiveness of white dominance and fear and loathing of minority groups. The civic fairness model argues that negative stereotypes may also serve a heuristic purpose for a far wider universe of people, "filling in the blanks" about whether immigrants are likely to meet criteria tied to civic fairness. Both of these interpretations imply that prejudice plays a role in the formation of opinions about immigration. They disagree about what kind of prejudice is at work: group-centric prejudice is motivated simply by one's (explicit or implicit) dislike of Latinos, whereas civic fairness-driven prejudice occurs because people *assume* that Latinos violate civic fairness norms. Accordingly, our goal now is to illustrate how civic fairness plays a role in the anatomy of ethnic discrimination itself.

Empirically, we test whether anti-Latino bias in White's immigration policy choices diminishes, remains unchanged, or increases in response to information that speaks directly to functional assimilation: labor market performance and English language ability. We expect to find significant bias where national origin cues are manipulated in isolation or where other information is sparse. If this bias reflects a group-centric motivation – that is, it is founded on deep-seated racial animus per se or "taste-based" recalling terminology we deployed in Chapter 2 – it should remain intact or even expand in response to such information. If it reflects the use of immigrants' ethnicity as a heuristic when alternative sources of information about civic fairness are in short supply, it should diminish. This is our fourth hypothesis, and its corroboration would suggest that anti-Latino bias is heavy on stereotyping and light on the kind of racial animus at the heart of group-centric models.

ETHNIC BIAS AND INFORMATIONAL CONTEXT

To anyone who has followed immigration politics in the last several years – or, really, ever – the limited evidence of ethnic bias in Americans' immigration choices we saw in Chapter 4 might seem unrealistic, to put it mildly. What about the overt racial demagoguery? What about casual references people make to "illegal Mexicans?" On the other side, what about the role of ethnic consciousness in rallying millions of immigrants and their co-ethnics to march on major cities?

Part of the answer is of course that group-centrism does play an important role in generating and mobilizing opinions about immigration, even if we are right that the influence of civic fairness is more widespread. But another part of the answer is context. In Chapter 4's conjoint experiment, respondents were presented profiles of immigrants that made a good deal of individuating information easily accessible. Respondents learned not only where the immigrants were from, but also whether they spoke English well, had family already in the United States, possessed education and labor market skills, and so on. In this rich information environment, people discriminated little, all else being equal, against Mexican immigrants versus those from other places. Similar patterns obtain wherever contextual information of this kind is available: we see them in other conjoint-based studies,[1] in experiments that have varied ethnic labels or racial cues such as skin color along with only one additional attribute such as English proficiency,[2] and in experiments in which only ethnic cues are manipulated but a substantial amount of other information is made explicit and held constant.[3] The upshot is that in information-rich settings, discrimination on the basis of Latino ethnicity (or other racial cues) is simply not all that prevalent.

Of course, ordinary citizens often lack such information when forming opinions about immigration, unless they happen to be employees of the State Department or, more likely, the Department of Homeland Security. If they did make choices in a context that mimicked this informational context, format, and environment (e.g., individually rather than in a group setting, in a normal emotional state rather than whooped up by a racist firebrand at a rally or just off a desert patrol with the Minutemen), we would have a reasonably good basis for believing that their choices would resemble those elicited in the conjoint.[4] Indeed, some clever real-world research on the Swiss case by Jens Hainmueller, Dominick Hangartner, and Teppei Yamamoto strongly suggests that conjoint analyses are quite good at mimicking patterns in a rare situation in which people voted directly on whether immigrants should have Swiss citizenship.[5]

But what if people have little to go on besides clues about ethnicity? Or what if ethnic cues had been placed front and center, rather than listed with a bunch of other attributes? A large body of research, much of which we canvassed in Chapter 2, suggests we would have found more bias.[6] For example, researchers have found that white Americans responded to an image of Asian immigrants

Ethnic Bias and Informational Context 127

more positively than did those exposed to an image of Latino immigrants.[7] Other research found greater support for immigration after a news story featured reports about Eastern Europeans versus Latin Americans.[8] And still other survey experimental research shows that whites consider a Mexican immigrant's overstaying a visa and flying a foreign flag as more serious than the same violations by British and Canadian immigrants.[9] In all three cases, contextual information was sparse and most everything aside from ethnicity was left to the imagination. And in all three, anti-Latino bias was evident.

What are we to make of these conflicting results? Recall the distinction we introduced in Chapter 2 between "taste-based" discrimination and "statistical" discrimination. The former refers to discrimination based on preferences about immigrants' racial group membership per se. Foundational treatments[10] were agnostic about where "tastes" come from, but certainly any and all group-centric motives are in play. Whites, for example, might prefer European immigrants to Latinos *because* they are white or *because* they are not Latino. The majority racial group may worry about its dominant or majority position, say, or simply feel that Latinos are intrinsically un-American or otherwise undesirable. The underlying motivation for symbolic racists, for example, is deep-seated emotional hostility toward Latinos, inculcated through early socialization, and concealed behind putative violations of civic fairness. Symbolic racism therefore predicts not only an effect of ethnic cues but also ethnic double standards *in the processing of auxiliary information*. As we discussed in Chapter 4, there was no evidence of such double standards in the conjoint.

Statistical discrimination, on the other hand, is based on beliefs about systematic differences in the personal attributes that members of different ethnic groups tend to possess (or lack). It is these differences that *really* matter to people, and ethnicity is just an easy stand-in for cognitive misers.[11]

Statistical discrimination sees anti-Latino bias as an outgrowth of stereotype-driven beliefs that immigrants from this group tend to violate norms tied to civic fairness. Prejudice enters the equation as a reflection of the prevailing stigma and stereotypes attached to Latino immigrants in American society. No small number of Americans apply them, in some cases unawares, to their fairness assessments. Such people may have little or no animus toward Latinos *qua* Latinos. Negative affect may exist but stem mostly from stereotypic beliefs – a contrast to the group-centrist idea that stereotypes are concocted to justify and reinforce negative group affect or at least would only take root in relation to an outgroup. Ethnic cues can, however, "fill in the blanks" in the absence of clear and pertinent information about civic fairness. Although we saw in Chapter 2 that group cues are usually accompanied by civic fairness cues in media communication about immigration, there are likely to be frequent instances in which this information is sparse, conflicted, or confusing.

Ethnic biases revealed by experiments that vary immigrants' national origin or race without much context might reflect either kind of discrimination. But the fact that they seem to shrink or vanish in experiments where people learn more about the immigrants they are evaluating is consistent with statistical discrimination against Latinos and not (or at least not straightforwardly) with taste-based discrimination on racial grounds per se. What is more, it is consistent with the idea that, when push comes to shove, values play a stronger role. The additional information about immigrants' personal qualities seems to be obviating or counteracting the automatic stereotyping of Latino immigrants as being less "worthy" on civic fairness grounds: unlawfully present, less educated, and less assimilated than immigrants from other ethnic backgrounds.

To help illustrate, imagine a white respondent who harbors deep-seated animus toward Latinos as a group. Such a person might perceive Latino immigration as a threat to traditional norms of American identity or her cultural heritage, view Latinos as outsiders whose traditions and norms are antithetical to "true Americanness," or simply feel an intense emotional dislike of Latinos that she has never reckoned with and perhaps is unaware of or refuses to acknowledge. This is an obvious instance of deep-seated racial animus: race is a matter of "taste," not a stereotype-based stand-in for missing information.

Now consider a different white respondent, someone with weak emotional attitudes toward Latinos as a group and who feels little sense of racial threat, cultural vulnerability, or disdain for symbols of Latino ethnicity. This is not to say that negative attitudes are absent altogether but only that they are low intensity, vague, or ambivalent. And, unlike our first example, the negativity is not so dominant or racially motivated that it prevents her from updating her beliefs in response to information. She may simply disbelieve accounts that go against the stereotypes she has absorbed through years of occasional exposure to media or everyday life – for example, the idea that immigrants' offspring almost universally do learn English – when she can see for herself how prevalent the use of Spanish is in certain parts of town. But she has no trouble believing that some Latinos, perhaps many of them, defy those stereotypes and do learn English and hold jobs that make them self-sufficient. She has no problem with giving Latinos who check those boxes the right to live in the United States legally. She is not looking for a reason, any reason, to deny this to Latinos even though she would extend it to Asians or Europeans, and she does not consider illegality a categorical "deal breaker."

Either person might discriminate when asked to make a decision about a Latino immigrant *in the absence of contextual information*. But we can learn a great deal more by observing how biases respond to information than we can infer from the existence of ethnic biases alone, in low-information contexts. To the extent that biased reactions to ethnic cues reflect nothing more than stereotypic beliefs about the "usual" tendencies of immigrants from different groups to assimilate and provide for themselves in the United States, we would expect information that goes against these beliefs to close the gap between whites' support for Latino immigrants and Asians or Europeans. But if whites are

Ethnic Bias and Informational Context

really, or also, tapping into deep-seated racial animus or threatened feelings toward Latinos, we would expect the ethnic cues to continue to hold sway.

Additional information might even *exacerbate* the bias for those who are strongly motivated by anti-Latino sentiment. Those hostile to Latinos ex ante might discount positive information about a Latino immigrant's steady record of work and ability to speak English, and glom onto negative information about legal status and low-skilled employment. This kind of biased information processing or "motivated reasoning" has a long legacy in psychological studies of "consistency bias" and shows up often in political choices between parties and candidates.[12] However, existing research provides no definitive answers about the degree of motivated reasoning at work in ethnic group-centric influences on choices about immigration policy. We know only that white Americans' immigration policy opinions display marked anti-Latino discrimination in some instances and not in others but not why or to what degree these biases are resistant to individuating information that should counteract prevailing stereotypes in an observer whose choices are not terribly clouded by emotional dislike of Latinos.

Of course, students of psychology may object that cognition and emotion are not as separable as our distinction between taste-based and statistical discrimination implies. People are not cold calculators who process information in an unbiased way and marshal facts and beliefs irrespective of emotional impulses. Many of those people who develop and hold onto negative beliefs about Latinos and make choices about immigration in ways that privilege certain stereotypes over others are surely engaging in "hot cognition,"[13] guided by negative emotions about Latinos or other racial fears and anxieties – even anger – as they form opinions about immigration policy.

One can accept this point in general without dismissing the possibility that some will hold beliefs accompanied by strong emotional animus that leads to motivated reasoning, while others may hold similar beliefs without the same emotional baggage, or are able to look past the emotional baggage in making choices about immigration policy. To the extent that stereotypic beliefs are accompanied by strong emotions that cloud respondents' fairness judgments, we would expect firm and unshakable ethnic biases. To the extent that they are not, however, people should discard these biases when confronted with clear and credible information that counteracts the stereotypes. Whether they do, when it comes to anti-Latino bias and immigration policy opinions, is an empirical issue, not something that can be deduced from any theory or inferred from the prevalence of stereotyping in public media or the public mind.

The rest of this chapter empirically tests whether whatever prejudice Americans harbor against Latinos is better explained by group-centric (e.g. "taste-based") considerations, or by stereotypes about violations of civic fairness norms. But before proceeding, we should distinguish statistical discrimination as applied here from the theories of symbolic racism described and tested elsewhere in this book. Both argue that prejudice and values are intertwined in American public opinion. Symbolic racism theory argues that values are deployed as rationales for taste-based discrimination, which results in bias against Latinos as long as people are furnished a normatively acceptable reason for expressing it. Civic fairness argues that values are a sincere basis for issue opinions but that people harbor stereotypes about the extent to which different ethnic groups tend to comply with liberal assimilationist precepts, which results in statistical discrimination in low-information contexts in particular.

EXHIBIT A: JOHN AND JANE, MEET JUAN, YUAN, OR JOHAN

We begin by introducing Jane and John Q. Public, to one of three immigrants, Juan, Yuan, and Johan. We describe them as young – thirty years old – and living in the country without legal permission going on two years. Just in case the names are not a sufficiently clear ethnic cue, we also make explicit each immigrant's country of origin (Mexico, China, and Germany, respectively). We tell them only these facts.

But our respondents probably also believe they "know" a lot more about Juan, Yuan, and Johan than these facts alone. Assuming that telling respondents where these immigrants come from activates prevailing stereotypes, Juan would be presumed less educated, more likely to consume public services, and less likely to know or learn English than Yuan and especially Johan.[14] Respondents who have learned these stereotypes could be less favorably inclined toward Juan than toward the other two immigrants even if they bore Latinos no particular ill will *qua* Latinos or harbored no deeper anxieties about racial change, the loss of white privilege or numerical dominance, and had no particular attraction to the idea of ascriptive racial hierarchy. Such people, in other words, would discriminate on civic fairness grounds against Juan because they stereotype him (and Latinos generally) as coming up short on that score.

Now, what happens when we *also* tell a random subset of our respondents that Juan/Yuan/Johan speaks English and has worked steadily in a particular occupation that does not require a high degree of technical skill or education. This added context provides reassurance that he has functionally assimilated to some degree and counters anti-Latino stereotypes about dependency. The nature of the occupation might also counteract the assumption that Yuan and Johan are working in a field that requires a high level of professional skill. But neither of these details would make Juan, Yuan, or Johan seem suspiciously uncommon to the point that the aim of the experiment should be obvious to respondents or lead them to think that they were weighing in on an exceedingly rare subset of immigrant.

We fielded our experiment around the hypothetical fates of Juan, Yuan, and Johan as part of an Internet survey of California voters recruited by SSI in the spring of 2015 (see Online Appendix for details). The sample was selected out of convenience and obviously does not represent the US public as a whole, but it is large enough (N = 2,267) to allow us to drill down in the data and look at effects among whites separately from Latinos – albeit only those who could

Exhibit A: John and Jane, Meet Juan, Yuan, or Johan 131

be interviewed in English – as well as to explore differences in effects by party identification and racial prejudice. If we find that even California voters exhibit anti-Latino bias, we should expect that this bias would be at least as large nationally. If information about immigrants' personal attributes counteracts these biases, then we will have at least shown that *some* substantial ethnic biases reflect stereotypes unaccompanied by deep-seated racial animus potent enough to subvert information processing and undermine civic fairness. This would support the hypothesis that *some* substantial degree of the prejudicial underpinnings of opinions about immigration policy are rooted in concerns about civic fairness and stereotypes that link beliefs about which immigrants are likely to conform to these norms to ethnic labels.

After answering a series of questions about unrelated topics in politics and current affairs, respondents were randomly assigned to read a short vignette about Juan, Yuan, or Johan. Critically, each respondent only read (and responded to) a single vignette about one of the three immigrants. Specifically, half of the respondents were randomly (and independently) assigned to read only that he is thirty years old and has been living in the United States illegally for approximately two years. The other half also read that he speaks English and had been working steadily as a waiter.

Figure 5.1 shows how much support for a green card each immigrant receives with and without the added information. Support for all three is quite high regardless of the information condition, possibly in part due to the sample (California whites) and possibly also due to the person-positivity bias (Sears 1983) in which people respond more favorably to individuals than to groups. However, consistent with research indicating that anti-Latino bias helps structure respondents' reactions to immigration policy, Mexican immigrants are at a substantial (eight to nine percentage points, $p < .05$) disadvantage relative to Germans and Chinese when the national origin cues are provided without additional reassurance about functional integration. Recall that this disadvantage exists *even though all three immigrants are portrayed as relatively recent arrivals and illegally present*, something that, if the literature on Latino stereotypes in the media is correct, our respondents would have been more likely to assume about Juan than the others.[15] If we had not provided this information – say, by describing Juan/Johan/Yuan only as "an immigrant" rather than as being "in the country illegally" – the initial gap in support between Juan and the other two immigrants might well have been larger.

The situation changes strikingly among those who learned that Juan/Yuan/Johan speaks English and has worked steadily as a waiter. There is no longer any trace, at least on average, of anti-Latino bias. Indeed, the information boosts support for Juan by over sixteen percentage points ($p < .05$), double the (also significant) increases in support for Yuan and Johan ($p < .05$). Learning that they are employed and speak English makes all three more popular among our respondents, but Juan benefits by so much *more* that the favorability gap between him and the others vanishes.

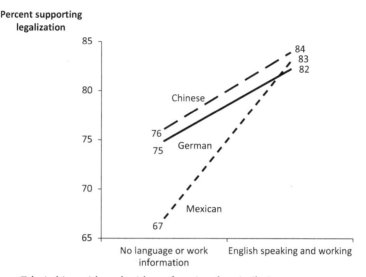

FIGURE 5.1 Ethnic bias with and without functional assimilation cues
Note: The figure displays the percentage of respondents who accepted immigrants from each national origin, with and without the information about functional assimilation. Mexicans were significantly ($p < .05$) less likely to be accepted in the no information condition. Differences across categories are not significant when the information is provided. The effect of the information is significantly ($p < .1$) greater on acceptance of the Mexican immigrant than the Chinese and German immigrants pooled together. Full tabulations are provided in the Online Appendix.

Let us revisit the theoretical possibilities that seemed plausible at the outset. First, the counter-stereotypic information might have been processed in biased fashion due to motivated reasoning. If the average bias against Juan among respondents reflected strong animus against Latino immigrants relative to whites or Asians, many respondents could have simply disregarded, dismissed, or down-weighted the positive information about Juan but warmed toward Yuan or especially Johan. Since all respondents evaluated only one immigrant, they would not have had to reveal any personal bias to the researcher by making this choice, or even acknowledge it to themselves. They could easily have reasoned to themselves that Juan was an illegal immigrant and adopted a categorical stance against "rewarding lawbreakers," as we showed in the previous chapter that many Americans do. This bias could reflect explicit prejudices respondents were aware of and willing to acknowledge or implicit prejudices that escape the respondent's own cognizance. In either case, the positive information about all three immigrants would have *increased* bias against Juan by boosting support for the other two by more than it boosted support for him. While some respondents may have reacted in this way, our sample overall clearly did not.

Second, the information might have boosted support for all three immigrants in equal measure. This is what we would expect if the average respondent weighed

Exhibit A: John and Jane, Meet Juan, Yuan, or Johan 133

both race and civic fairness considerations as separate ingredients in attitude formation. In that scenario, both considerations – I dislike the idea of letting in more Latino immigrants and would prefer more Europeans or Asians, and I also like the idea of letting in immigrants who speak English and work – would each be taken into account independently in assessing each immigrant. The assumption in this model is that the information matters equally regardless of the hypothetical immigrant's ethnicity. Or, equivalently, it assumes that the ethnic cues matter to the same degree regardless of the availability of the additional information. But we can clearly see that the data belie these assumptions. Only in the low information environment is there anti-Latino bias on average, and the information matters a good deal more to assessments about Juan than evaluations of Yuan or Johan.

This brings us to the third, civic fairness-based model, which assumes that ethnic biases reflect the automatic application of stereotypic concerns about how immigrants from different groups conform to norms of civic fairness, in this case functional assimilation through speaking English and holding a job. Here, the counter-stereotypic information should reduce the initial ethnic bias by addressing some of these stereotypic concerns head-on and obviating respondents' tendency to "read them in" to ethnic cues. In other words, it should have a greater average effect on assessments of Latino immigrants than Asian or European ones. The results fit this model quite well: there is substantial anti-Latino bias in low information environments that is reduced as respondents process the additional information – in this case reassurance that basic civic fairness criteria are being met – that we provide to them.

This is not to say that *none* of the respondents in the sample is fundamentally motivated by deep-seated anti-Latino bias. Some may well have discounted uncongenial information about Europeans and emphasized negative information about Latinos. Others may have continued to weigh Latino ethnicity as a constant negative consideration though also responding favorably to the information. But this is not the tendency we observe *on average*. For any who do continue to harbor biases against Latinos once the information is provided, there are as many who favor them to an equal degree. More to the point, if some in our sample responded to the information by preserving or increasing anti-Latino bias, there must also be many who erased this anti-Latino bias by harboring particular sympathy toward Latino immigrants.

We find similar patterns among Latinos, Asians, and whites. Non-Hispanic whites who got the national origin cues with little elaboration discriminated against Juan (67%), relative to Johan (73%) and to a smaller degree also Yuan (71%). Those who got the additional information that the immigrant speaks English and works as a waiter did not so discriminate (81% for Juan, 81% for Yuan, and 79% for Johan). Among Latinos, support for all three immigrants was markedly higher than among whites in all conditions, more so among respondents who did not receive the information. Caution is in order due to the small sample (minimum N = 60 per condition among Latinos) and the fact that the survey was only of registered voters and conducted in English, which surely fails to represent Latinos in the state generally. Latinos who did not receive the employment and language information were actually less likely (p < .1) to accept Juan (78%) than Yuan (88%) or Johan (88%), while those who did receive this information were slightly more favorable toward Juan (95%) than Yuan (90%) or Johan (94%). The sample of Asians is even smaller (minimum N per experimental condition = 38) and no more representative. However, there is some evidence that Asians favored Yuan (75%) over Juan (60%) and Johan (63%) in the uninformed condition. The information boosted support for all three immigrants, to 83% for Yuan, 69% for Juan, and 80% for Johan but did not close the gap in support between Yuan and Juan.

Breaking down the results among whites by party affiliation, as shown in Figure 5.2, suggests that the responsiveness to information is not uniform.

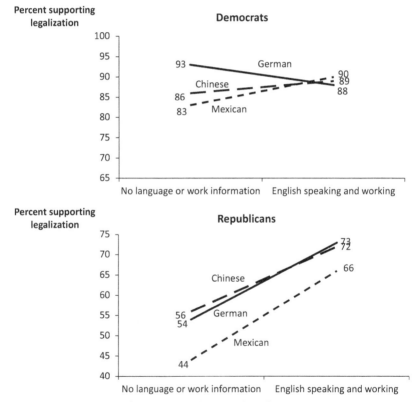

FIGURE 5.2 Ethnic bias, information, and party identification
Note: The figure displays the percentage of respondents who accepted immigrants from each national origin, with and without the information about functional assimilation, by respondents' party identification. None of the effects of information within party across national origin differs significantly due to smaller sample sizes. Full tabulations, including standard errors, are provided in the Online Appendix.

Exhibit B: Groups, Not Individuals

Predictably, Democrats are considerably more favorable to all three immigrants in both conditions than are Republicans. However, they show an initial bias in favor of Johan over Juan that is almost as large as Republicans'. The information about employment and language completely erases this bias among Democrats. Republicans are in fact even more responsive to the information across all three groups than are Democrats, and the initial bias against Juan shrinks by nearly half among those who learn about the immigrants' English proficiency and occupation. However, there is still evidence of anti-Latino bias among Republicans who got this information. Whether this enduring bias reflects specifically racial animus in the sense of taste-based discrimination or stereotyping that the design did not address and that is particularly relevant to Republicans' opinions cannot be ascertained from these data.[16]

EXHIBIT B: GROUPS, NOT INDIVIDUALS

Although our Juan/Yuan/Johan experiment followed a format used by a great deal of research on this topic, corroborated the existence of significant anti-Latino biases, and seems also to affirm our conjecture about the source of divided results in the existing literature, it is important to determine whether there is something specific to how we did it that is driving these findings. We might especially worry that asking respondents to make a choice about *one particular immigrant* makes it easier for them to set aside prejudice and acknowledge that some members of disliked groups are viewed as exceptional. On that basis, they can extend a benefit to that particular individual without having to reckon with the possibility of benefiting the group as a whole. Respondents in our survey might have thought to themselves "Juan is not like the other Latino immigrants. He is really doing things the right way. Let's give him a break."

We conducted a second experiment on a joint Field Poll – Institute of Governmental Studies survey of California registered voters to address these concerns (see the Online Appendix). We wanted to see if white bias against Latinos as a group would exist when little information about a policy was available but dissipate in the face of policy-specific information about requirements for learning English, holding a job, and passing a background check. If so, we could be more confident that the results in the Juan-Yuan-Johan experiment were not simply catching people giving Juan the benefit of the doubt by virtue of his (perceived) atypical attributes. People also tend to rate individuals that they see as positive outliers within their groups especially highly. Juan may get credit from many whites not only because he speaks English and holds a job but because in having these attributes, he sets himself apart from the stereotypic images of his group. He has succeeded against the odds.

As in our experiment in Chapter 3, we randomly assigned some respondents to weigh in on a proposal that would allow 100,000 additional immigrants from Latin America into the United States annually, and others about a proposal that would admit the same number from Europe. Half of the respondents

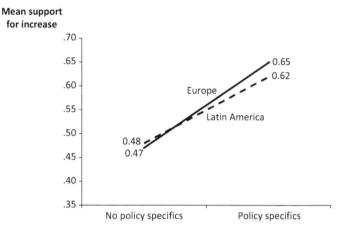

FIGURE 5.3 Ethnic bias and information, groups rather than individuals
Note: Displays the mean support on the seven-point dependent variable scale (recoded 0–1 where 1 is strong support) for the policy related to Latin America and Europe, with and without policy specifics, drawn from the IGS-The Field Poll Study. The differences by origin are not statistically significant overall or within either information condition. The effects of the policy specifics were statistically significant ($p < .05$) for both the Latin America and Europe proposals, and the effect was not different between the two. Full tabulations are displayed in the Online Appendix .

learned only this number and the region of origin. The other half also received information about policy specifics, namely that the immigrants would have to have held a job, know English or enroll in English classes, and pass a criminal background check. The dependent variable, support for the policy, was measured on a 7-point scale ranging from strong, somewhat, and slight support, to neither support nor oppose, to slight, somewhat, or strong opposition. We rescaled this variable to run from 0 to 1, where 0 is strongly oppose (most restrictionist) and 1 is strongly support (most expansionist).

Figure 5.3 displays the results for the full sample. Unlike in the Juan-Yuan-Johan experiment, both unelaborated policies divide the public and receive more opposition than support (full tabulations available in the Online Appendix), with means just under .50. Also unlike the earlier experiment, there is no evidence that respondents are any more hostile to immigration from Latin America than from Europe. Adding the policy specifics substantially increases support for the policy and does so equally for immigration from Europe and Latin America. In the aggregate, there is no evidence of anti-Latino bias and considerable evidence of ethnically even-handed responsiveness to the policy-specific information.

It should come as no surprise by now that information about functional assimilation boosts support for admitting immigrants. Things get interesting when we examine white and Latino respondents separately. These results are displayed in Figure 5.4. White respondents in fact favor the European proposal

Exhibit B: Groups, Not Individuals

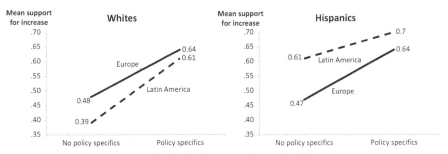

FIGURE 5.4 Groups versus individuals by respondent ethnicity
Note: Displays the mean support on the seven-point dependent variable scale (recoded 0 to 1 where 1 is strong support) for the policy related to Latin America and Europe, with and without policy specifics, drawn from the IGS-The Field Poll Study, for non-Hispanic whites and Hispanics. The differences by origin are statistically significant ($p < .05$) for both groups when no policy specifics are provided and insignificant for both when the policy specifics are provided. The effects of the policy specifics were statistically significant ($p < .05$) for both the Latin America and Europe proposals for both whites and Hispanics; however, the effect of the policy specifics did not differ significantly between the Europe and Latin America proposals among whites. This difference was statistically significant among Hispanics. Full tabulations are displayed in the Online Appendix.

significantly more than the Latin American proposal when no policy specifics are provided: evidence once again that, without much else to go on, whites fall back to a biased position. But those who also learned about the policy specifics expressed almost identical levels of support for the two proposals. This again points to statistical discrimination based on stereotyping of Latin American immigrants as less assimilated, economically self-sufficient, or law-abiding. With these concerns addressed in the policy-specific information, the perceived utility of such stereotyping diminishes and the anti-Latino bias dissipates.

Unlike in the previous experiment, Latinos in the sample, which in this case did include a minority that took the survey in Spanish, displayed favoritism for Latin American immigrants. It turns out that the degree of in-group favoritism is much larger among those who did take the survey in Spanish than among those who took it in English, who evince no bias at all, perhaps a reflection of stronger pan-ethnic attachments among the former group. The favoritism appears to shrink when policy specifics are provided, though this narrowing of the gap is not statistically significant. One way to interpret this result is that Latinos widely evaluate immigration policies in group-centric ways when the information provided gives them little to go on other than immigrants' national origin background and presumed ethnicity. But they clearly take much else strongly into account when information about functional assimilation is provided, and this additional information seems to reduce reliance on ethnic ingroup favoritism as a basis for decision-making.

Breaking down the results among whites by partisanship (not shown but results tabulated in Online Appendix) reveals similar patterns to those we found with Juan/Yuan/Johan. White Democrats exhibit a significant preference for the Europe plan in the unelaborated condition, but this bias vanishes with the policy specific information. White Republicans exhibit an even larger bias toward the Europe plan at baseline and respond more substantially than Democrats to the information. Although this bias narrows marginally with the information, it remains statistically significant. This again raises the possibility that anti-Latino bias reflects different tendencies in different types of people. Among white Democrats, it seems not to reflect any deep-seated taste-based racial animus toward Latinos but instead a tendency to rely on automatic stereotypes of Latinos as less assimilated or economically self-sufficient when other information is not available. Among Republicans, taste-based discrimination may be more widespread.

Still, this more persistent bias among Republicans is not so overpowering that it makes them on average unreceptive to information. Keep in mind that a program that would *increase* immigration by 100,000 annually from Latin America receives almost as much support as opposition among these respondents when the policy specifics are provided. Nor do we see white Republicans using the information as a rationale to increase their favorability toward the Europe policy by *more* than toward the Latin America policy in response to the policy specifics.

The findings in this second experiment also help allay concerns about ceiling effects. In the Juan-Yuan-Johan experiment, support for all three immigrants was very high. We might have worried that Juan "caught up" among respondents who learned about his personal qualities in part because baseline support for Yuan and Johan couldn't get much higher. In this experiment, both policies engender a good deal of opposition at baseline, as would be expected from a public that tends to prefer reducing rather than increasing immigration in the abstract (again, see Chapter 3). Thus there was plenty of room for the European proposal to gain support and leave the Latin American proposal as far or further behind. But this is not what we observe.

Of course, California voters might be different from others, more accepting of immigration and diversity, at least provided that civic fairness criteria are met. Perhaps so, though the separate analysis of whites and Latinos and white Democrats and Republicans helps address this concern. A skeptic might object that the overall level of support for *increasing* the level of immigration is unrealistic, at least as a reflection of Americans' immigration policy opinions as a whole. But few polls have asked questions quite like the ones in our second experiment, and, as we showed in Chapter 3, those that have, including our own question on the Lucid and YouGov surveys reported in that chapter as well as the December 2011 Fox News poll we described in Chapter 3 (which did not even reference immigrants' English proficiency), yield strong support for increasing immigration when cues about functional assimilation are provided.

Exhibit B: Groups, Not Individuals

Conflation of Latino Ethnicity with Immigration Redux

This chapter has focused on how introducing information influences the effects of ethnic cues, examining a clash of predictions between the group-centrism perspective and civic fairness. As a bonus, the data from our SSI experiment in this chapter also gives us a second chance to examine how attitudes toward Latinos are correlated with support for Latino and non-Latino immigrants. In Chapter 4, we saw that the Latino feeling thermometer independently (over and above attitudes toward other groups) predicted support for immigrants from all national origin backgrounds, not only those from Latin America. We conjectured that this relationship obtains because measures of attitudes about Latinos as a group in effect solicit attitudes about immigration in general, both legal and illegal. And we noted that the naïve interpretation of these statistical associations as a reflection *only* of the influence of the group attitude on the policy opinion would overstate the influence of group-centrism on opinions about immigration policy. These correlations would also reflect the application of anti-immigrant sentiment, originating in any number of sources, to attitudes about Latinos as a group.

Figure 5.5, plots the predicted probability that each immigrant in the vignette experiment is supported against the Latino and Asian feeling thermometers. These predicted probabilities are drawn from a logistic regression

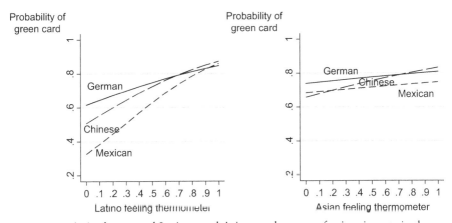

FIGURE 5.5 Attitudes toward Latinos and Asians and support for immigrants in the vignette experiment

Note: The figures display the model-predicted probability that each immigrant is given a green card in the SSI California experiment described earlier by national origin. The model is a logistic regression in which the dependent variable is whether an immigrant was given a green card, and the regressors were dummy variables indicating randomly assigned national origin, each interacted with the Latino, Asian, and white feeling thermometers. Full tabulations of these results are provided in the Online Appendix. See Chapter 4 for more elaboration.

model in which the dependent variable is whether the described immigrant was supported for inclusion in the program, and the independent variables are feeling thermometers for whites, Asians, and Latinos (we did not have a feeling thermometer for blacks in this survey), each interacted with the national origin cue treatments. The results presented here are similar to the ones in Chapter 4. In addition to promoting bias against Latinos relative to Germans and also possibly relative to Chinese, "cold" feelings toward Latinos seem to capture generalized opposition to illegal immigration. By contrast, the feeling thermometer measuring feelings toward Asians again seems not to reflect people's feelings about illegal immigrants. In the previous chapter, we saw that it did seem to reflect people's attitudes about legal immigration. We did not illustrate how these probabilities vary against the white feeling thermometer, but, interestingly, warmer feelings toward whites, all else being equal, reduces support for all three immigrants in approximately equal margins. This may mean that the white feeling thermometer is picking up general ethnocentrism.

CONCLUSION

Stereotypes of Latinos as "unassimilated" immigrants who do not learn English and drain the nation's fiscal coffers are likely to be intertwined with at least some negative emotional content for most people who harbor them. Such people will surely report more negative feelings about Latinos and Latino immigrants than they do toward other groups. There is no sharp separation between negative group affect and negative stereotypes.

There is, however, a meaningful difference between (1) a public that forms opinions about immigration largely based on whatever desirable or disqualifying attributes they think members of various racial groups tend to have and (2) a public that is fundamentally concerned about preserving white racial dominance and is loath to admit more members of a subordinate racial minority group because it dislikes that group per se or feels its own dominant position threatened. Existing studies have generally not broached this distinction and, we would say, adopted the second view without sufficient justification.

Our aim in this chapter was to adjudicate between these two characterizations of anti-Latino bias, using the distinction between taste-based and statistical discrimination as ideal types to guide our inquiry. Most of the literature on this topic has assumed that ethnic animus or threat is the fundamental driver of these biases and the civic fairness concerns that people cite in order to justify restrictive policy stances are at least in part veneer, a cover for prejudicial feelings that cannot be expressed openly. We find instead that much anti-Latino bias in white Americans' immigration policy opinions rests on a foundation of apparently *sincere* concern about civic fairness, mediated by ethnic stereotypes perpetuated in media and political rhetoric. Instead of permitting negativity toward Latinos to induce selective processing of information about

Conclusion

functional assimilation, many respondents in our surveys clearly discriminate much less against Latino immigrants when armed with this information.

At a minimum, these experiments – and all others discussed in this book – should dispel the idea that citizens are unwittingly at the mercy of ethnic prejudice and unable to update their opinions in response to information that clarifies how policy alternatives relate to their professed values. It points, instead, to the centrality of beliefs, information and values in the formation of opinions about immigration. Beliefs may be accurate, but they are often grossly distorted. Either way, they clearly draw on ethnic identification as a heuristic. The availability of more direct information about functional assimilation reduces the value of this heuristic and, hence, also the ethnic biases. Further research is needed to determine to what degree the residual biases, especially among white Republicans, are fundamentally resistant to information or whether they reflect stereotypes that our particular interventions did not counteract.

The dark side of civic fairness is that it can be expressed through ethnic stereotyping in low information environments and most likely also in contexts where information is ambiguous or contested. The more encouraging result is that these biases are responsive to the sort of information that, we showed in Chapter 2, public debates over immigration routinely make available. Here we see evidence both of the promise and limitations of the American ethos – its tendency to resolve conflicts between prejudice and values in favor of values but also the reality that prejudice and ethnic bias remain prominent features of mass politics nevertheless. Whether the glass is half empty or half full, it is clear that the degree of anti-Latino bias in white Americans' immigration policy choices varies with the availability of information about functional assimilation. This illustrates that the civic fairness framework can offer a compelling interpretation of ethnic biases that are often taken as prima facie evidence of group-centrism.

6

Assimilation, Civic Fairness and the "Circle of We"

The previous chapters demonstrated that liberal assimilationist norms are among the most powerful influences on American public opinion about immigration. Here, we examine two competing accounts of why this is so. As in the earlier chapters, we adjudicate between civic fairness and group-centrism. But having repeatedly shown that support for assimilation generally overrides *ethnic* group-centrism, we turn our attention to a different variety of group-centrism – one predicated on feelings of attachment to fellow members of the *national* ingroup and solidarity with immigrants who are seen as belonging within it.

We begin by elaborating on how each of these accounts explains the premium that Americans put on assimilation, and follow by linking assimilation to people's decisions about whether immigrants should have access to social benefits and political rights. This leads to an experimental test of the fifth hypothesis developed in Chapter 2, which has two parts: (1) cues about civic fairness strongly influence opinions about immigration policy even if they do not engender feelings of communal solidarity and identification with immigrants and (2) cues about types of cultural assimilation that are tangential to mass perceptions of civic fairness weakly affect opinions about immigration policy even if they do engender such feelings. In the course of testing this hypothesis, we also reconfirm Hypotheses 1 and 3 by illustrating that civic fairness cues exert a strong influence, even in the presence of ethnic cues, and that civic fairness cues are applied evenhandedly to immigrants from different ethnic groups. Separately, we once again corroborate our second hypothesis, which is that responsiveness to cues about civic fairness is correlated with measures of individual-level commitment to abstract values (in this case legalism and egalitarianism).

As an alternative way of disentangling group-centrist and civic fairness perspectives on assimilation, we then turn to our sixth and final hypothesis:

142

Civic Fairness, Group-Centrism, and Support for Assimilation 143

We explore whether assimilationist norms matter more among those who express strong attachment to the nation than among those who express weaker attachments.

The findings we present have broader relevance to what is known as the "progressive's dilemma" – the challenge of maintaining public support for a robust welfare state as countries become more ethnically diverse through immigration *without* enacting drastic reductions to immigration or immigrant rights.[1] A standard prescription has been for elites to redefine the national community in more inclusive terms. Our inquiry raises the possibility that *even successful efforts to do so* may not have the intended effect unless they address the values and norms that most strongly influence mass perceptions of civic fairness.

CIVIC FAIRNESS, GROUP-CENTRISM, AND SUPPORT FOR ASSIMILATION

Allowing for some give and take,[2] assimilation is a process by which immigrants adopt the host nation's mores and folkways – conventionally, though not always,[3] meaning those of its mainstream. Civic fairness and group-centrism posit different explanations for the importance of assimilation in public opinion about immigration and, by implication, for the types of assimilation that should carry the most weight.

Viewed through the lens of civic fairness, assimilation derives its importance from Americans' commitment to the values of individualism and legalism. In particular, these values heighten the importance of *formal* and *functional* assimilation. As we saw in Chapter 2, Americans also see other aspects of cultural assimilation as desirable.[4] But dimensions of assimilation that are linked in people's minds with self-sufficiency and the rule of law are regarded as far and away the most essential. Though often tempered by egalitarianism and humanitarian exigency, norms of functional and formal assimilation shape Americans' judgments about what immigrants owe, and are owed by, the host country and, hence, their opinions about immigration policy. Crucially, these normative judgments override feelings of group affinity and solidarity with immigrants when the two conflict.

Viewed through the lens of group-centrism, assimilation influences public opinion about immigration because it erodes and eventually eliminates group boundaries between a national "us" and a foreign "them."[5] In effect, from a group-centrist standpoint, assimilation matters because it turns immigrants from outsiders into adopted members of a national community. Immigrants who assimilate enough to be categorized as fellow members of the American "Circle of We"[6] evoke horizontal attachment. These feelings are expected to override abstract values (and more parochial identifications such as race and ethnicity) when the two conflict.

144   *Assimilation, Civic Fairness and the "Circle of We"*

In Chapter 2, we showed that this view is endemic in the literature on national identity and its political relevance. We also distinguished horizontal attachment from "vertical attachment" to the nation and its symbols and ideals. As we explained there, vertical attachment is also a component of national identity – one's sense of one's identity *as* American as distinct from one's identification *with* other Americans. But the influence of vertical attachment to the nation on political attitudes is not, on its own, group-centric as we have defined the term throughout. Recall that group-centrist theories root political choice in the impulse to benefit ingroups and sometimes harm outgroups. Choices based on horizontal attachments to fellow members of the national ingroup are group-centric because they are predicated on precisely this. But choices based on vertical attachment to the nation need not be. Commitment to American symbols and ideals may instead be seen as requiring the *evenhanded* application of national values and *refusing* to bend the rules in order to benefit fellow members of the "Circle of We" or keep strangers at bay. Given the semantic confusion that often arises in connection with multidimensional concepts such as "identity," which can have both normative and group-centric components, it is important to underline that the primary influences we consider in this chapter are *horizontal* attachments to the national community versus the political values associated with the liberal tradition. Put differently, we want to adjudicate between civic fairness and group-centrism, not between civic fairness and "national identity" or "Americanism," since these terms are often defined in ways that subsume traditional American values.

HORIZONTAL ATTACHMENT VERSUS CIVIC FAIRNESS IN DECISIONS ABOUT BENEFITS AND RIGHTS

In this chapter, we focus on the choices Americans make about which, if any, noncitizens should be eligible for social benefits and official participatory rights (i.e., voting, running for public office, and jury service) in the United States.[7] We choose this case for two reasons. First, it is an issue that is inherently about assimilation. Becoming a citizen is a type of assimilation in and of itself. It is also a process that requires various auxiliary forms of assimilation. In the United States, these include learning the dominant language, pledging loyalty to the host country, forswearing other national allegiances, and passing a test about the nation's history, political system, and civic creed that evidently stumps no small number of native-born Americans. Therefore, to inquire about what Americans see as the operative difference between citizens' and noncitizens' deservingness of benefits and rights is to ask which of these dimensions of assimilation matter to them in this way and why.

Second, immigrants' eligibility for rights and benefits has been a major focus of a large comparative literature arguing for the importance of national community, cohesion, and solidarity to sustaining ample and "inclusive" welfare

Horizontal Attachment versus Civic Fairness in Decisions 145

state institutions. Thus, we are choosing a case that is widely seen as congenial to the group-centrist perspective. If horizontal attachment predominates over civic fairness in any domain of immigration policy, its influence should be clearly evident here.

By way of background, most recent controversy in the United States has centered on noncitizens' eligibility for welfare benefits and access to government social insurance (Social Security and Medicare). The issue came to a head in the 1990s. California Republican Governor Pete Wilson made the ostensible fiscal burdens associated with immigrant dependence on social services his signature issue, a strategy that paid electoral dividends in the short run but has saddled the GOP in the state with an anti-immigrant reputation ever since.

Much of Proposition 187, the heart of Wilson's campaign, was later struck down by federal courts. But Wilson's campaign increased the visibility of these issues nationally. By 1996, President Bill Clinton had concluded that he had no choice other than to work with the Republican Congress on legislation that would cut immigrants' access to federal benefits, weakening these provisions as much as he could. The rallying cry for these efforts – "immigration yes, welfare no" – sought to decouple opposition to an aspect of immigration that was seen as violating individualist norms of civic fairness (self-sufficiency) from opposition to immigration in general. President Clinton signed two pieces of legislation in 1996 that limited immigrants' access to welfare benefits. The Personal Responsibility and Work Opportunity Reconciliation Act imposed a five year waiting period before noncitizens could access the new Temporary Assistance for Needy Families (TANF), Supplemental Nutrition Assistance Program (SNAP, or food stamps), and other forms of government assistance. States were allowed to choose whether to finance the restoration of benefits to some noncitizens, leading to a federalist patchwork of benefits regimes.[8] The Illegal Immigration Reform and Immigrant Responsibility Act put in place the Systematic Alien Verification for Entitlements (SAVE) program, allowing local, state, and federal agencies to electronically verify the identity and eligibility of benefits claimants.

Polling from that time suggests that limitations on noncitizens' access to social benefits were very popular with the American public.[9] Twenty years later, it is clear that the majority of Americans remain opposed to expanding their eligibility. Most support restrictions on legal immigrants' eligibility for welfare, entitlements, subsidized health insurance, and other benefits. Many would deny legal permanent residents who are not citizens these benefits altogether, and an overwhelming majority would withhold them from undocumented immigrants.[10]

Debates about whether noncitizens should be able to participate officially in the political process have received less attention. But they are a new frontier in progressive advocacy for immigrant rights. These advocacy efforts seek to restore a long legacy of noncitizen voting and political participation in nineteenth century America. The United States, like other countries, had reasonably well-developed laws concerning the rights of "denizens" or foreigners who had something less than a complete claim on membership in the state but were nonetheless officially entitled to certain rights and protections.[11] At present, a handful of localities but no states have approved measures that would enfranchise noncitizens. California, ever a trendsetter in contemporary American immigration politics, came close to granting noncitizens the right to serve on juries. The legislature approved it, but Governor Jerry Brown vetoed it, arguing that jury service, like voting, is a "quintessential" prerogative of citizens – a sentiment that seems to echo the emphasis on formal assimilation that we argue explains why much of the public would likely support the governor's decision.

Sparse polling indicates scant support for noncitizen voting, jury service, and public office holding. In a 2013 poll we conducted (see Online Appendix for details), more than three-fourths of a sample of California registered voters opposed legal immigrant noncitizen voting or service in city council elections and on school boards and service on juries. Even in the liberal bastion of San Francisco, voters twice rejected a ballot measure to allow noncitizens with children in local public schools to vote in school board elections before narrowly approving it in 2016.[12]

The first question to ask, then, is why so many people draw a bright line between the rights of citizens and legal immigrant noncitizens? One possibility is that people who generally dislike immigrants, foreigners, or nonwhites take the opportunity to deny legal immigrants the rights and benefits that they grudgingly accept naturalized citizens must be given. But, recalling Chapter 1, many of the same people who broadly support legal immigration nevertheless oppose granting more extensive sets of rights and benefits to legal immigrants who have not become citizens. Generalized negativity toward immigrants, foreigners, and racial minorities obviously cannot explain why so many of those who welcome legal immigrants would still restrict their access to benefits and rights. Nor can generally positive attitudes toward these groups adequately explain support for making them eligible: as we saw in Chapter 1, a substantial minority of those who would like legal immigration reduced nonetheless believed legal immigrants should be given "equal rights."

In keeping with group-centrist theories that emphasize group-specific prejudice, people might assume that immigrants from some ethnic backgrounds naturalize less often than others. For example, people might imagine that legal immigrants who do not become US citizens are disproportionately Latino. It is in fact true that the rate of naturalization is lower among Mexican immigrants who are eligible to become US citizens than it is among most other groups (including other Latin American immigrants).[13] But it seems doubtful that the ethnic stereotypes about naturalization among legal immigrants would be anywhere near as pervasive and accessible as stereotypes associated with illegality. And we found in Chapters 4 and 5 that attitudes about Latinos did not emerge as main drivers of *differentiation* between legal and illegal immigration policy.

Horizontal Attachment versus Civic Fairness in Decisions 147

In the group-centrist view we focus on in this chapter, citizenship matters because it indicates that an immigrant has become "one of us," a member of the national community, and an object of horizontal attachment. Naturalization per se may be seen as a salient marker of shared identity and membership in the national community and therefore engender feelings of social solidarity. Or it may be assumed that immigrants who naturalize have also assimilated in other ways, and these auxiliary dimensions of assimilation may be the proximate source of horizontal attachment. Some auxiliary dimensions may fall into the categories of functional assimilation – adapting, learning English, and integrating enough to be able to provide for oneself. But, importantly, others may fall outside the functional and formal assimilationist norms that guide perceptions of civic fairness – feeling American, loving the country, and adopting American cultural customs in private, for example. The key provisos are that the group-centrist perspective does *not* see a strong role for dimensions of assimilation apart from those that influence feelings of horizontal attachment, and it *does* see a strong role for dimensions of assimilation that do inculcate such feelings.

The civic fairness framework instead suggests that the importance of citizenship derives from its connection to values. Most clearly, naturalization is itself a type of formal assimilation, the prioritization of which we have linked to legalistic values. It should therefore matter even when other dimensions of assimilation that might be associated with citizenship in people's minds (and ethnicity) are held constant. In addition, people may harbor doubts about whether legal immigrants who have not become citizens are complying with norms of functional assimilation by learning enough English and becoming self-sufficient. These indirect effects are also consistent with civic fairness. But unlike the group-centrist view, the civic fairness perspective sees at most a weak role for auxiliary forms of assimilation that are *not* part and parcel of formal and functional assimilation. And it predicts a strong influence of information about formal and functional assimilation irrespective of whether this information also promotes horizontal attachment.

Tailored to the case at hand, our two-part fifth hypothesis is as follows: (1) cues about formal assimilation strongly affect support for extending benefits and rights to immigrants even if they weakly influence feelings of horizontal attachment and (2) cues about dimensions of assimilation that are not directly tied to the values of legalism and individualism (i.e. not functional or formal assimilation) weakly influence opinions about providing immigrants benefits and rights even if they strongly influence feelings of horizontal attachment. Testing this hypothesis requires isolating the effect of various dimensions of assimilation, some tied to civic fairness and others immaterial to it, from one another and from ethnic cues. Testing the hypothesis also requires measuring not only policy support as a dependent variable but also horizontal attachment.

148 *Assimilation, Civic Fairness and the "Circle of We"*

Cooperative Congressional Election Study (CCES) Vignette Experiment

To this end, we embedded an experiment in the 2015 CCES module, which also included the follow-up to the "Green Card Experiment" presented in Chapter 3. We showed our respondents a short vignette that described a hypothetical immigrant living in the United States. In the vignette, five of the hypothetical immigrant's attributes were randomly varied: (1) Mexican vs. French national origin; (2) five- or ten-year length of residence in the United States[14]; (3) citizenship and legal status – whether the immigrant was illegally present, legally present but not a citizen, or had become a US citizen; (4) level of cultural assimilation – whether the immigrant feels attached to the United States or his country of origin and has learned English well or little English, this latter stipulation introducing a potential confound that we address in a follow-up study later[15]; and (5) whether the immigrant paid taxes scrupulously or hid income from the IRS, a signal of law-abiding behavior that is not part and parcel of formal assimilation (since it is not connected to the process of joining the polity), which we introduced here as a way of decoupling official legal status from broader compliance with the law. In all manifestations of the vignette, we made the immigrant an auto mechanic.

After reading the vignette, respondents answered three distinct sets of questions about the immigrant "and others like him." The first of these tapped horizontal attachment. Specifically, we asked whether respondents would view such an immigrant as "truly American" (a hallmark in the national identity literature that emphasizes horizontal attachment), as someone who would belong in their community, and as someone who would fit in well in their neighborhood.[16] The second queried eligibility for certain government benefits, including government-subsidized job training programs, health insurance, Social Security, and unemployment benefits. The third included questions about eligibility for certain official democratic rights including voting in local elections, holding local public office, and serving on a jury. The questions, all of which offered response options on a five-point strongly agree–strongly disagree scale, were as follows:

Identity: Do you agree or disagree – people like [Juan/Claude] have the qualities of a person I would think of as...

- Truly American
- Someone who could really belong in my community
- The sort of person who would fit in well in my neighborhood

Benefits: Do you agree or disagree – people like [Juan/Claude] should be eligible for...

- State unemployment benefits if they lose their jobs
- Government-subsidized health insurance programs
- Federally funded job training programs
- Social Security

Horizontal Attachment versus Civic Fairness in Decisions 149

Polrights: Do you agree or disagree – people like [Juan/Claude] should be permitted to...

- Vote in local elections
- Serve on a jury
- Serve on a school board

The battery that respondents answered first was determined at random. Those who first received the horizontal attachment battery were subsequently asked the questions about rights and benefits in random order. Those who first received the benefits or rights battery were subsequently asked the other battery of policy questions and then asked the identity questions last. We re-scaled each of these dependent variables to run from 0 to 1, where 1 is the most "inclusive" response. We then created three scales – *attachment*, *benefits*, and *polrights* – by taking the mean of the measures in each battery. We want to know how the attributes we manipulated in the vignettes influenced each of these scales among respondents who encountered each scale first. We focus on responses to the first battery each respondent encountered because it is the least likely to reflect a positive or negative response set about the immigrant that develops after the details of the case have been forgotten. However, it turns out that the differences in the degree to which treatments affect each outcome remain and are only modestly attenuated even when we include respondents' sequential answers to all three indexes (see the Online Appendix).

How, then, does our fifth hypothesis fare? Table 6.1 shows the results of three ordinary least squares (OLS) regressions (one for each scale) that we use to estimate the effect of each treatment in the vignette on each index. One clear takeaway is that formal assimilation per se only weakly influences feelings of horizontal attachment. To give some specific examples, a noncitizen who is legally present, pays his taxes dutifully, and manifests signs of cultural assimilation (speaking English and feeling American) averages a score of .77 on the "truly American" item, .86 on the "fits into neighborhood" item, and .88 on the "belongs in community" item (all falling between .75 or "somewhat agree" and 1 or "strongly agree"). Even for an illegal immigrant, the respective figures are .69, .78, and .78. Clearly, then, lack of citizenship (and even legal status) does little, on average, to preclude feelings of horizontal attachment, at least as we measure them here.[17]

Consistent with the hypothesis, however, people do weigh formal assimilation heavily in making choices about eligibility for benefits and rights. Consider the distributions for rights and benefits conditional on legal status. There, the legally present, assimilated, tax-paying noncitizen averages .65 for unemployment benefits, .57 for subsidized health insurance, .60 for Social Security benefits, and .60 for subsidized job training (above .5 or "neither agree nor disagree" but considerably below "somewhat agree"). For illegal immigrants, the respective averages are .53, .49, .51, and .49. When it comes to beliefs about who should be eligible for democratic rights, the differences are even starker.

150   Assimilation, Civic Fairness and the "Circle of We"

TABLE 6.1 *Determinants of horizontal attachment and public opinion about eligibility for benefits and political rights*

	Horizontal Attachment	Benefits	Political Rights
Mexican (vs. French)	−.02	.06	−.05
	(.02)	(.04)	(.04)
10 years in United States (vs. 5)	−.01	.04	.00
	(.02)	(.04)	(.04)
Citizen (vs. Legal permanent resident)	.07[*]	.18[***]	.45[***]
	(.03)	(.05)	(.04)
Illegal (vs. Legal permanent resident)	−.09[**]	−.10[*]	.05
	(.03)	(.05)	(.04)
English and US flag (vs. Fr./Sp. or foreign flag)	.23[***]	.06	.14[***]
	(.02)	(.04)	(.04)
Scrupulous about taxes (vs. not)	.25[***]	.27[***]	.09[*]
	(.02)	(.04)	(.04)
Constant	.38[***]	.23[***]	.19[***]
	(.03)	(.05)	(.05)
N	605	297	343
R^2	.30	.24	.31

Note: This table displays the estimated effect of each independently and randomly varied treatment in the vignette experiment on each index among respondents who answered that battery of dependent variable questions first. For a tabulation that includes all respondents for each index, irrespective of order, see the Online Appendix. Standard errors in parentheses [*] $p < 0.05$, [**] $p < 0.01$, [***] $p < 0.001$. Each dependent variable index is rescaled to run from 0 to 1, where 1 is most supportive of benefits or rights for immigrants and highest level of shared identity.

Legally present noncitizens who speak English, display the American flag, and pay their taxes average only a .35 (somewhat disagree is .25) when it comes to the right to vote in local elections, .41 for serving on a jury, and .42 for serving on a school board. Taken together, we see that noncitizens can evidently meet most citizens' conception of what it means to be "truly American" and to belong in their communities, yet still fall short of what many believe ought to be required to receive benefits and political rights.

Turning to the second part of the hypothesis, markers of cultural assimilation that do not speak directly to an immigrant's self-sufficiency or compliance with official rules and procedures – have a far weaker effect on these policy opinions than on horizontal attachment. Americans are more likely to identify with those who seem more culturally assimilated to mainstream American life, just as many studies of the normative boundaries of identity have shown. But these dimensions of assimilation have no discernible *independent* influence on judgments about eligibility for benefits and a relatively small influence on eligibility for political rights. That this cultural assimilation treatment had a

Horizontal Attachment versus Civic Fairness in Decisions 151

significant impact on the *polrights* index may be attributable to its reference to English, a potential confound that we address in a follow-up experiment discussed subsequently. Although the civic fairness framework emphasizes the liberal tradition of American political culture and the association people make between speaking English and economic self-sufficiency, support for linguistic assimilation has also been tied to the republican tradition that emphasizes civic duty.[18] People may associate speaking English with the ability to carry out the participatory responsibilities of citizens. Alternatively, an immigrant's perceived national loyalty may loom larger when it comes to the question of civic responsibilities than other aspects of immigration policy. But the main implication for Hypothesis 5 is that attributes that engender classification as co-national and a sense of shared identity translate much more weakly into greater support for benefits or democratic rights. Legalistic judgments based on civic fairness criteria appear to overpower many Americans' conceptions of social belonging and feelings of horizontal attachment to immigrants.

We have been focusing on the distinction between civic fairness and horizontal attachment, but it is important not to lose sight of the fact that these results also reconfirm hypotheses we examined in previous chapters. Consistent with Hypothesis 1, we find that a clear cue about civic fairness (formal assimilation) strongly influences policy opinions over and above the influence of other potentially correlated factors and in the presence of clear ethnic cues. Further inspection of the results (available from the authors) found no evidence that the importance of formal assimilation varied by the immigrant's national origin background, in keeping with the evenhandedness stipulation of Hypothesis 3.

The results also once again challenge the idea that immigrants' ethnicity per se is a major basis for Americans' immigration policy choices. Consistent with what we showed in Chapters 4 and 5, ethnicity (or at least its proxy, country of origin) doesn't seem to matter much when respondents have other clear information germane to civic fairness. The other information we provide in the experiment may counteract stereotypes of Latino immigrants as less skilled or assimilated and more likely to be present without permission. For those keeping score, we were also able to reproduce quite closely the conflation between anti-Latino sentiment and "anti-immigrant" positions in this study that we illustrated in Chapters 4 and 5. This again corroborates the conjecture that measures of group attitudes toward Latinos and Asians have generalized feelings about immigration "baked into" them, which means that their strong empirical association with measures of immigration policy opinions is not straightforwardly interpretable as evidence for ethnic group-centrism. To spare the reader another "redux," we have included graphical illustration and discussion of this result in the Online Appendix.

Given how often length of residency has been invoked in partisan debates about US immigration policy – in the mid-1990s as a criterion for benefits eligibility for legal immigrants and in the mid-1980s and again more recently for legalization for those illegally present – it is surprising that it does not register in these results.[19] It is possible that by the time an immigrant has been in the United States for five years, an additional five years' tenure does not foster any greater sense of belonging. Or perhaps information elsewhere in the vignette provided more direct information about assimilation that made length of residence seem less relevant. One other point of note is that general law-abiding behavior is not necessarily processed the same way as formal assimilation, which pertains specifically to following rules and procedures on the path to immigrating and joining the polity. Predictably, respondents feel more solidarity with those who deal honestly with the government in their finances and use this attribute to judge whether people deserve to reap public benefits in times of distress. But formal assimilation is the far greater influence on eligibility for rights, with relatively few evidently using this behavior to judge whether people should be able to participate in the official channels of the democratic process.

To summarize, the results are consistent with our fifth hypothesis. Of course, the distinctions people draw between general affect for an immigrant or horizontal attachment and moral deservingness are not perfectly sharp in real life, and they certainly will not separate like oil and water in an experiment of this kind. But we see that formal assimilation matters greatly to judgments about immigration policy even where it only weakly influences feelings of solidarity and communal fellowship with those who are seen as belonging in the "Circle of We." And cultural assimilation that does not so directly signal self-sufficiency and compliance with legal norms and procedures registers weakly in policy judgments even though it powerfully affects horizontal attachment.

Further inspection of the results in this experiment illustrates once again that legalistic values and norms of formal assimilation promote "categorical response," or the tendency to make all-or-nothing judgments about policy on the basis of rigid application of principle. In Chapter 4, illegal immigrants were three times as likely as legal immigrants to be so judged, we argued, because "illegality" per se encourages a rigid and moralistic outlook that puts formal assimilation above all else.

In the case at hand, civic fairness entails viewing citizenship status as a necessary and sufficient condition for benefits and rights, even if it is not a necessary or sufficient condition for horizontal attachment. Thus, eligibility of immigrants who hold a particular formal status for rights and benefits will often be judged "categorically" even if feelings of identification *with* are expressed with more grey area and responsiveness to immigrants' other individual qualities. The difference is that legalistic values will lead many people to see formal assimilation as a *necessary* condition for legal entitlement to benefits and rights, an absolute barrier, whereas feelings of horizontal attachment are not likely to be cut off sharply by any single, official threshold.

Figure 6.1 amply corroborates these expectations. The top panel pertains to immigrants of all three official statuses pooled together – naturalized citizens, legally present noncitizens, and illegal immigrants. Below that panel, we break

Horizontal Attachment versus Civic Fairness in Decisions

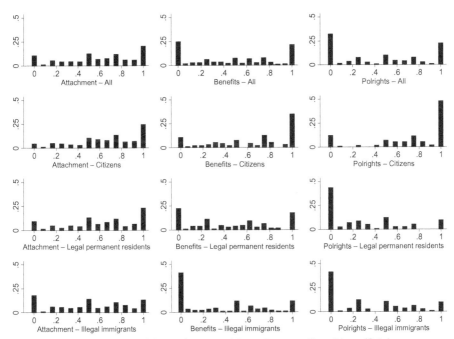

FIGURE 6.1 Distribution of dependent variable scales overall and by official status
Note: The figure displays the full distribution of each dependent variable index for the pooled set of immigrant profiles described in the CCES vignette (top panel), naturalized immigrants, legal immigrant noncitizens, and illegal immigrants. Categorical responses are captured by the bars over values of 0 and 1 for each index. The figure illustrates that far more people adopt categorical stances across the citizenship divide when it comes to policy choices about benefits and rights than when it comes to self-reported feelings about horizontal attachment.

out the distributions by official status. Since English-speaking ability, length of residence in the United States, patriotic sentiment, employment, and scrupulousness with which the subject of the vignette pays taxes are all randomly assigned across official statuses, any differences in respondents' reaction to status cannot be ascribed to these otherwise potentially confounding attributes. Rather, they reflect differences in how people process the questions themselves.

As is readily visible, questions about benefits and rights eligibility do tend to evoke "all-or-nothing" categorical response far more than is manifested on the horizontal attachment index. To underline this point, the threshold for categorical response is high. People had to strongly agree with all three or four questions in each battery or strongly disagree with all of them. Overall, 31% of respondents scored a 0 (11%) or a 1 (20%) on the identity scale, while 47% were at the extremes of the benefits scale (25% categorically rejecting benefits and 21% categorically endorsing them), and a whopping 55% were at the extremes of the political rights scale (32% categorically opposed and 22% categorically in favor). This is consistent with the idea that citizens' attention to formal assimilation in forming policy opinions is tied to simple and rigid legalistic precepts about whom government is obligated to assist and whose rights it must provide and protect.

Subsetting by immigrant legal status further illustrates the influence of formal assimilation on the prevalence of categorical policy opinions but not horizontal attachment. Moving from citizens to legal noncitizens to illegal immigrants gradually shifts scores on the attachment scale downward. When it comes to benefits, there is overwhelming categorical support for access by naturalized citizens and overwhelming categorical opposition to access for illegal immigrants, with opinion about legal noncitizens sharply divided between categorical supporters and opponents. Categorical judgments are even starker when it comes to political rights; for citizens, they are even more overwhelmingly supported categorically while for legal and illegal immigrant noncitizens, they are overwhelmingly rejected. On the whole, it is difficult to reconcile these results with the theory that citizens' opinions about whether noncitizens should receive benefits and rights are primarily a byproduct of feelings of social solidarity with immigrants who are categorized as belonging within the national community. These opinions instead seem to reflect legalistic judgments about whose well-being and rights the government is obligated to secure, an influence that is consistent with the civic fairness framework but is difficult to square with group-centrism.

Lucid Labs Follow-up

In a follow-up experiment embedded in the May 2018 Lucid Labs survey (see Chapter 3), we replicated the key results from this first exhibit and addressed a potential confound in our initial experiment in the CCES. Specifically, as noted earlier, our cue about cultural assimilation also mentioned that the immigrant spoke English well or had not learned much. Though we told respondents that the immigrant was employed and implied his economic self-sufficiency, it could have been this reference to functional assimilation, not the more diffuse and private attachment that the immigrant is said to feel toward America or his country of origin, that influenced the *attachment* index so strongly and also, more weakly, support for extending political rights.

Respondents in the experiment were assigned to read a brief passage about a legal immigrant whose citizenship status and attachment to the United States or his homeland were varied randomly and independently. The immigrant's spoken language, occupation, age, arrival year, legal status, and national origin were all noted in this passage and held constant across treatment conditions. The wording of the passage, with experimental manipulations indicated within square brackets, was as follows:

Now consider a legal immigrant from Mexico who came to the U.S. five years ago and [*citizenship randomization:* is not a US citizen/recently became a US citizen]. He is thirty

Horizontal Attachment versus Civic Fairness in Decisions

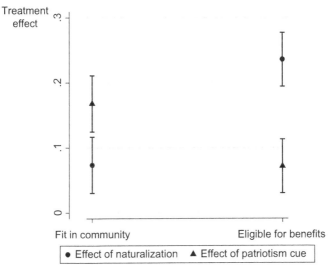

FIGURE 6.2 Influence of cues about immigrant patriotism and naturalization on perceived fit in community and support for benefits eligibility
Note: The figure displays the effect of the naturalization and patriotism treatments (with 95% confidence intervals), which were randomly and independently varied, on the degree to which respondents agreed that the immigrant in question would fit into their community and on whether the immigrant should be eligible for public benefits. Respondents were asked only one of these two dependent variables, at random. The full tabulation is included in the Online Appendix.

years old, speaks English, and works as a mechanic. He is proud of [*patriotism randomization*: his Mexican heritage and displays a Mexican flag outside his home / America and displays an American flag outside his home].

Participants were then assigned at random, with equal probabilities, to answer one of two questions. One question asked about benefits eligibility: "If he were to fall on hard times, do you think that he should be able to receive government assistance such as unemployment benefits and food stamps while he gets back on his feet?" The second asked about subjective belonging: "Do you feel that this immigrant would fit well in your community?" In both cases, the response options were yes (1), no (0), and not sure (.5).

As Figure 6.2 shows, this design successfully recovers the key patterns from the more elaborate vignette experiment in the CCES. Naturalization per se, above and beyond the other information provided and held constant in the experiment, only very modestly boosts perceived fit in community but dramatically increases the belief that the immigrant ought to be eligible for benefits. Also in keeping with the results of the CCES experiment, informing respondents about the immigrant's private feelings of attachment to his adopted or native land has a much larger impact on their feelings about whether he belongs

156   *Assimilation, Civic Fairness and the "Circle of We"*

in their communities than it does on their opinions about whether he should be eligible for public benefits. Both treatments influence both responses, but they influence them to much different degrees, as would be expected if assimilationist norms derived their influence on policy judgments from their connection to perceptions of civic fairness more than from their impact on feelings of group solidarity with immigrants.

Opinions Are Structured by Legalism and Egalitarianism

Why, then, do cues about formal assimilation matter so much in these policy opinions even when they do not much influence horizontal attachment? In the civic fairness framework, liberal assimilationist norms derive their importance from their connection with abstract values. When it comes to formal assimilation, we saw in Chapters 2 and 4 that legalism and egalitarianism play an especially pivotal role. Although these measures are not available alongside our two vignette experiments, our 2013 SSI survey (see Chapters 3 and 4) provides a way to examine this influence in the context of opinions about whether noncitizens should be eligible for benefits and rights that citizens can receive.

The SSI survey included multiple measures of values, including legalism and egalitarianism. It also included a battery of questions that asked whether immigrants who had naturalized, legal immigrant noncitizens who had been in the country at least five years, legal immigrant noncitizens who had been in the country less than five years, and illegal immigrants should have access to various public benefits: welfare, food stamps, reduced in-state university tuition, emergency room care, and publicly subsidized health insurance. This allows us to observe where, if anywhere, people draw the line on immigrants' eligibility for these benefits. As the previous experiments would suggest, citizenship status again emerges as the key barrier. Averaging across all of the specific benefits, only 28% of the SSI sample would award as many or more benefits to legal resident noncitizens in the country at least five years as they would to immigrants who had naturalized. Fully 36% of the sample would award all of these benefits to citizens and none to these long-resident noncitizens, with another 13% making an allowance only for noncitizens' access to one benefit (usually emergency room care). By contrast, 74% of the sample said it would grant the same or fewer benefits to legal immigrants living in the United States at least five years as to those more recently arrived. About 60% drew no average distinction between illegal immigrants and recently arrived legal immigrants, and only 8% took the position that recently arrived legal immigrants should have access to all of the benefits and illegal immigrants to none. Indeed, the main dividing line in people's judgments on these matters is naturalization, and it is also in this case the major source of categorical opinion.

We analyze the predictors of this distinction, a proxy for people's appraisal of the importance of formal assimilation as a condition for receiving benefits, using the same specifications as described in Chapter 4. Our dependent variable is the difference between the proportion of the benefits awarded to citizens and

Horizontal Attachment versus Civic Fairness in Decisions 157

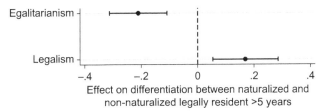

FIGURE 6.3 Legalism and egalitarianism predict differentiation between citizens' and legally resident noncitizens' eligibility for public benefits
Note: The figure displays the coefficient and 95% confidence interval estimated in an OLS regression in which the dependent variable is the difference between the average proportion of benefits the respondent believes naturalized citizens should be able to receive and the average proportion that legal resident noncitizens who have been in the country at least five years should be able to receive (theoretical range: −1 to 1). The data source is the national SSI survey from 2013. Apart from the dependent variable, the models include the same variables and specification as those used in Figure 4.2 in Chapter 4. Full tabulation of results is provided in the Online Appendix.

the proportion awarded to legal immigrant noncitizens in the country at least five years, a group that is mostly eligible for citizenship but has not naturalized. This difference measure ranges from −1 to 1 since 9% of the sample said they would award more benefits to noncitizens than to the citizens.[20] Our expectation was that legalism would predict higher scores and egalitarianism lower ones, using specifications identical to the ones reported in the note to Figure 4.2 in Chapter 4, where we analyzed the relationship between legalism and egalitarianism and opinions about a path to citizenship for illegal immigrants and legal admissions. Figure 6.3 shows that these values also predict opinions about whether noncitizens should be able to receive benefits. Both effects are significant at $p < .01$. All else being equal, highly legalistic individuals who score near the top of the scale would award an average of about one benefit less to long-resident noncitizens than to citizens compared to those who score near the bottom of the scale. Highly egalitarian respondents differentiate by about one benefit less compared to those near the bottom of the equality scale.

Of course, these two variables are not the only predictors of differentiation on the basis of naturalization. The full regression results are displayed in the Online Appendix, and they show that a variety of other factors come into play, including age, liberal-conservative ideology, humanitarianism (which curiously predicts *more* differentiation), and authoritarianism.[21]

Notably, feeling thermometer measures of positive affect toward whites predict more differentiation, whereas the same targeted toward Latinos and Asians predict less differentiation. Here again, prejudice is correlated with more restrictive policy opinions even though our CCES vignette experiment showed no net effect of ethnic cues. Recalling our earlier discussions, possible reasons for this are that measures of ethnic prejudice are themselves capturing abstract positivity or negativity toward immigrants (a problem of discriminant validity that we observed in Chapters 4 and 5 and earlier in this chapter), tapping into ethnic stereotypes that are counteracted by information about civic fairness (Chapter 5), and, of course, also identifying a highly prejudiced minority of the population that does prefer to withhold rights and benefits from noncitizens on the basis of deep-seated ethnic animus and ingroup favoritism toward whites.

Nonwhites also differentiate less than whites, and, unlike most of the other results we have described in this book, further inspection shows little evidence that legalism and egalitarianism influence nonwhites' choices the way they do those of whites. It may be that the perception of citizenship as a barrier to formal membership carries more weight among whites and has been more tied to the values we investigate here. Whether and why this is so are questions that merit further research, but we speculate that it has some relation to a long history of racial exclusions that limited full citizenship to whites.

"But It's Still about Groups!"

Before proceeding, we must anticipate a common reaction to these results – the objection that people's concern about formal assimilation is still indicative of group-centrism because naturalization is the act of joining a group. Insiders relative to the political community are being distinguished from outsiders, after all, so why is that not ingroup favoritism and outgroup derogation?

It may be a sign of just how dominant the group-centrist paradigm has become that this reaction arises as often as it does. But there are many different kinds of groups, and not all are sensibly interpreted in the light of psychological theories of social identity and intergroup relations. We would not invoke these theories to explain compliance with the rights and duties arising from and exclusive to membership in a charter organization. Presumably ingroup loyalty and outgroup animosity do not explain why the members of a homeowner's association pay dues and follow mutually agreed on rules while withholding benefits from nonmembers. Making its members feel closer to one another may matter at the margin, but these connections are likely to be a matter of personal friendship rather than shared group identity. It is unlikely in any case to make members overlook chronic nonpayment of dues or violations of its rules. By the same token, making people feel closer to those in neighboring communities is unlikely to make the members want to award them the full range of benefits afforded members.

Naturalization seems to matter to Americans' immigration policy opinions because it is associated with membership in the state, a legal association, and compliance with its formal norms. Formal citizenship is at most a weak source of the kinds of feelings of shared national identity and social solidarity that are the catalysts of group-centrism. And the types of assimilation that do promote the acceptance of immigrants into the social nation, the "Circle of We," and do engender horizontal attachments among its members, register relatively little in policy opinions.

ATTACHMENT TO THE NATION AND THE INFLUENCE OF ASSIMILATIONIST NORMS

Another strategy for teasing apart civic fairness from horizontal attachment is to examine whether the importance of assimilationist values depends on people's self-described attachment to the national community. From a group-centrist point of view, people demand assimilation because they view immigrants who have assimilated as "one of us," members of the national community. If this is true, assimilationist values should be more important to those who themselves strongly identify with this ingroup. The civic fairness model, instead, regards the emphasis that Americans place on assimilation as part and parcel of a pervasively endorsed "contract"[22] – the terms that immigrants are expected to meet as a condition of coming to the country and sharing in the rights that its government secures. This logic leads to our sixth hypothesis: if these relationships are predicated on horizontal attachments to others in the national community, they should be more potent among individuals who identify strongly with the national ingroup. In contrast, our expectation is that the assimilationist values that are central to Americans' conceptions of civic fairness should influence these opinions regardless of the strength of people's own sense of attachment to the nation.

We therefore turn to individual differences in national attachment as a potential source of variation in the relevance of these criteria to policy opinions. For evidence, we draw on the 2004 and 2014 General Social Surveys. They are useful for several reasons. First, they include rich batteries of questions about immigration that have been used by others to illustrate that conceptions of national community are associated with opinions about immigration,[23] and that we drew on in Chapters 1 and 4. Allowing us to move beyond our focus to this point in the chapter on benefits and rights for noncitizens, the GSS also includes questions about whether legal immigrants should have the same rights as citizens but also on the preferred level of immigration and whether more effort should be made to exclude illegal immigrants (see Chapter 1 for more details).[24] Second, the GSS also includes two measures of national attachment – pride in and feelings of closeness with America. This permits us to construct a two-item index of attachment to the nation.

Third, the GSS includes a battery of items asking respondents how important various attributes are to making someone "truly American," and our use of these measures clearly requires further comment. Taken at face value, these measures delineate the national ingroup on the basis of various attainable and ascriptive attributes. That is, most analysts who study them take them to be markers of a social community, with all the horizontal attachment this entails. But read another way, the questions about attainable attributes are more generally an indicator of the importance people give to various assimilationist norms. We see no reason to assume that people would answer all that differently if they were asked, "What kinds of things should immigrants say and do once they have moved to this country?"

Before getting to the meat of our sixth hypothesis, it is worth establishing which of these assimilationist norms are actually independently associated with opinions about immigration policy. To examine this, we analyze the relationship between the truly American items and opinions about each of the three policies asked in the 2004 and 2014 GSS. Specifically, the dependent variables are the three questions about immigration policy, each rescaled to run from 0 to 1, where 1 is the most restrictive position. Each of the "truly American" items is also rescaled to run from 0 to 1, where 0 means that the respondent said the particular criterion was unimportant and 1 means that the respondent believes it is "very important." These items are all asked so that more agreement indicates stronger endorsement of a given criterion. There is overwhelming support for assimilationist criteria but also considerable support for ascriptive criteria such as American nativity and being Christian.[25] Instead of classifying these items into separate indexes, we simply include them all in the regression models separately in order to see which, in particular, are influential. The index of emotional attachment to America averages items soliciting feelings of pride in America and closeness to America and is also rescaled to run from 0 to 1, where 1 represents the strongest degree of attachment. We also control for party identification, age, education, sex, race, and Hispanic ethnicity.

As Table 6.2 shows, easily the strongest predictors of these three policy opinions are the items concerning linguistic assimilation and citizenship (i.e., functional and formal assimilation). The other predictors have surprisingly weak and inconsistent effects. The citizenship item has strong effects on the two dependent variables that involve questions of formal status – excluding illegal immigrants and equal rights for noncitizens – and no significant effect on the level of admissions. Speaking English has strong effects across the board. Respect for laws and institutions is significantly *negatively* correlated with opposition to immigrant admissions but has no effect on the other two variables. The nativity item predicts more opposition to the two items that concern restriction of entry but has no effect on the rights item, which pertains to rights for legal immigrants who are already here.

These findings alone reinforce the idea that not all widely endorsed norms of assimilation play a major role in structuring immigration policy opinions: functional and formal assimilation stand apart not only for their nearly universal acceptance but for their powerful influence. Yet mere consistency with civic fairness does not rule out that group-centrism is at work. As we stated at the outset, it might be that the distinctive power of these particular norms stems from the fact that they engender feelings of horizontal attachment (although the previous experiments suggest that citizenship, at least, is a *weak* source of such feelings). If this group-centrist interpretation is correct, compliance with these norms should matter most, and engender the strongest feelings of horizontal attachment, among Americans who are most strongly identified with the nation. Shared identity is a two-way street. Becoming part of the "Circle of We" would be expected to promote strong feelings of social solidarity among

TABLE 6.2 *Norms of American identity and immigration policy opinions*

	Level of Immigration	Exclude Illegal Immigrants	Equal Rights for Noncitizens
Truly American Items			
Citizenship	.03	.08[**]	.07[*]
	(.03)	(.03)	(.03)
English	.13[***]	.23[***]	.12[**]
	(.04)	(.03)	(.04)
Feel American	.05	.05	.01
	(.03)	(.03)	(.03)
Lived in America	.02	−.02	.04
	(.03)	(.03)	(.03)
Respect laws/institutions	−.07[*]	−.03	−.00
	(.03)	(.03)	(.03)
Christian	−.00	−.01	.03
	(.02)	(.02)	(.02)
Nativity	.07[**]	.05[*]	.01
	(.02)	(.02)	(.03)
Other Covariates			
National Attachment Index	.02	.07	.01
	(.04)	(.04)	(.04)
Age	.00	.00[***]	.00[***]
	(.00)	(.00)	(.00)
Education	−.01[***]	.00	−.00
	(.00)	(.00)	(.00)
Female	−.00	−.03[**]	.00
	(.01)	(.01)	(.01)
Party identification	.06[**]	.13[***]	.06[**]
	(.02)	(.02)	(.02)
Black	−.04[*]	−.03	−.01
	(.02)	(.02)	(.02)
Other race	−.09[***]	−.04	−.08[**]
	(.02)	(.02)	(.02)
Hispanic	−.09[***]	−.18[***]	−.08[***]
	(.02)	(.02)	(.02)
Year = 2014	−.02	−.03[*]	.06[***]
	(.01)	(.01)	(.01)
Constant	.55[***]	.25[***]	.18[**]
	(.06)	(.05)	(.06)
N	1639	2071	2089
R^2	.117	.206	.088

Standard errors in parentheses
[*] $p < 0.05$, [**] $p < 0.01$, [***] $p < 0.001$
Note: The table displays the results of OLS regression analyses of each of the three immigration policy dependent variables included in the 2004 and 2014 GSS. For more detail about these items, as well as descriptive statistics, see Chapter 1 and the section of the Online Appendix that pertains to Chapter 1.

those who themselves strongly identify with this ingroup but weaker feelings of solidarity among those who more weakly identify with it. But if these assimilationist norms matter because they speak to pervasive conceptions of civic fairness, it should not make much difference whether respondents feel strongly or more weakly attached to the national ingroup – our sixth hypothesis.

To gauge this, we include an interaction between each of the "truly American" items in Table 6.2 and the index of emotional attachment to America. The question is whether those who are more strongly identified with the national ingroup place more weight on these norms, especially those that directly relate to functional and formal assimilation and have proved most influential. We display the full results of these models in the Online Appendix but summarize the key relationships here in Figure 6.4. To make a long story short, there is no significant interaction between the importance given to speaking English or being a citizen and respondents' own degree of attachment to the national ingroup.

If assimilationist values were more important to those who were strongly identified with the American nation, we would expect to see the gray lines, which show the estimated relationship between support for functional and formal assimilation among those with the strongest level of American national identity, consistently having a steeper upward slope than the black lines, which show the same estimated relationship for those who report the weakest sense of national attachment. In fact, this pattern only materializes in one out of the six graphs (for the level of immigration and support for linguistic assimilation), and the difference in slopes is not close to statistical significance. In four of the graphs we see precisely the opposite pattern. Assimilationist norms seem to influence policy opinions *more* among those who are *less* emotionally attached to the nation, though these differences in slopes are not statistically significant.

There is no evidence, in other words, that assimilationist norms resonate more strongly in the immigration policy opinions of those who themselves identify most strongly with the national community.[26] This non-effect is consistent with our sixth hypothesis. It implies once again that assimilationist norms influence policy opinions not so much because they define the boundaries of a national ingroup that engenders feelings of horizontal solidarity but because these norms reflect bedrock beliefs about fairness that Americans tend to espouse and apply irrespective of their feelings of shared identity and community with immigrants.

Of course, there is reason to be cautious about the results from any one study. Responses to the attainable items among the "true American" battery that we used to measure support for various assimilationist norms are highly skewed toward the "important" end of the scale. The national attachment index is also quite skewed toward stronger attachment. All of these measures may reflect some acquiescence bias since they are all worded so that "high" response categories indicate more support for assimilation and more attachment to the national ingroup. And there are moderate correlations between all

Attachment to Nation and Influence of Assimilationist Norms

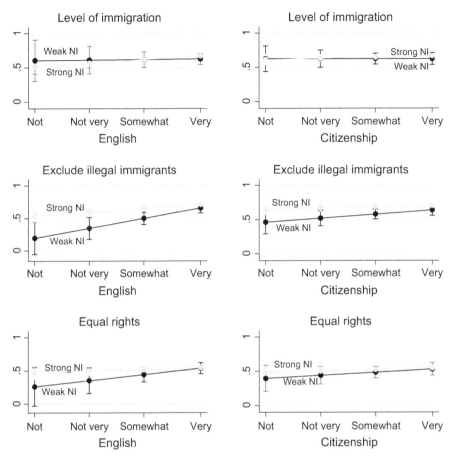

FIGURE 6.4 National attachment and the influence of support for functional and formal assimilation on immigration policy opinions

Note: The figure displays the model-estimated mean support for each immigration policy dependent variable in the GSS at each level of the speak English (functional assimilation) and citizenship (formal assimilation) "truly American" items. The models are OLS regressions in which the immigration policy items are the dependent variables (all rescaled to run from 0 to 1, with 1 the most restrictive) and the regressors are each of the "truly American" items, recoded 0–1 (1 indicates highest importance), interacted with the index of national attachment, also rescaled 0–1, where 1 indicates highest national pride and feelings of closeness with other Americans. The model also includes controls for standard demographics, partisanship, and liberal-conservative ideology. See the Online Appendix for full tabulations of these results. Upward slopes on the grey lines indicate that the truly American item in question promotes more restrictive opinions about the dependent variable in question among those who have a strong sense of national attachment. Upward slopes on the dark lines indicate a positive relationship between the "truly American" item and restrictive policy opinions among those with a weaker sense of national attachment. Full tabulations are provided in the Online Appendix.

164 *Assimilation, Civic Fairness and the "Circle of We"*

of these measures, although the variance inflation factor in no analysis was high enough to suggest cause for concern about multicollinearity. We would have preferred to use measures of assimilationist norms that did not refer to American national identity and measures of national attachment that explicitly tap into horizontal feelings of solidarity *with* fellow members of the national ingroup, but found none in existing data sources. The absence of evidence isn't evidence of absence, especially when the scales are not perfectly discriminating or necessarily well suited to the competing accounts. Still, the results dovetail with the experimental findings described earlier in the chapter and lend further support to the idea that civic fairness accounts better than horizontal attachment for the paramount importance of liberal assimilationist norms in American public opinion about immigration.

IMPLICATIONS FOR THE "PROGRESSIVE'S DILEMMA"

Lest the exploration of civic fairness and horizontal attachment as sources of support for liberalizing or tightening immigrant admissions and rights regimes seem like too much "inside baseball," it is important to pause and consider the political implications of each perspective. Nowhere are these implications more evident than in debates over the "progressive's dilemma."

Milton Friedman famously said, "It's just obvious you can't have free immigration and a welfare state."[27] His point was strictly economic. Were immigration unlimited and immigrants given full and immediate access to the panoply of benefits that developed liberal democracies furnish their citizens, more immigrants from poor countries would come to take advantage of them and deplete the fiscal coffers.[28] More recently, scholars have explored a socio-political dimension to this progressive's dilemma. The premise is that citizens' feelings of national solidarity and social cohesion are essential sources of public support for the welfare state. To the extent that the demographics of mass migration and "deep diversity" chip away at those feelings of shared group identity and community, they put these institutions in jeopardy.[29] This dilemma may go beyond the social safety net. In the United States and elsewhere, opposition to immigration often goes hand-in-hand with distrust in governing institutions, dissatisfaction with the functioning of democracy, and even weak support for the political system.[30] Just as the eligibility of large numbers of "outsiders" to receive social benefits may reduce support for the welfare state, their exercise of democratic rights may reduce the popular legitimacy of the democratic process and its outputs.

Here again, even though the vernacular is different, we find the same underlying (and group-centrist) assumption about the cardinal importance of horizontal attachment. People's baseline preference for "homophily" and tendency to "hunker down" in the face of ethnic diversity[31] are virtually taken for granted as primary influences on public opinion in this domain. Some researchers even go so far as to write about the welfare state as if it is indistinguishable

Implications for the "Progressive's Dilemma" 165

from the social "we." Keith Banting and Will Kymlicka, for example, write about the sources of "welfare solidarity."[32] The opposite of "welfare solidarity" is "welfare chauvinism." These terms imply that social affinity and social exclusion, which rest on definitions of the boundaries of community and categorizations of a national "us" and a foreign "them," are conceptually indistinguishable from the policy opinions that they are argued to predict.

One way of dealing with the progressive's dilemma is to limit immigration or, since many immigrants are already here, immigrants' access to public benefits and democratic rights. A second possibility is to persuade citizens to view the national community more inclusively so that they regard immigrants as "one of us" rather than "strangers." This would naturally entail weakening the remnants of ascription in mass conceptions of national identity. But it would also entail convincing people to develop the sort of "fellow-feeling" toward immigrants, irrespective of their _cultural_ likeness, that citizens ostensibly now feel toward people whom they regard as true conationals. Redefining public conceptions of the national ingroup in this way, the thinking goes, will promote stronger feelings of shared group identity and social solidarity with immigrants. These feelings will counteract the threat that diversity otherwise poses to social cohesion and, in turn, increase public support for including immigrants in the social safety net and the political system.

Virtually all of the literature in this realm prescribes the second solution, in effect advocating that we need to foster a sense of common nationhood that is strong enough to bind, yet inclusive enough that socially diverse immigrants may easily join. How feasible is this? Recent public opinion work shows that expressions of national identity go hand-in-hand with welfare chauvinism and other manifestations of anti-immigrant sentiment.[33] Elite-led efforts to promote new norms of nationhood and community have often met with public resistance, as the widespread public backlash to multiculturalism that has roiled European democracies and animates conservative hostility to "political correctness" in the United States have shown.[34] Multiculturalism is only one approach to solving the problem of e pluribus unum, but any attempt to redefine popular conceptions of "us" and "them" that ignite feelings of communal kinship is sure to be an uphill battle. Primordial group attachments based on common appearance, language, myths of ancestry and descent, and cultural practices tend to be stubborn.[35] Moreover, efforts to redefine national identity generally erect new social barriers that exclude successive groups of immigrants. As just one example, Protestant America became Christian America and then Judeo-Christian America. But atheists and Muslims are still left on the periphery in many people's conceptions of Americanism.

Still, suppose it were feasible to make Americans follow the biblical commandment to love the stranger as one born among you.[36] Would this weaken the public's reliance on perceptions of civic fairness as a barrier to policy inclusivity? If these policy choices are really group-centric and predicated on feelings of community solidarity, selective altruism, and ingroup favoritism and outgroup animus, then the answer should be yes. But the predominance of civic fairness over group-centrism in the studies we have described in this chapter suggests that they might be futile unless accompanied by changes in the prioritization of competing values and their perceived relevance to immigration policy issues. That is to say, messages about greater inclusivity would not change people's policy opinions unless they directly addressed citizens' perceptions of civic fairness.

CONCLUSION

In the final chapter of *Idols of the Tribe*, Harold Isaacs writes that "It remains the essence of the American theory and largely, indeed, of the American fact that one is 'American' only as an individual."[37] Isaacs was taking issue with multiculturalism and the idea that groups, rather than individuals, should be the locus of rights. But our discussion in this chapter suggests that Isaacs' point holds true also when it comes to many Americans' national identities. Of course, these identities constitute an important group identity for many people, with its various symbols, stories, emotive bonds, and language. And there is no doubt still pressure to conform culturally to the mainstream, albeit one that evolves rapidly and absorbs aspects of the cultures of immigrant groups even as they blend in.[38] But to be American is in large part also the right to remain an individual, to freely associate or to eschew association provided one accords the same right to others. Commitment to civic fairness and its "American" values and norms entails fealty to ideals that are held and prioritized by individuals as individuals. These commitments – not a sense of blind loyalty to a national "us" against a foreign "them" – are the primary basis on which the public makes choices about immigration policy.

To review the particulars, research on the sources of mass opposition to including immigrants in the welfare state and the democratic process ties policy exclusion to social exclusion and prescribes the redefinition of the national community to promote feelings of solidarity with immigrants that ostensibly translate into more support for immigration and immigrant rights.

The inquiries we have described in this chapter suggest that this approach might bear quite limited fruit in the realm of policy opinion if unaccompanied by a massive public rethinking of the importance of formal assimilation to mass perceptions of civic fairness. Cultural assimilation, we have shown, can indeed evoke feelings of solidarity and shared identity with immigrants. But those feelings evidently do not translate into much impact on people's policy opinions. And the type of assimilation that most affects people's policy opinions in these domains seems little tied to whether people feel close to immigrants, believe them to be "truly American," or see them as fitting into their communities. Support for formal assimilation appears to be group-centric only in the most trivial sense that one who acquires membership of any form is in effect joining a group. But the conception of the group that seems to be most salient to

Conclusion

people is more akin, as we have said, to legal association than an "imagined community"[39] that commands emotional loyalty, purveys self-esteem, and generates fellow feeling.

Of course, the nation does also have these characteristics of social groups, and they are reinforced constantly through "banal" repetition of exposure to symbols of national unity and pride.[40] These more group-centric aspects of national identity and patriotism are surely crucial influences on a great many choices that citizens make. They are likely preeminent in times of war, national crisis, or moments of national ceremony such as the inauguration of a president. And they doubtless influence some attitudes about immigration as well, as others have shown, over and above the norms of civic fairness we have highlighted.[41]

But horizontal solidarity does *not* seem to be the main reason that norms of formal and functional assimilation guide so many Americans' opinions about immigration policy. The importance of these norms derives from values, and their impact on policy opinions is no stronger among those who are particularly attached to the national community. The priority that Americans accord citizenship as a requirement for the perquisites of membership probably stems from a great many sources, including uncritical and perhaps unconsidered acceptance of a simple and long-standing precept. In keeping with the civic fairness framework we outlined in Chapter 2, we show that it is strongly tied to the competition of legalistic and egalitarian values, much as in our exposition of public opinion across the legal–illegal divide (Chapter 4).

On a practical level, while these results complicate the prospects of group identity engineering to bring about public support for more inclusive policies, they also suggest other approaches that might be more promising. One might, for example, appeal to other legalistic arguments as a way to counter the prevailing assumption, as Jerry Brown put it, that "voting is a quintessential prerogative of citizenship."[42] Could this assumption be dislodged? In a 2013 survey of Californians fielded by SSI, we tested the strength of two different arguments for allowing noncitizens to serve on juries, serve on a school board, and vote in city council elections. Support for all of these things was very low at baseline – never in excess of 25%, even in California. One argument sought to evoke feelings of solidarity and community. It noted that many noncitizens are longstanding residents and integral parts of our communities. This argument was a flop. The level of support for these policies barely budged. A second argument adopted a legalistic rationale that we thought might have special resonance in a country founded on the mantra of "no taxation without representation." We told people that noncitizens are required to pay taxes and are subject to the laws. This argument nearly doubled support for including immigrants in these policies. Of course the influence of a one-sided argument may not tell us much about how things would work out in an extended political debate. But it does mean that opposition to noncitizen political participation is not intransigent and that it is at least responsive to normative considerations about what is fair.

On a theoretical level, distinguishing the influence of civic fairness from accounts of nationalism predicated on both horizontal attachment once more demonstrates that values are capable of competing with and overriding group-centrism in shaping public opinion about immigration. And it furnishes another illustration of the American ethos at work: where creedal values conflict with group-centric impulses, it is conceptions of civic fairness that tend to prevail.

7

Conclusion

Stephen Hawking's *A Brief History of Time*[1] begins with a famous anecdote about a "little old lady" who challenges a scientist's public lecture on astronomy, insisting that in fact the earth is flat and rests on the back of a giant tortoise. When the scientist asks what holds the tortoise in its place, the lady is ready for him: "You're very clever, young man, very clever ... but it's turtles all the way down!" Too often, it seems to us, both the guiding assumption and core insight of sociopsychological accounts of mass opinion is that "it's groups all the way down."

The resort to group-centrist explanations for public opinion is pervasive, long-standing, and often on the mark.[2] Politics provides ample "linking information" that connects policy proposals to ideas about which groups will be harmed, and which will benefit. Accordingly, we find in the literature group-centrist explanations for people's positions on affirmative action and other race-related policies,[3] foreign policy,[4] and support for civil liberties and the war on terror.[5] We find these explanations in recent accounts of party identification,[6] gaining strength as partisan polarization has become the dominant feature of American politics. In the previous chapters, we have critically examined what should be an easy case for group-centrism: the notion that ethnic or nationalistic understandings of "us" and "them" control citizens' opinions about immigration.

We know that ethnic and national identities can matter a great deal to people, and that when these identities are poked, prodded, or threatened, this can cause backlash against "outsiders." There are, and have always been, nativists among us aggrieved by influxes of foreigners who look, sound, and act different from "true Americans" and convinced that large groups of people do not have and cannot acquire the attributes necessary to become "one of us."[7] Motivated by prejudice and the desire to preserve (or restore) their place in a racial order, they think about immigration and act in precisely the kinds of ways that intense group-centrism might evoke. They anxiously expose themselves to "alternative facts" that preserve their worldview.[8] They flock to news websites and spew hatred and bigotry in the comment sections under the articles they find there. They scream at Latino workers in eateries simply because they were speaking Spanish to one another.[9] Group-centrist explanations may well provide a reasonably complete account of the attitudes and behavior of this vocal and sometimes influential minority.

Yet this is not most Americans, we have shown, or even really that many. The vast majority are, as we have argued, motivated primarily by fealty to the kinds of high-minded values that populate two centuries' worth of work on American political culture. The majority want immigrants to assimilate *formally* by arriving legally and getting citizenship and they want them to assimilate *functionally* into American society by working hard and speaking English. Sometimes they are willing to make exceptions to these rules on humanitarian grounds or in the interest of egalitarian values, sometimes not. Their beliefs are commonly laden with racial stereotypes and biases, but not with overpowering and deep-seated racial animus strong enough to derail clear counter-stereotypic information when it is available. When push comes to shove, most Americans resolve conflicts between prejudice and values in favor of their values, applying them in an even-handed manner across groups.

We began by illustrating in Chapter 1 that group-centrist models of public opinion cannot adequately account for the ambivalent nature of most Americans' attitudes about immigration and immigration policy. The great majority of people express moderate, uncertain, and somewhat conflicted views about immigration generally. The great majority also take the "pro-immigrant" position on some contemporary controversies and the "anti-immigrant" position on others, the puzzle that motivated our inquiry. Critically, this was true even when the policies in question called to mind the same immigrant group. And it remained true even among segments of the population whose ethnic identities and attitudes might have predisposed them to more uniform and extreme positions.

It is worth underlining as well just how deeply at odds this portrayal is with the common view that America is now in the grip of a large nativist faction that elected Donald Trump president *mainly* because they wanted him to turn back the clock on immigration and rising ethnic diversity. To be sure, Donald Trump's campaign rhetoric was more unabashedly nativist than any in recent memory by a prominent politician, and his surprise victory over Hillary Clinton made him the most powerful outspokenly nativist politician in American politics since Henry Cabot Lodge roamed the Senate. Yet it is difficult to ascertain the degree to which Trump's hardline policies are appealing because of hostility and fear toward immigrants per se and to what extent his policies reflect a signal to his base that he is not beholden to the political establishment and its norms of political correctness.[10] Tellingly, however, even most of Trump's own core supporters are not committed to hardline immigration policies: a recent

Conclusion

Monmouth poll, for example, conducted well into the Trump presidency, found that only about one in five Trump voters would be "very upset" if Trump became more moderate on immigration issues, and half of his supporters would actually be either "very" or "somewhat" satisfied if Trump softened his position.[11]

In Chapter 3 we demonstrated that the public's general lean toward restricting legal admissions gives way in the face of information that primes functional assimilation and humanitarianism. Even overtly prejudiced respondents (as such things are usually measured) respond favorably to subtle primes that cue considerations about civic fairness. This remains true even when explicit ethnic group cues are available and even when people are made aware that taking a "pro-immigrant" stance on the policy questions we ask them about will sustain or expand a status quo that involves a very large volume of annual admissions. In short, what distinguishes abstract restrictivism from operational openness in immigration policy is the salience of civic fairness criteria in people's minds.

Chapter 4 showed that civic fairness explains why people's opinions about legal and illegal immigration so often diverge. This case is especially useful not only because of its high salience in current political debates, but also because it allowed us to set up a fair playing field on which to test the relative influence of group-centrism versus civic fairness. From the former perspective, most of the public's special hostility to illegal immigrants stems from deep-seated hostility to Latinos, coupled with an assumption that illegal immigrants are disproportionately likely to belong to that ethnic group. We argue instead that much of this reaction derives from the perception that illegal immigrants have violated a civic norm by coming to the country illegally, irrespective of their ethnic background. On the other side of things, the emergence of contestation over the rights and status of illegal immigrants has taken on the character of a social movement that demands equality. This framing has caused many strong egalitarians' support of a path to citizenship for illegal immigrants to outstrip their support for expansive legal admissions. In short, the values of legalism, egalitarianism, and functional assimilation seem to explain why Americans so often hold different types of opinions about legal and illegal immigration policy. Prejudiced respondents are more likely to be against immigration generally than unprejudiced ones, but prejudice in and of itself turns out to provide little leverage in differentiating Americans' opinions about legal and illegal immigration policy. And although naturally standard measures of prejudice are strongly correlated with virtually all opinions about immigration, we showed that it is important to be wary of what standard correlational techniques are really telling us. Measures of prejudice may come too close to capturing attitudes about immigration or immigration policies themselves, in which case researchers are to a degree predicting anti-immigrant sentiment with itself.

Chapter 5 assessed competing explanations for anti-Latino bias in Americans' immigration policy choices, which emerges in some experimental studies but not others. The civic fairness interpretation of these biases is that they reflect the use of ethnic cues as heuristics that provide information (often incorrect, however) about whether a policy is consistent with individuals' conceptions of civic fairness. Here, anti-Latino bias is akin to 'statistical discrimination,' without need for animus against a group per se. The group-centrist interpretation, on the other hand, is that these biases reflect outgroup derogation motivated by a desire to withhold a benefit or enhanced status from a disliked racial group or one that is seen as threatening to whites' group position. The critical test lies in whether and how respondents react to "stereotype-correcting" information that addresses concerns about civic fairness. A pair of experiments showed first that in low-information settings – when, for example, ethnicity is salient without any accompanying context – anti-Latino bias is easy to elicit. An emphasis on creedal values is no panacea for prejudice in this domain. These experiments also showed, however, that these biases greatly dissipate among those who are reassured that whatever immigrant or immigrant group respondents were evaluating met basic criteria tied to civic fairness. The contribution of the civic fairness perspective in this context is that it suggests something definite about what kinds of stereotypes are at work and why they matter. Stereotype disconfirmation takes on extra power, it turns out, when it invokes liberal assimilationist principles regarding work ethic, legal status, and citizenship status, because these are closely tied to principles of civic fairness that most Americans endorse.

Chapter 6 shifted attention from varieties of group-centrism that emphasize ethnic and racial identity to those predicated on feelings of attachment to the national community and solidarity with immigrants who are perceived to have joined the "Circle of We." We illustrated that citizens' reliance on liberal assimilationist norms to determine whether to support immigrants' access to social benefits and political rights is not dependent on their degree of "we-feeling" or shared group identity with immigrants. That is, the evidence demonstrates the limited influence of horizontal attachment and the strong influence of values. There are two key pieces of evidence. First, Americans are, on average, quite willing to extend social benefits and political rights to immigrants they do not feel attached to and to withhold them (often categorically) from those they do; the key factor is not shared identity or ingroup solidarity, but rather formal assimilation, and its influence is tied to the abstract values of legalism and egalitarianism. Second, the intensity of respondents' own attachments to the nation does not alter the effect of support for norms of functional and formal assimilation on various opinions about immigration policy. Most Americans hold assimilationist values, and most are nationalists. But the distinctive relevance of formal and functional assimilation to their opinions about immigration policy does not depend much on how attached they are to the national community.

These findings suggest taking a fresh look at the prospects for social solidarity in an era of "deep diversity." It is axiomatic among those who study the consequences of diversity in the United States and Western Europe that

Remaining Questions 173

"social cohesion" and a sense of national community are necessary preconditions for equal treatment and a robust welfare state.[12] From this point of view, ethnic tensions can only be eased once a new affective tie is forged between immigrants and natives. Yet when put to the empirical test in public opinion, the prospects for identity engineering of this kind appear dim: nationalism of virtually any kind translates all too easily to anti-immigrant sentiment among natives, and identities based on multicultural or cosmopolitan values are too thin a gruel to nourish meaningful social bonds. Civic fairness, however, does not presuppose the primordial need for "identification with" beyond bare allegiance to the rules. Thus, civic fairness, more than solidarity with immigrants, may be the unavoidable way station on the road to building support for expanded immigrant admissions and rights.

On the whole, our findings indicate that, at least when it comes to immigration, values supersede group-centrism for most people, most of the time. Americans' opinions are complex and varied, they respond heavily to information about assimilation and context and little to racial and ethnic identities per se, ethnic biases are common but seldom insurmountable, and values override nationalistic feelings of solidarity that accrue only to those who are seen as fellow ingroup members. In other words, when prejudices and blind group loyalties come into direct conflict with higher values that Americans profess to cherish, values usually win out.

This quite obviously does not mean that prejudice and identity politics will become only mild forces in American public opinion and society any time soon or that they have a negligible impact on the way that many Americans now think about immigration. In fact, we have repeatedly shown that the opposite is true. But those influences, we have argued, fall short of the overriding power and psychological centrality that would obtain if much of the public were truly in the grip of potent unacknowledged beliefs in ascriptive hierarchy. In the domain of immigration policy, at any rate, the moralism and rationalism that Gunnar Myrdal saw as central to the American ethos are prevailing far more than the bulk of writing on this subject would suggest. Most ordinary citizens do take stock of manifest inconsistency between their creedal values and group-centric impulses, and they resolve this tension in favor of their creed.

REMAINING QUESTIONS

The inquiries in this book suggest three main avenues for future research. First, does the power of civic fairness and group-centrism vary across public reactions to different immigrant groups, and, if so, how and why? Second, more broadly, to what extent does the civic fairness framework lead us to rethink prevailing approaches to the study of politicized group identity in mass politics? Third, are the influence and content of civic fairness that we have elaborated throughout this book distinctively American?

174   *Conclusion*

Cross-Group Variation

The studies in this book focused for the most part on immigrants with European, Latino, or Asian backgrounds, which we cued in several experiments by referring to national origin. Across these groups, for which we often used national origin as a proxy for pan-ethnicity, the standards of civic fairness were for the most part applied evenhandedly. A broader question is whether this result depends in part on which immigrant groups people have in mind. Put differently, under what conditions do citizens judge policies directed at a particular immigrant group through the lens of civic fairness rather than group-centrism?

We noted a number of times that Americans' reactions to cues about religion, and Islam in particular, seemed to have a distinctively resilient impact. This raises the issue of what we termed "Muslim exceptionalism" – the idea that attitudes toward Muslims might be better characterized than attitudes toward other immigrant groups by group-centrist theories and less well by civic fairness. Recall the conjoint experiment presented in Chapter 4, where our respondents were persistently more opposed to allowing hypothetical Muslims to immigrate than they were Christians and nonreligious people, even as other ethno-racial characteristics had only trivial influence. Indeed, a large and growing literature tackles the issue of anti-Muslim sentiment both in the United States and beyond.[13] There, the debate is less about whether such biases exist or whether their basis lies in social identity, but rather whether people react negatively to Muslims as a *sui generis* category stereotypically associated with terrorism,[14] as part of a broader ethnocentric tendency, or as part of a "band of others" that also includes other non-ethnic marginalized groups in society.[15]

Evidence from a couple of recently published studies indicates that anti-Muslim hostility runs deeper than fears about terrorism alone, but it is not altogether clear yet to what extent that depth encompasses the influence of group-centrism and civic fairness. In a separate conjoint analysis of choices about illegal immigrants we reported elsewhere,[16] the preamble specifically stated that the immigrants in question would have to pass a background check in order to qualify for a hypothetical legalization program. This proviso, which should reduce concerns about letting individuals linked to terrorism into the country, did nothing to soften the negative response to Islam: Muslim immigrants were equally disadvantaged relative to Christians in that study just as they were in the study reported in Chapter 4.

A second study, which one of us conducted in collaboration with Richard Johnston, Stuart Soroka, and Jack Citrin, examined the roots of anti-Muslim sentiment in a somewhat different way. There respondents were asked about whether they supported people's rights to wear religious garb in a variety of "public" settings.[17] Respondents saw either a Christian woman wearing a crucifix, a Muslim woman wearing a hijab, or a Muslim woman wearing a niqab. The results showed that Americans (as well as Quebeckers and English

Remaining Questions

Canadians, who were also surveyed as part of the study) are substantially less tolerant of the right to wear religious symbols in public places when primed to think about hijabs and niqabs than they are when primed to think about the crucifix. We think it unlikely that this is a response to terrorist threat per se, since the question focuses on religious liberty and the object of attention is female. It is also unlikely to be *racial* prejudice in the narrowest sense, since the face and skin tone of the woman in question was held constant for all respondents. And the well-documented public resistance to certain "strong" multiculturalist accommodations[18] cannot easily explain such strong resistance to distinct dress codes or the major gaps in tolerance across religions.

Some of this more stubborn discrimination likely relates to the importance that Christianity holds to a large minority of Americans as an essential component of national identity, and in this sense it would seem to be group-centric. Indeed, in a 2016 poll by the Pew Research Center, a considerably higher percentage of Americans (32%) said that being Christian is very important to their conception of national identity than did British (18%), Canadians (15%), Australians (13%), Germans (11%), French (10%), Spanish (9%), Dutch (8%), and Swedes (7%).[19] Unlike race and ethnicity, and "customs" more generally (see Chapter 2), religion may thus remain a distinctively formidable ascriptive barrier to acceptance of immigration in the United States. It is, moreover, impossible to miss the parallels between some of the rhetoric circulating about Islam nowadays and the virulent anti-Catholicism of the mid-nineteenth century Know Nothing movement. Consider the following passage from Thomas Whitney's (1856) widely read *A Defence of the American Policy*: "To believe that a mass so crude and incongruous, so remote from the spirit, the ideas, and the customs of America, can be made to harmonize readily with the new element into which it is cast, is, to say the least, *unnatural* ... [immigration] is unquestionably the 'Grecian Horse' of the American Republic" (165–166). And compare it to the slightly less eloquent statement from Candidate Trump, "This could be the all time great version, modern day, of the Trojan horse, folks ... And just so you understand I have many Muslim friends."[20]

There is still, for all that, a case to be made that the kinds of considerations about civic fairness that have animated our book are also driving public attitudes toward Muslims, even if they are often predicated on stark misperceptions. For one, many concerns about Muslim immigrants and immigration point to perceived violations of established liberal norms. Some of these derive from concerns about gender equality, whereas for others a major issue is Shari'a law and Muslims' (assumed) desire to live within the host society but by a different set of rules. Like much of what we discuss throughout this book, some of this concern likely boils down to group-centrism, and some of it is likely tied to stereotyping and concerns about both public safety and egalitarian norms.

While empirical research on this topic is only now gaining steam, we can provide some tentative evidence in favor of a civic fairness component. In a separate study one of us recently published with Soroka and colleagues, we plumbed a similar question to the one that preoccupied us in Chapter 6: when it comes to access to social benefits, what matters more, race or citizenship? Our setup was a vignette study that varied, at random, both the immigration status (born in the country versus immigrated as an adult)[21] and ethnicity (white versus Muslim). Because "Muslim" is not a racial category per se, we cued it with a combination of name and skin-tone morphed images of the kind widely used in this literature. Respondents were asked to determine whether John (or Sulaiman) should have the right to unemployment benefits.

Notably, both white (John) and Muslim (Sulaiman) receive high (and indistinguishable) levels of support when they are described as being born and raised in the country. Immigrants are substantially less likely to be viewed as deserving of this benefit, and within that category, it didn't matter much at all whether people encountered John or Sulaiman. Taken together, then, even if much of the reaction to Muslims in the United States is nativistic in character and driven by group-centric considerations, there is reason to believe that civic fairness also plays a role.

Where does this leave us? Research on public opinion has often noted that people who are prejudiced against one group are more likely to be prejudiced against others as well.[22] But this obviously does not mean that all negative feelings are of the same type, origin, or intensity. One of the important tasks for future research is to shed more light not only on why but also how some immigrant groups, at some times, come to evoke sharply nativist responses among large segments of the public while others largely do not. A sensible approach would be to compare directly the negativity that people feel toward different groups of immigrants in the presence of different sets of additional cues pertaining to civic fairness.

What our analyses indicate is that such a comparison permits a richer assessment, characterization, and diagnosis than simply demonstrating that ethnic biases are ubiquitous. For example, we have shown that at least some of the bias against Latino immigrants, while deeply problematic from a normative standpoint, responds to clear information. This is no panacea, but it is an indication that fundamentally group-centric hostility is not so widespread and overpowering that it dominates people's policy opinions – and, as a result, we observe quite a bit of openness by most Americans to certain types of policies that would greatly expand immigration and immigrant rights.

There is a good deal to indicate that a far larger portion of the American public harbors much more inflamed and intensely hostile attitudes toward Muslims. Why is this so? One possibility is that, as Higham pointed out, nativist reactions tend to reflect not only the latent suspicion of "the other" that people commonly feel but also broader social anxieties about security, prosperity, and stability.[23] The strong association in people's minds between Islam and terror or violence or even the existential clash of civilizations pique such anxieties far more than the diffuse "threats" that Latino immigration has

Remaining Questions 177

been argued to pose to whites' numerical, cultural, and political dominance.[24] Accordingly, many Americans may have developed deeply ingrained group-centric orientations toward Islam that are ripe for exploitation by politicians reciting nativist refrains.

The Nature of Prejudice and the Conceptualization of Group Identity

More broadly, our study raises important questions about the nature of prejudice and the conceptualization of group identity that merit further scrutiny. We saw, especially in Chapter 5, that many Americans make decisions about immigration on the basis of stereotypes and stereotyping. It is common to treat such stereotyping as of a kind with negative group affect. In *Us Against Them* (2009), for example, Kinder and Kam treat both relative feeling thermometer ratings respondents assign to different ethnic groups and agreement with negative stereotypes as functionally equivalent measures of an ethnocentric tendency (46–48).

There is no question that negative affect and negative stereotyping often go together, but it is not always so clear what this means. In some cases, deep-seated racial animus may be the wellspring of stereotyping and, in such cases, stereotypes may be rigid, stubborn, and difficult or impossible to counteract. But in other cases, such as the one we examined in Chapter 5, discrimination may arise from negative stereotypes that are held *without* a great deal of animus, making biases more tractable to information. Here, culturally learned stereotypes are likely to feed emotional negativity, but such negativity is far likelier to be surmountable. A population that reasons primarily on the basis of "statistical discrimination" strikes us as much less self-evidently nativist than one motivated by bigotry. "Prejudice with adjectives" – modern, implicit, aversive, covert, symbolic – clearly play a powerful role in American mass opinion. But it is important to differentiate the influence of outgroup hate from more pliable stereotypes.

Future research should also clarify concepts that are often introduced with far too little precision about which types of citizens they pertain to and why. The idea of racial "dog whistle" politics is a case in point. Its original meaning, as we understand it, was a rhetorical gesture to outright racists that is sufficiently veiled that it does not rile those who reject racism. This is a coalition-building tactic if, for example, a politician wishes to make statements that appeal to racists without offending those who dislike racism. Mitt Romney's rhetoric about "self-deportation," for example, could pass the smell test for principled or pragmatic restrictionists but also energize a nativist minority whose reasons for embracing this idea were quite different. But a different spin on the dog whistle idea is that it instead sugarcoats a racist message sufficiently to let it fly under the egalitarian radar defenses of very many Americans and appeal to the bigoted impulses that prevail in the deep recesses of their minds. In this interpretation, Mitt Romney's "self-deportation" rhetoric appealed to a much broader swath of the public on the basis of its racial implications. Our research suggests that the first interpretation is more plausible than the second. The different interpretations imply radically different understandings of most Americans' psychological motivations, but researchers seldom clarify which meaning of "dog-whistle politics" they have in mind or make a clear case for the more cynical view.

Moving beyond prejudice, the multiple roles of "social identity" in public opinion need to be better elaborated and disentangled. More than ever, it seems to us, group identities – most often partisan or racial identities, though also class and gender – have become a go-to explanation for public attitudes about politics. Recent work goes so far as to identify "single-issue identities" as attitudes distinct from issue opinions. There is surely a good deal of value and insight to be gained from an enterprise relating the innate human need for categorization to mass politics. And "groups all the way down" may indeed accurately describe some aspects of public opinion. But illustrating a static or changing link between some dimension of self-identification and an attitude about politics should be the beginning of an inquiry, not the end. It is important to probe how robust these links are and how easily they are derailed by additional cues or information that speaks to values and interests rather than self-categorization alone. And we should pay more attention to *why* group attitudes and issue opinions are linked. Group identities can serve as a heuristic guide to opinion formation for a variety of reasons, only some of which are consistent with the centrality of prejudice or ingroup loyalty, let alone the assumption that social identities are "unmoved movers."

Defenders of group-centrist approaches might respond that insisting on the need for a meaningful emotive bond between ingroup members to catalyze deep-seated prejudice is setting ablaze a straw man. After all, one could conceive of a "thin" version of identity that does not require strong social ties. One might speak of "whiteness" or "Americanness" as identities that people find important, even without recourse or reference to an underlying social tie to other ingroup members. Social identities are multidimensional, and group-centrism as we have defined it is only one channel through which they influence mass politics.

This is true, but it only underlines the importance of careful attention to which dimension of which identities are activated in different political contexts and why. Given that psychological motivations that range from self-interest to group-centrism to principled and evenhanded application of values can be interpreted through the lens of "identity," scholars should be clear about what theoretical leverage is gained by invoking this concept and what functions it is being ascribed. In some cases, it may add little and lead to confusion. We are reminded of the response that Pierre-Simon Laplace reportedly gave when Napoleon asked him about the absence of God in his model of the solar system: "I had no need of that hypothesis."

American Exceptionalism?

Our focus in this book has been on American public opinion. Future research might fruitfully consider whether and how civic fairness comes into play outside that context. A substantial part of the canon on American political culture focuses on characterizing American *exceptionalism*. Richard Hofstadter famously claimed that America was unique in that it was "not to have ideologies, but to be one."[25] Some other countries have their political cultures rooted in *jus sanguinis*, and even other more or less ideologically defined nations may prioritize different values from those that prevail in the United States. Does it make sense, then, to assume that the influence of civic fairness as we've described it here stops at the American border?

Here we are limited to some informed speculation. Moreover, even in-depth studies are deeply complicated by both cross-national differences in the composition of the immigrant stock and the configuration of party systems, among other things. In discussing Muslim exceptionalism, we have noted that the relevance of civic fairness cues to immigration in the United States does seem to vary by ethnic group. And multiparty systems amplify the unabashedly xenophobic and racist issue frames that appeal to a minority of citizens in all countries.

With these caveats in mind, it is at least plausible that many of the elements of civic fairness we have described here would resonate outside America as well. For one, notwithstanding its putative "exceptionalism," Americans do not hold the trademark on liberal-assimilationist values nowadays, and references to such values often find their way into elite-level European debates. As one relatively recent example, consider the 2010 bill passed in France banning all face coverings in public places. What is noteworthy is not that such legislation is so widely supported,[26] but that the *rationales* that political elites from both sides of the political spectrum espouse for them are so often liberal and liberal-assimilationist in character; both Nicolas Sarkozy, who as center-right president oversaw the passage of the bill, and Francois Hollande, the socialist who eventually unseated him, favored the ban because the burqa is illiberal and degrading to women.[27] This is most certainly not to say that such concerns are the *only* ones underpinning hostility to Muslims in Europe or that they are genuine and not a socially acceptable veneer for ethnoreligious hostility. The point is, just as with the American case, that there is a prima facie case that values are also at play, which, at the very least, warrants closer investigation.

We also know that European political elites have moved away from the rhetorical embrace of "multiculturalism" to demand "civic integration" from immigrants.[28] This is true in the rhetorical sense, as when former British Prime Minister David Cameron called for remodeling British national identity around what he called "muscular liberalism." It is also true in policy, as access to citizenship has become more contentious in many states[29] and, increasingly, many countries have made it contingent on immigrants' functional

180   *Conclusion*

assimilation.[30] Certainly, then, political elites in Europe have set the stage for assimilationist norms to play a prominent role in European public opinion.

Is the public listening? Comparative research on public opinion has followed the same general trajectory outside the United States as inside, beginning with (largely unsuccessful) attempts to validate *homo economicus* and following with the ascendance of sociopsychological models.[31] So far, scads of comparative public opinion research on this topic reveals relatively little "exceptional" about Americans in terms of national identity and anti-immigrant sentiment.[32] Most of this work has examined things from a group-centrist point of view, although we do have some examples of Europeans rejecting immigrants on the basis of perceived values conflicts, even if the prevailing view of the politics behind these value conflicts is fundamentally group-centrist.[33]

What seems clear from all of this is that Europeans, just like Americans, react negatively when they perceive immigration policy as opposed to the values that they believe should guide political life. As in the American case, some of this is probably ethnoracial and group-centric, and there is certainly a hard nativist core concentrated among Europe's assortment of extreme-right political parties. But it seems likely that a big part of this is values-centric, turning on concerns of cultural assimilation that cannot be boiled down to simple "us versus them" thinking. Of course, some of this could just be racism masquerading as values, something that will need to be determined by future research.

But the ideas we have explored also provide a basis for future research that might look more closely at similarities and differences in the values frames that have been applied to immigration in the United States and elsewhere as well. Perhaps certain values associated with American exceptionalism (e.g., legalism and individualism) have more resonance in opinion about particular facets of immigration policy here than elsewhere. It is also worth probing the implications of some of the starkly different views about cultural assimilation that we described in Chapter 2 – for example, the fact that vastly fewer Americans than Western Europeans and considerably fewer even than Canadians and Australians say that shared customs are essential for full membership in the nation state. This difference suggests that while support for assimilation may be strong across liberal democracies that receive large volumes of immigration, Americans' greater streak of cultural libertarianism may foster support for a thinner version of liberal assimilationism that is largely restricted to the functional and formal components we have considered here. Elsewhere, the demand for cultural integration along many dimensions may be greater than in America, and it may play a larger role in shaping immigration policy opinions. America, after all, has been a "democracy in cupidity, rather than a democracy in fraternity."[34]

PUBLIC OPINION AND IMMIGRATION POLICY

In the prologue to this book, we tabled a discussion about a puzzle in contemporary immigration politics. The public is far more exposed to immigration

Public Opinion and Immigration Policy 181

debates than it used to be, and elected officials seem more responsive to public pressure in this domain than they have been at any time since the Second World War, possibly ever. Yet the direction of policy still *seems* curiously "disconnected" from the majority will. Of course, part of the explanation has to do with the usual counter-majoritarian suspects in American politics. Pro-immigrant ethnic and business lobbies remain well funded and well organized, influential elites remain by and large committed to a cosmopolitan vision that embraces diversity and globalization, and Michels' Iron Law of Oligarchy still applies. Still, there have been efforts to reduce legal immigration, which have generally failed to gain much public interest or traction. Moreover, the interests appear to side with the people when it comes to illegal immigration – all parties involved, including a strong majority of the public, support a path to citizenship – yet the status quo persists.

However, once we get beyond broad brushstrokes and appreciate the complexity of public opinion about immigration, rooted as it is in perceptions of civic fairness, a resolution comes into focus. When opinion-policy congruence is assessed relative to Americans' opinions about specific policies, rather than on the basis of their general positivity or negativity about immigration, it becomes easier to see parallels between what the public thinks and what the government does or does not do.

The contours of mass opinion about immigration policy comprise what V. O. Key called a "permissive consensus" in support of the expansionary status quo when it comes to legal admissions. The public's diffuse preference for less immigration falters in response to even subtle primes. Few citizens are stably or intensely committed to major reforms. Most acquiesce to the status quo even if they are not so happy with it. Elites are unlikely to succeed in drumming up strong support for restricting legal immigration under such conditions. If elites manage to enact cuts to legal immigration, it will likely be for reasons other than majority demand. Americans do harbor doubts about immigration and tend to reject the most permissive of policies, but there seems to be considerable latitude in the types of policies that most Americans will accept. Moreover, there is widespread belief that, while the status quo produces some undesirable effects, it is nevertheless preferable or at least no worse than the restrictive alternatives that would scale it back. Most of the public is willing to accept a wide range of admission levels and even, we have shown, to *expand* annual intakes, provided these policies are seen as consistent with civic fairness.

This proviso is important. There are limits to what people will accept, and these limits tend to parallel public conceptions of civic fairness that are anchored in the values we have highlighted. These limits are tested when a large percentage of the public becomes convinced that immigration policy is violating their standards of civic fairness. In the early 1990s, for example, the share of Americans saying they wanted immigration reduced jumped to about two-thirds, vastly higher than at any other time in more than fifty years of polling on this question. Researchers at the time often read this as a reaction to the sheer volume of immigration and a desire for less of it.[35] This research correctly appraised public policy as out of sync with public opinion, but it may have misdiagnosed the crux of the disconnect. After all, the stock and flow of immigration continued its rise virtually unabated after 1965, but support for cutting immigration has declined fairly steadily ever since. By 2018, Gallup[36] found that only slightly more than one-third of the public wanted the level of immigration reduced.

What quelled the public's discontent? While it is impossible to say with certainty, the onset of this steady decline in support for cutting immigration strikingly coincides with the national welfare reform of the mid-1990s. This reform addressed a concern that was central to the restrictionist campaigns of that era – namely that noncitizens were consuming public benefits. Of course, neither side was completely happy with the outcome of the Clinton-era reforms, with conservatives believing cuts to immigrant eligibility should have been more extensive and liberals feeling them to have been draconian. But by imposing restrictions that most Americans support and punting the issue to the states, that law has preempted much further agitation on this issue. Efforts to portray immigrants as welfare dependent have not gone away, but they have become more sporadic, and those who would rebut them are armed with the fact that the country already places sharp limits on the kinds of benefits that noncitizens can receive.[37] Thus, policy moved in the direction of mass conceptions of civic fairness not by reducing the level of immigration but by addressing one of the major reasons that people believed at that time that it ought to be reduced.

The issue of welfare benefits for noncitizens is an example of how perceptions of civic fairness – in this case, the norms of functional and formal assimilation – can create what V. O. Key termed "opinion dikes" that check and channel the evolution of public policy. Other such opinion dikes have come up throughout the course of this book. For example, our exploration of how public opinion has responded to initiatives that would dramatically scale back refugee intakes and drastically cut the level of family-based immigration suggests that these might be especially difficult reforms to legislate unless there are similar humanitarian goals at play on the other side of a compromise proposal.

Opinion dikes came perhaps most clearly into play in our investigation of the distinctive opinions that many people have about whether to normalize the status of illegal immigrants. A large minority categorically opposes such legalization programs, a stance that is tied to legalistic values. Although egalitarian values lead the great majority of Americans to support giving at least some illegal immigrants a way to become legal residents and, eventually, American citizens, legalistic considerations about "rewarding lawbreakers" pull a large number in the other direction. The particular rigidity of many of these opinions surely contributes to the grassroots pressures that have kept many Republicans – and some Democrats – wary about supporting policies that would be swiftly derided as "amnesty."

Public Opinion and Immigration Policy

Opinion dikes that stand in the way of comprehensive immigration reform proposals that include a pathway to citizenship for illegal immigrants are not limited to categorical opinion. When asked more detailed questions about such reforms, we noted that Americans widely support conditions and stipulations connected to functional and formal assimilation that would in effect run these initiatives aground by excluding larger numbers of illegal immigrants than advocates will countenance. For example, many people believe that immigrants who qualify for a path to citizenship should have to return home and apply legally, in effect "getting in line." This condition would defeat the purpose of addressing the situation of people who have by the millions become inextricably tied to their communities. Others reject the idea of extending benefits to those who qualify for legalization and demand strict policies governing immigrants' proficiency in English, both part and parcel of functional assimilation. Such rules and restrictions appear in most legislation – another testament to democratic responsiveness in immigration policy making – but when it comes to how strict and sweeping they should be, it has been hard to thread the needle. At the same time, mass deportation is not only viewed as impractical by most of the public but also inhumane, a clear violation of most contemporary Americans' perceptions about what is fair. With policy changes currently blocked on all sides, an unpopular status quo persists despite pressure from entrenched lobbies.

These are not the only opinion dikes that obstruct the flow of immigration policy making in the directions that activists on either side of the political spectrum would like. Other research suggests, for example, that certain "hard" multiculturalist policies such as quotas in employment or political representation and "cultural maintenance-style" bilingual education in public schools evoke similarly strong opposition that has constrained the enactment of some of the kinds of policies that political elites have favored.[38] These kinds of policies may encounter such strong resistance in large part because they run against the grain of the norm of functional assimilation and its underpinnings in the beliefs in economic individualism that are central to mass perceptions of civic fairness.

It is harder to change public policy in the United States than it is to maintain it, so opinion dikes are at their strongest when they reinforce the status quo. An intense minority, that is to say, can block changes that have diffuse or weakly articulated majority support. It can even buck the preferences of powerful lobbies. As a result, despite all the clamoring from grassroots activists for change of various kinds, the US immigration system has remained in a period of relative stasis for more than twenty years. The contours of mass opinion help sustain that stasis. Were policy to change in the near future, a reasonable expectation is that it would follow a path of relatively weak public resistance and navigate a path somewhere within the broad latitude of arrangements that the majority of Americans accept.

The direction of immigration policy will therefore depend in large part on the stability of the contours of mass opinion that we have examined. A concern is that the resurgent nativism in the country's political discourse could return American public opinion about immigration to racially uglier times. So far, however, there is little indication of a restrictionist turn in mass opinion. Indeed, many of the surveys we have used in this book were collected well into Donald Trump's campaign and administration. It is in this very context that we find perceptions of civic fairness continuing to predominate. Predictably, a steady barrage of restrictionist rhetoric has made Republicans slightly less sanguine about immigration than they were only a few years ago. But these shifts are more than offset on some measures by an ongoing rise in supportive attitudes about immigration among Democrats and Independents. As of early 2019, support for *increasing* immigration was at an all-time high in the Gallup time series, while support for decreasing it matched the all-time low. Positive appraisals of the effects of immigration have also hit all-time *highs*.[39] Support for a pathway to citizenship for illegal immigrants is at least as high as it has ever been and may have *risen* since 2015.[40] Restrictionists may continue to win some elections, but they appear to be losing these debates in a rising tide of tolerance and egalitarianism.

These developments suggest that the standards by which Americans judge their country's immigration policies are evolving along with their perceptions of civic fairness. But as priorities change and values take on new significance, Americans' fealty to the ideals of individualism, equality, and the rule of law remains resilient. As long as this is true, the story of immigration politics in America will continue to be a story about how a nation of immigrants understands the meaning of its creed.

Notes

PROLOGUE

1 Hofstadter 1948; Hartz 1955; Huntington 1981; Tocqueville 2000[1835].
2 Tocqueville 2000[1835].
3 Isaacs 1975, pp. 1–2.
4 Ibid, p. 212.
5 Smith 1993, 1999.
6 Citrin and Sears 2014.
7 See, e.g., Chua 2019 as well as the essay by Sullivan 2017. *New York Magazine*.
8 Feldman 1988; Feldman and Zaller 1992; Chong 1993; Alvarez and Brehm 2002; Peffley and Hurwitz 2002.
9 See, among many others, Stouffer 1955; Prothro and Grigg 1960; McClosky 1964; Free and Cantril 1967; Kinder and Sears 1981; Bobo 1983; Ellis and Stimson 2012.
10 Among many examples, see Converse 2000[1964]; Nelson and Kinder 1996; Sides and Gross 2013; Tesler 2016.
11 As a rough indication, a JSTOR search for peer-reviewed articles in political science that contain the words "social identity" and "public opinion" in any search fields generated 63 between 1986 and 1995, 161 between 1996 and 2005, and 363 between 2006 and 2015. The prevalence of articles that contained the words "core values," the term of art, and "public opinion" was initially higher but then stagnated, with 98 articles between 1986 and 1995, 202 between 1996 and 2005, and 264 between 2006 and 2015.
12 Achen and Bartels 2017.
13 Others have used the terms "group interest or "group-centrism" in ways that would include the use of group-related information as a heuristic source of information about the values at stake. Converse (2000)[1964], for example, defines his third "level of conceptualization," labeled "group interest," as follows: "respondents who failed to rely upon any such over-arching dimensions [of conventional left-right ideology] yet evaluated parties and candidates in terms of their expected favorable or unfavorable treatment of different social groupings in the population"

(p. 14). His two primary examples are hostility to the Democratic Party because "it's trying to help the Negroes too much'" and support for the Republican Party "because farm prices might be better with the Republicans in office." The second is quite obviously a case in which perceived group interests have an instrumental value. The first might reflect intrinsic concerns about the well-being of groups (dislike of blacks or concerns about the dominant status of whites) or underlying values such as individualism that do not amount to a coherent left-right ideology of the sort Converse explores. Nelson and Kinder (1996) explicitly label group-centrism "an efficient *heuristic* [their emphasis] that conveniently reduces the complexity of policy to a simple judgmental standard" and summarize Converse's position in terms that allow for the intrinsic or instrumental valuation of group benefits: "converting questions on policy into a judgment on the *moral qualifications* [emphasis ours] of the groups involved" (p. 1056). Their experimental interventions are designed to accentuate the stereotypic moral failings of various beneficiary groups.

14 Sherif, White, and Harvey 1955; Tajfel and Turner 1979; Mason 2018.

15 Dawson 1994; Masuoka and Junn 2013.

16 An excellent overview of these perspectives on ethnicity, in particular, can be found in John Hutchinson and Anthony D. Smith's (1996) reader, *Ethnicity* (Oxford University Press).

17 Anderson 1991[1983].

18 However, our definition does not *necessarily* encompass citizens' involvement in interest groups that push a given social or economic agenda unless the participants value the well-being of the group itself rather than its political aims. Of course, group-centrism may motivate participation in interest groups, but in this instance the interest group is a vehicle for the expression of group-centrism rather than the group that itself commands allegiance.

19 Chong and Levy 2018.

20 Converse 1964.

21 Kinder and Kam 2009.

22 Ibid.; Masuoka and Junn 2013; Abrajano and Hajnal 2015; Jardina 2019; Sides, Tesler, and Vavreck 2018.

23 See, e.g., Hartman, Newman, and Bell 2014; Pérez 2016.

24 McClosky and Zaller 1984, p. 17.

25 Smith 1993; Schildkraut 2011.

26 Smith 1993.

27 Myrdal 1996[1944]. It is Myrdal's conceptualization of the American ethos that inspires this book's title (for more detail, see Chapter 1, note 42).

28 Lyndon Johnson called in 1965 for "an immigration law based on the work a man can do and not where he was born or how he spells his last name," a reference to plans to repeal the 1920s national origins quotas that had effectively ended the last great wave of immigration. Bill Clinton's 1995 address reflected a quite different read on the public's mood. He called for tougher measures against illegal immigration. The handful of references to immigration between the two were indirect or devoid of policy content. Ronald Reagan's 1984 and 1985 State of the Union addresses contain passing references to refugees who found financial success in America. George H. W. Bush's 1990 address stated that "Our nation is the enduring dream of every immigrant who ever set foot on these shores, and the

Notes on pages xvi–xvii 187

millions still struggling to be free." Several written addresses submitted to Congress referenced immigration briefly. For example, Jimmy Carter's 1980 written address mentions the issue of refugees from Latin America without elaboration.

29 Reagan viewed immigration as an important safety valve for surplus Mexican labor, which he thought would help ward off communist revolution south of the border.

30 For an excellent overview of these policies and the politics that gave rise to them, see Daniel Tichenor's (2002) *Dividing Lines*. In brief – the 1965 Hart-Celler Act jettisoned racist national origins quotas that Congress had adopted only forty years earlier in favor of a framework that remains to this day. It designated over half a million annual visas for immigrants seeking to be reunited with family in the United States and over 100,000 for the recruitment of skilled foreign labor. The 1986 Immigration Reform and Control Act (IRCA) granted legal status to almost 3 million previously undocumented immigrants. Provisions for sanctioning employers who "knowingly" hired unauthorized workers proved to be a paper tiger. Salutary neglect remained the nation's de facto illegal immigration policy, and by the mid-2000s there were an estimated 12 million undocumented immigrants living in the country. Capping off the period was the Immigration Act of 1990, which added another 200,000 annual visas and appended a 55,000 green card "diversity lottery."

31 The labeling of American ethnic groups is both complex and politicized. For the sake of clarity and consistency sake, we will refer to the largest racial/ethnic groups in America throughout this book as "whites," "blacks," "Latinos," and "Asians."

32 Gary Freeman's "Modes of Immigration Politics in Liberal Democratic States" (1995) is a particularly influential version of this argument. Adopting James Q. Wilson's theory of regulatory politics, he proposed that the economic and cultural costs of immigration were spread too thinly across the citizenry to prompt grass-roots mobilization. Mass opposition to immigration would therefore remain scattered and unorganized, leaving the arena to the machinations of entrenched pro-immigrant lobbies. Postwar elite norms against rhetoric that smacked of racism or nativism further held any incipient populist backlash at bay. See also Daniel Tichenor's *Dividing Lines* (2002, p. 17), Peter Schuck's "The Disconnect between Public Attitudes and Public Policy on Immigration" (2007), and Christian Joppke's "Why Liberal States Accept Unwanted Immigration" (1998).

33 See Gimpel and Edwards (1999). The Personal Responsibility and Work Opportunity Act (1996) cut welfare benefits. The Illegal Immigration Reform and Individual Responsibility Act (1996) hired additional border agents, mandated more sophisticated surveillance equipment, strengthened employer sanctions, and expedited deportation procedures. Both enjoyed bipartisan support and were signed by a Democratic president. See, for example, Schrag (2010, pp. 170–174).

34 Tichenor 2009.

35 Skocpol and Williamson 2016.

36 Wong 2017.

37 See, e.g., Peters and Parker 2015.

38 In a recent example, Democrats have come under pressure from Dreamer activist groups to avoid conceding even token enforcement measures or truncated rights for legalized immigrants to sponsor family members in exchange for the preservation of the Obama administration's Deferred Action for Childhood Arrivals (DACA) program, which the Trump administration announced it would let lapse in September

188   *Notes on pages xvii–4*

2017 and whose fate, at the time of this writing, is in the hands of the courts. See Shear and Alcindor 2017.
39 See, e.g., Krogstad 2015.
40 Key 1961.

1 WHAT DO AMERICANS WANT FROM IMMIGRATION POLICY, AND WHY?

1 Kopan and Agiesta 2017.
2 See the Online Appendix for a full list of these questions by survey and year, with response distributions.
3 For more detail and full correlation matrices, please see the Online Appendix. Responses to the item asking whether respondents prefer that government provide many more services even if taxes increase or many fewer services to keep taxes low are measured on a seven-point scale. Specific spending items are social security, science and technology, public schools, crime prevention, welfare, child care, aid to the poor, and the environment. The median correlation between the abstract preference for more services or lower taxes and the specific spending items in 2012 was .43. The median pairwise correlations between the specific items is .27, and the range is from .07 to .52.
4 Among various other writings by M. Lind, see The Open-Borders "Liberaltarianism" of the New Urban Elite, September 15, 2016.
5 Haidt 2016.
6 Attitudes about immigration, like many other political attitudes, are powerfully shaped by elite communication transmitted through mass media (Brader, Valentino, and Suhay 2008). Generations of Americans have come of age in an environment in which elite discourse frames immigration generally as a source of the nation's strength and central to its heritage while also focusing regularly on illegality, fiscal distress, crime, and political failure (Abrajano and Hajnal 2015). Content analyses of immigration news find a mix of positivity and negativity overall and in almost all outlets including the more partisan, predictable slants notwithstanding (Haynes, Merolla, and Ramakrishnan 2016). Research may even depict more one-sidedness than is truly characteristic of the coverage by overlooking mixes of positivity and negativity within stories. Haynes et al. (2016), for example, code stories as "positive" if they are at least 55% positive in tone, according to their classification scheme, and "negative" if they are at least 55% negative in tone. They do not report the percentage of stories that are more highly skewed, or the percentage that fall in the neutral zone, but this classification procedure allows for a great many stories that are quite mixed even if slanted enough to count as positive or negative.
7 The 2014 GSS asked respondents whether they agree strongly, agree, neither agree nor disagree, disagree, or disagree strongly with the following statements: Immigrants (1) take jobs away from American citizens, (2) are good for the American economy, (3) undermine American culture, (4) make America more open to new ideas, and (5) increase crime rates. Sixty-eight percent of the sample expressed positivity on more items than negativity, 9% are on balance neutral, and 23% issued more negative than positive responses. The "take jobs" item elicited the most negativity, with 36% agreeing against 42% disagreeing. But when it came to impact on the economy as a whole, 54% agreed that immigration was a positive and only 19% disagreed. Similarly, pro-immigrant assessments prevailed when it came to culture,

Notes on pages 4–5

too; 60% disagreed that immigrants undermine American culture while only 18% agreed, and fully 66% agreed that immigrants make Americans more open to new ideas and only 13% disagreed. Only 21% of the sample agreed that immigrants increase crime rates while 54% disagreed, a pattern that was not reversed in subsequent polling well into the 2016 election despite Donald Trump's rhetoric about immigrant criminality. Eighty-seven percent of the sample had at least one positive assessment and 49% at least one negative assessment.

8 Converse 2000[1964]; Zaller 1992.

9 The interwave correlations between opinions about the level of immigration hovered around .5, considerably lower than a number of hot-button social or "moral" issues such as abortion, suicide, gay marriage, and marijuana legalization, lower than issues that pertain to government aid to blacks, and roughly on par with questions about how much government should spend on particular priorities – not typically thought of as deeply held attitudes for most Americans.

10 There are five response categories, three "pro" and two "anti," so the probability of choosing the "pro" side in any one wave is 3/5 and the "anti" side 2/5 for a respondent choosing at random. Respondents choosing at random would therefore have a $(3/5)^3 = .22$ chance of falling on the "pro" side every time and a $(2/5)^3 = .06$ chance of falling on the "anti" side every time, yielding a .28 probability of being on the same side of the issue in each of the three waves. If we assume that everyone who switches sides is answering more or less at random, we can back into an estimate of about 46% of the public that has at least some stable preference on one *side* of the matter or the other, excluding the small percentage of respondents who do not provide a response.

11 Schuck 2008.

12 Scheve and Slaughter 2001; Hanson, Scheve, and Slaughter 2007.

13 See, e.g., Citrin et al. 1997; Hainmueller and Hiscox 2010; Hainmueller and Hopkins 2014. There are undoubtedly instances where narrow and immediate material goals override the influence of norms, values, and identities in shaping opinions about immigration, but, as with other political issues, they appear to be confined to the relatively uncommon situations in which the stakes are clear, large, and certain. See Malhotra, Margalit, and Mo 2013 for an example. For more on self-interest in public opinion, see Citrin and Green 1990; Chong, Citrin, and Conley 2001.

14 Wong 2017.

15 Converse 1964; Nelson and Kinder 1996. See also Hainmueller and Hopkins 2015.

16 Citrin, Levy, and Wong 1990; Theiss-Morse 2009; Wong 2010. Other accounts of Americanism (e.g., Schildkraut 2011) are more agnostic about whether "Americanism" derives its force from group-centric impulses to favor fellow members of the national community and keep "strangers" at bay or from commitment to a set of values one feels obligated to "as an American" to uphold, even if so doing results in short-term costs to "us" or benefits to "them." We will elaborate on this distinction briefly in Chapter 2 and more extensively in Chapter 6.

17 See, e.g., cf. Kinder and Sears 1981; cf. Greenwald and Banaji 1995; Brader et al. 2008; Kinder and Kam 2009; Masuoka and Junn 2013; Hartman, Newman, and Bell 2014; Pérez 2016.

18 Tajfel and Turner 1979.

19 Sherif et al. 1954; Bobo and Hutchings 1996.

190   *Notes on pages 6–13*

20   Chavez 2008; Ramakrishnan, Esterling, and Neblo n.d.
21   See, e.g., Clement and Nakamura 2017.
22   This is a common and straightforward definition of ethnocentrism (Kinder and Kam 2009). Analyses come out very similarly when we emphasize "white identity" (viz., whites who say that their race is "extremely" or "very important" to their identities) as opposed to out-and-out prejudice.
23   Fully 40% supported a path to citizenship, compared to 13% who wanted temporary work visas and 48% who favored deportation; 22% opposed the wall, with another 23% who neither supported nor opposed it.
24   See, e.g., Masuoka and Junn 2013.
25   The 37% of whites in the 2006–2010 GSS panel who reported that they would be more supportive of a relative marrying a white person than a black, Hispanic, or Asian person hold *less* stable opinions over time about the appropriate level of immigration (average r = .44 among the three waves of the 2006–2010 GSS) than those of unprejudiced whites (.60). Indeed, only 14% of prejudiced whites said in all three waves of the survey that immigration should be reduced a great deal. Opinion stability is marginally higher among whites (average interwave correlation = .57) than Hispanics (.43) and blacks (.27). Among the 47% of Hispanics who located themselves at the extreme high on both an item measuring pride in ethnicity as well as on an item about the importance of ethnicity to one's identity, stability was in fact markedly *lower* (.25) than among those who located themselves lower down (.59).
26   Carmines and Stimson 1980.
27   Converse 1964; Zaller 1992; Ellis and Stimson 2012.
28   Lane 1962; Hochschild 1981; Feldman and Zaller 1992; Chong 1993.
29   See, among many others, Rokeach 1973; McClosky and Zaller 1984; Tetlock 1986; Hurwitz and Peffley 1987; Feldman 1988; Feldman and Zaller 1992; Chong 2000; Alvarez and Brehm 2002; Goren 2005;Jacoby 2006; Chong and Druckman 2007.
30   Hartz 1955; Tocqueville 2000 [1835].
31   Citrin et al. 1990; Schuck 2003; Huntington 2004; Theiss-Morse 2009; Wong 2010; Schildkraut 2011; Wright, Citrin, and Wand 2012.
32   Pantoja 2006.
33   Newman et al. 2015.
34   Bansak, Hainmueller, and Hangartner 2016.
35   Bloemraad, Silva, and Voss 2016.
36   See Pantoja 2006; Campbell, Wong, and Citrin 2006; Wright et al. 2012 among the very few exceptions.
37   Soto 2012.
38   Ngai 2004.
39   Haney-Lopez 2003, 2014.
40   Hajnal and Rivera 2014; Abrajano and Hajnal 2015.
41   Rubin 2017.
42   The term "American ethos" is commonly used to refer to core American values and beliefs, particularly freedom and equality (e.g., McClosky and Zaller 1984). Both these values play an important role in our account. But Myrdal was clearly talking about a more general outlook, a quintessentially American *character trait* that sustained Americans' commitments to these values and others.
43   Myrdal 1996[1944].

Notes on pages 14–21 191

44 Smith 1993, p. 549.

45 Citrin 2009.

46 Fuchs 1990, p. xv.

47 Our research here is limited to immigration, and generalizing is always a perilous enterprise in the study of mass opinion. But a broader question our inquiry raises is whether public debates that appeal to competing values and interests are futile when it comes to the broad range of political issues that have been "racialized" by media coverage and elite discourse. Welfare policy, for example, has long held clear racial overtones to white and black Americans alike. Research on public opinion before and during Barack Obama's presidency reaches the dispiriting conclusion that racialization and racial polarization extended to a broader range of issues, such as health care, because Obama's race and sponsorship were so salient to ordinary citizens. See, e.g., Gilens 1999; Tesler 2016.

48 Graham, Haidt, and Nosek 2009.

49 Chong 2000.

50 Kinder and Sears 1981; Citrin and Green 1990.

51 Sears and Citrin 1982.

52 Walzer 1984; Carens 1987; Macedo 2011; Pevnick 2016.

53 Hartz 1955.

54 As in other realms of public opinion, self-interest is likely to have the greatest influence when the material stakes of a political choice are clear, large, and certain (Citrin and Green 1990).

55 See, e.g., Tesler 2016, pp. 21–28.

56 Schrag 2010; Albertson and Gadarian 2015.

57 Gest 2018; Mutz 2018.

58 Hofstadter 2008[1952], p. 3. What he called the "Paranoid Style" is not always directed at immigrants and immigration per se, though Hofstadter links it explicitly to the same nineteenth century nativist movements treated in Higham's *Strangers in the Land* (2002[1955]). And, what is more, the anti-Communism that interested Hofstadter was a major element of immigration policy debates during the "Red Scare" and the early Cold War (e.g., Daniels 2004, pp. 27–58, 113–128).

59 Chavez 2008, pp. 79–84.

60 See, e.g., Brader et al. 2008; Masuoka and Junn 2013; Valentino et al. 2013; Hartman et al. 2014; Abrajano and Hajnal 2015; Pérez 2016.

61 See, e.g., Theiss-Morse 2009; Wong 2010; Schildkraut 2011; Citrin and Sears 2014.

62 Druckman, Peterson, and Slothuus 2013.

63 Masuoka and Junn 2013.

64 Research on public support for values suggests a great deal of similarity across racial groups with some important differences. Rokeach (1973) found that whites and blacks for the most part endorsed similar sets of values, but an important exception was equality. Citrin and Sears (2014) find pervasive support for assimilationist norms among whites, blacks, and Latinos. Research by Pérez and Hetherington (2014), however, indicates that authoritarian values have distinct impacts among blacks and whites.

65 Mendelberg 2001; cf. Huber, and Lapinski 2006; Valentino, Neuner, and Vandenbroek 2018.

66 Collingwood, Lajevardi, and Oskooii 2018.

192   *Notes on pages 22–26*

67 Hochschild 2016.
68 Vance 2016.
69 Citrin and Sides 2008; Ceobanu and Escandell 2010 .

2 CIVIC FAIRNESS AND GROUP-CENTRISM

1 The term values is generally used for overarching precepts or notions about worthy and unworthy aims and behavior whereas the term "norms" refers to more domain-specific rules governing choice and behavior. We therefore describe the criteria of formal and functional assimilation as norms but their underpinnings in individualism and legalism as values. Similarly, we describe as values the egalitarian and humanitarian orientations that frequently soften people's insistence on assimilation.
2 Rokeach 1973; McClosky and Zaller 1984; Feldman 1988.
3 Schwartz 1994.
4 Stenner 2008.
5 Rokeach 1973; Jacoby 2006.
6 See, e.g., Chong and Druckman 2007. It is not crucial to our theory that people's commitments to these values be acquired early in life and stable through the lifecycle. We do assume, however, that these values are sincerely held and, as an empirical matter, sufficiently stable and important to structure opinions about specific immigration policy controversies, a more or less necessary assumption in any research that sees values as a source of constraint in mass or elite opinion (cf. Jacoby, Searing, and Tyner 2016). Although "values [may] serve as the building blocks for political ideologies" (ibid.), we treat them as distinct cognitive schemas that need not relate to one another in any coherent way among ordinary citizens.
7 Converse 2000[1964]; Feldman 1988.
8 McClosky and Zaller 1984. Many of these appeals differ across partisan lines. The salience and prioritization of values is therefore likely to be shaped by partisan identities (Goren 2005). Our analyses in the coming chapters do not manipulate partisan cues directly, but we do ensure that our claims about the influence of values obtain above and beyond survey respondents' partisan identities. It is not possible to resolve, on the basis of our analyses, whether values would continue to exert the sorts of independent effects we observe even if the parties took clearer and more uniform positions on immigration controversies (Tichenor 2002). However, our studies focus on a period in which the parties have polarized considerably on a number of immigration policy controversies (Wong 2017).
9 Research that has found Americans to be unresponsive to information that corrects their misperceptions about immigration is only superficially at odds with this contention. When people are told that they have overestimated the percentage of the US population that is foreign born or the percentage of the immigrant population that is illegally present, they do not, on average, become more supportive of preserving or expanding the level of immigration (Hopkins et al. 2019). This finding does not undermine the present claim because the particular information provided in the experiment (how many immigrants or illegal immigrants there really are estimated to be) has no direct or obvious bearing on most Americans' conceptions of civic fairness.
10 Zaller 1992.

Notes on pages 27–31 193

11 Lane 1962; Rokeach 1973; Hochschild 1981; Chong 1993.
12 Conflicts between strongly held values may also account for the instability of some immigration attitudes over time (cf. Hochschild 1981; Feldman and Zaller 1992), though Jacoby (2006) argues that most citizens are able to rank order their values and resolve situations when two values are "tied" without great difficulty.
13 Taylor and Crocker 1982; Bargh 1999.
14 Lippmann 2011[1922], p. 52.
15 Ibid., p. 46.
16 Chavez 2008.
17 Tetlock et al. 2000.
18 Salins 1997.
19 cf. Paxton and Mughan 2006.
20 Salins 1997.li XXX
21 For a good general discussion, see Noah Pickus' *True Faith and Allegiance* (2011, pp. 76–125).
22 Jindal 2015.
23 Schuck 2003.
24 Franklin, 1919.
25 Clear norms are a matter of near consensus among opinion leaders and are contrasted with contested norms. See McClosky and Zaller 1984.
26 The previous national identity module, in 2003, also included Canada and Australia. Even in the other "Anglo-American settler societies," agreement with the statement was markedly higher than in America, though lower than in most of Europe.
27 Citrin and Sears 2014.
28 On the resonance of multiculturalist ideology in contemporary American public opinion, see Citrin and Sears (2014).
29 See Neuman (1993) and Zolberg (2006) for discussions of colonial and state-level immigration policy making as well as early federal restrictions on immigration that adopted this language.
30 See, e.g., the Pew Research Center's 2016 report *Americans Stand Out on Individualism.*
31 Citrin 2009.
32 Schildkraut 2005.
33 See, e.g., Hartman, Newman, and Bell 2014.
34 Newman, Hartman, and Taber 2012; Enos 2014; cf. Hopkins 2015, who finds that immigrants who speak accented English enjoy more support than those who speak English fluently.
35 Wong, Levy, and Citrin 2017.
36 To avoid fatigue in responding to these many items, we assigned respondents to rate the importance of a randomly selected set of four items.
37 Gottlieb and Maske 2017.
38 Citrin and Sears 2014.
39 The correlation between the individualism index and "learn English" item was .30 and between individualism and "work hard" was .34. The only other strong correlation with individualism was the standing for the national anthem item (r = .31). The next highest correlation with individualism was "know basic

facts about American history" (r = .16) and "politics" (r = .15). All the other correlations were .1 or lower, and many were significantly negative.

40 Creation and use of the Systematic Alien Verification for Entitlements system (SAVE) by agencies that grant federal benefits was mandated by the 1996 Illegal Immigration Reform and Immigrant Accountability Act.

41 We return to this topic in Chapter 6.

42 Sassen 2001; but see Zolberg 1999; Bosniak 2000.

43 In the 1994 GSS and the 1992 and 1996 American National Election Study (ANES), Americans supported at least a one-year waiting period for legal immigrants to be able to receive public benefits by approximately 3 to 1 and 4 to 1, respectively. There is little polling on noncitizens' access to official forms of political participation, but a UC Berkeley Institute of Governmental Studies poll of California registered voters in 2013 (see Online Appendix for details) found similar levels of opposition to permitting noncitizen jury service, voting for city council or school board, and running for local office.

44 Tocqueville 2000[1835].

45 Lévy 2005.

46 Shklar 1964.

47 Ibid.

48 Hartman et al. 2014; Pérez 2016.

49 See, e.g., Dorf 2017.

50 This has been a point of controversy in recent municipalities that have considered extending limited franchise to noncitizens. See, e.g., Chason 2017.

51 *Los Angeles Times* 2014.

52 Citrin et al. 1997; Pantoja 2006.

53 As we will see in Chapters 3 and 4, illegal immigrants tend to receive "cold" ratings on feeling thermometer measures even though most polls find a substantial majority of the public opposes large-scale deportation and supports giving them a way to become citizens.

54 Hartz 1955.

55 And, to continue the passage from Bernard-Henri Lévy's essay quoted earlier, they are also central to the way we drive. He goes on to complain of "this other detail, perhaps even more bothersome, which says a lot about the anthropology of American automobile customs: in Europe the point of having a road with several lanes is to reserve one for slow cars, so that the fast ones, the ones in a hurry, which often happen to be the prettiest and most expensive cars, can drive as fast as they like in the lane reserved for them; here that is not the case. Both lanes are being used at the same speeds. Quick and slow, big and little, and thus, whether you like it or not, rich and poor, powerful and weak – all use their lane of choice interchangeably. If you're late, make sure not to blow your horn at the asshole who's blocking your way and who in France would comply and move over. You can shout, 'Get out of the way, moron, and let me pass' all you like; that would make him give way in France. Here, not only will he not give way, not only will he keep going at his imperturbable pace, sure of his right of way, but you'll see through his window, if you finally manage to pass him, his indignant, alarmed, incredulous look – 'Hey! Big and little, we're all in this together! This is an automobile democracy!' A real lesson, in the field, of equality of conditions where we French flaunt our social

Notes on pages 37–43

195

distinctions, our privileges. And a real example, once again, of the perspicacity of Tocqueville, who, more than a century before the birth of the highway, noted that 'the first and liveliest of the passions inspired by equality of status' is 'the love of equality itself.'"

56 Bartels 2008.

57 McClosky and Zaller 1984.

58 Sears, Sidanius, and Bobo 2000; though note that in his critical essay in this same volume, Schuman, who coined the term, reminded readers that he had intended it to refer specifically to the divergence between support for racial equality and opposition to *antidiscrimination* policy, namely fair housing – *not* to the idea that many supporters of racial equality opposed policies that aimed to make *outcomes* more equal.

59 Carter 1977.

60 Wong 2017.

61 Feldman and Steenbergen 2001.

62 Pantoja 2006; Newman et al. 2015.

63 Chavez 2008; Valentino, Brader, and Jardina 2013.

64 Linddara 2018.

65 Our query in Lexis-Nexis was immigration or immigrant or migration or migrant or undocumented or green card or illegal alien.

66 This includes references to alternative forms of official status, including H1-B and guest worker programs, EB-5 "investor's visas," T-visas, U-visas, and other special statuses.

67 The quote is from a tweet published by President Trump on August 6, 2018. The full text is: "Democrats want Open Borders and they want to abolish ICE, the brave men and women that are protecting our Country from some of the most vicious and dangerous people on earth! Sorry, we can't let that happen! Also, change the rules in the Senate and approve STRONG Border Security!" See Trump 2018.

68 Mitchell, Kiley, Gottfried, and Matsa, 2014.

69 Brewer (1999) provides a good general discussion. As it turns out, Dostoevsky's "Underground Man" is largely correct in his assessment that "knavery goes so easily with feeling" (1994[1864], p. 94).

70 Campbell et al., *The American Voter* (1960), or Converse's "The Nature of Belief Systems in Mass Publics" 2000[1964] are good early statements of this view.

71 See, for example, Kinder and Sanders' *Divided By Color* (1996), or Tesler's *Post-Racial or Most Racial?* (2016). For an opposing view tracing seemingly race-dominated attitudes to ideological principles, see Sniderman and Carmines' *Reaching Beyond Race* (1999).

72 The most fully fleshed out exposition of this idea is probably Rogers Smith's *Civic Ideals* (1999). That said, interested readers confront an embarrassment of riches here, and can find similar views expressed in John Higham's *Strangers in the Land* (2002 [1955]), Ari Zolberg's *A Nation by Design* (2006), Lawrence Fuchs' *The American Kaleidoscope* (1990), Susan Martin's *A Nation of Immigrants* (2011), Roger Daniels' *Guarding the Golden Door* (2004), and Peter Schrag's *Not Fit for Our Society* (2010) among others.

73 Early work in this tradition includes Milton Gordon's seminal *Assimilation in American Life* (1964) and Nathan Glazer and D. P. Moynihan's *Beyond the Melting Pot* (1963). More recent scholarship refining and in some cases challenging

196   *Notes on pages 43–46*

the models of assimilation laid down in these studies includes Richard Alba and Victor Nee's *Remaking the American Mainstream* (2009), Mary Waters' *Ethnic Options* (1990), and Alejandro Portes and Ruben Rumbaut's *Immigrant America* (2006).

74 On pervasiveness, even a cursory glance at the literature reveals our willingness to identify with others on the basis of shared characteristics, even arbitrary ones (blue eyes versus brown, Kandinsky or Klee, and "Eagles" versus "Rattlers," to name a few). On mechanism, the early work tracing back to William Graham Sumner pointed to material conflict over resources. Social Identity Theory, by contrast, emphasizes the self-esteem people draw from identifying with others (Tajfel and Turner 1979). Whatever their immediate psychological precursors, it seems uncontroversial that the need to "identify with" in this way results from humans' innate sociability as a species, and, in a grander sense, the evolutionary advantage that this afforded us (Brewer 2007). Finally, on prejudice-reduction, the paradigmatic work is without a doubt Gordon Allport's *The Nature of Prejudice* (1954).

75 Not unlike *Lucky Jim*'s Christine Callaghan, who tells the eponymous protagonist that she sees only "two great classes of mankind, people I like and people I don't" (1999 [1954], p. 143).

76 There is some debate over this point, which we return to later.

77 Abrajano and Hajnal 2015.

78 Ibid.

79 Bobo and Hutchings 1996; Sidanius and Pratto 1999; Masuoka and Junn 2013; Hartman et al. 2014.

80 Bobo, Kluegel, and Smith, 1996; Sears and Henry 2005.

81 See, e.g., Masuoka and Junn 2013. Approximately 10% of the US black population is foreign born, however, leading to complex dynamics of identity formation and complicating standard binary models of group relations applied to black-white interactions in the United States (Greer 2014).

82 Kinder and Kam 2009.

83 Hopkins 2015; Valentino et al. 2013.

84 Kalkan, Layman, and Uslaner; Sides and Gross 2013.

85 cf. Greenwald and Banaji 1995; Pérez 2010, 2016.

86 For more on the emotional triggers for ethnocentrism, see Banks (2014).

87 Pérez 2016.

88 Hartman et al. 2014.

89 Hyman and Sheatsley 1964; Schuman 1997.

90 For a thorough discussion of different perspectives on symbolic racism, see Sears et al. 2000.

91 Hartman et al. 2014.

92 Anderson 1991 [1983].

93 Key works in this tradition include Hans Kohn's *The Idea of Nationalism* 2005[1944], Benedict Anderson's *Imagined Communities* (1991 [1983]), and Ernest Gellner's *Nations and Nationalism* (1983), to name just a few. In *The Lion and the Unicorn,* George Orwell claimed that "[o]ne cannot see the modern world as it is unless one recognizes the overwhelming strength of patriotism, national loyalty. In certain circumstances it can break down, at certain levels of civilization it does not exist, but as a *positive* force there is nothing to set beside it. Christianity and international Socialism

Notes on pages 46–49 197

are as weak as straw in comparison with it" (Orwell 2002 [1941], p. 291). For an excellent overview of these ideas, see Citrin and Sears 2014, Chapter 1.

94 Billig 1995.
95 Gellner 1996.
96 Of course, nationalism has its dark side. The point for our purposes, however, is that its more virulent aspects are directed to those *outside* the national community.
97 Berlin 1997 [1979], p. 595; see also Kohn 2005[1944].
98 Citrin and Sears 2014.
99 It is worth recalling here the distinctions we drew in Chapter 1 between "narrow" or "immediate" group-centrism and the possibility of what might be termed "enlightened group-centrism." Just as enlightened self-interest, or self-interest properly understood, can include acting on behalf of the community and eschewing one's narrow self-interest, people may hew to values because they believe them to be conducive to the long-term interests of fellow group members – even when doing so incurs shorter run costs to the group. Moreover, just as people may understand their self-interest broadly, to include the satisfaction that comes from abiding by moral precepts, they may view the interests of their group broadly to include faithfulness to its norms. Just as studies that pit egocentric against sociological models of human behavior often restrict the domain of self-interest to the narrow and immediate (and often material, though that is not a restriction we make), we have deliberately excluded these more remote and indirect ways in which people may pursue their group's interests through adherence to its values and norms from our definition of group-centrism.
100 See Citrin and Sears 2014.
101 Federalist Paper 2 famously defines the United States as "one united people – a people descended from the same ancestors, speaking the same language, professing the same religion, attached to the same principles of government, very similar in their manner and customs." As Fuchs (1990) points out, John Jay was exaggerating the degree of homogeneity in America at that time in the service of arguing for a constitution that would empower a far stronger central government.
102 MacIntyre 1981; Walzer 1984.
103 Lipset 1960; Lipset and Raab 1978; Huntington 2004.
104 Miller and Ali 2014, p. 4.
105 Freud 1968 [1933], p. 73.
106 Archetypical examples of each school of thought are Habermas, J. (1994), Kymlicka 1995, and Miller 1995.
107 For a critical perspective on this literature, see Levy 2017.
108 Miller 1995, p. 140
109 Schildkraut 2014, p. 443.
110 See, for example, the opening chapters of Deborah Schildkraut's *Americanism in the Twenty-First Century* (2011), Citrin and Sears' *The Politics of Multiculturalism* (2014), Cara Wong's *Boundaries of Obligation* (2010), and Elizabeth Theiss-Morse's *Who Counts as an American?* (2009).
111 Deborah Schildkraut's *Americanism in the Twenty-First Century* is one exception. It portrays American national identity both in terms of affect (particularly attachment to "the nation") and norms, some of which overlap with civic fairness (Schildkraut 2011). But while the book is explicit about the fact that *others* have

Notes on pages 49–61

made the argument, Schildkraut does not take a position on the importance of horizontal attachment.

112 Citrin and Sears 2014, p. 31.

113 Wong 2010, p. 6 [emphasis ours].

114 Theiss-Morse 2009, pp. 22–23.

115 As we noted earlier, linguistic assimilation can be seen as a "civic" or "ethno-cultural" attribute, depending on whether Americans insist on it because they see it as crucial to political participation and economic upward mobility or because they yearn for a common culture that revolves around the English language. We therefore follow the clearer ascriptive-attainable typology that one of us has previously advanced (Wright 2011) to separate nativist conceptions of national identity that are fundamentally closed to many people based on qualities that are more or less immutable from liberal conceptions of national identity that are in principle open to anyone.

116 Hainmueller and Hopkins 2015.

117 See, e.g., Sniderman et al. 1989; Gross and Kinder 1998; Chong and Levy 2018.

118 The sides of this debate are well represented in Sears et al. 2000.

119 Hartman, Newman, and Bell 2014.

120 Ibid.

121 Pérez 2010; 2016.

122 The distinction traces to Gary Becker's "taste-based" models (e.g., 1957), and the limited information decision-making models developed by Kenneth Arrow (1972) in response. See Guryan and Charles (2013) for a recent review.

123 Tetlock et al. 2000.

124 Masuoka and Junn 2013; Hainmueller and Hopkins 2014; Hartman et al. 2014; Ostfeld 2015; Pérez 2016; Wright, Levy, and Citrin 2016; Valentino et al. 2017.

125 Citrin and Sears 2014.

126 Hainmueller and Hopkins 2015.

3 FUNCTIONAL ASSIMILATION, HUMANITARIANISM, AND SUPPORT FOR LEGAL ADMISSIONS

1 Muste 2013.

2 This number is a moving target, however. The 30% figure was reached in 2019, continuing a rapid trend toward more support for *increasing* immigration. This percentage is roughly triple the share of Americans who supported more immigration twenty years earlier, when the sharp rise in support for increased admissions began. Although this chapter emphasizes the sources of disconnect between abstract support for restriction and particular support for policies that would preserve or increase the level of immigration, it is worth keeping in mind that the two have been converging. The trends suggest that this convergence is occurring because abstract restrictivism is diminishing: during the period of heightened public attention to immigration, abstract attitudes about the level of immigration are becoming more like the accepting and permissive opinions people have tended to express about specific legal admissions policies.

3 Shepard 2017.

Notes on pages 61–83

4   See Pew Research Center (2018), Shifting Public Views on Legal Immigration into the U.S.: Support for Increasing Legal Immigration Now Outstrips Support for Decreasing It.
5   Schuck 2008.
6   Fox News 2011.
7   Gallup Organization 2013.
8   Bloemraad, Silva, and Voss 2016.
9   For descriptive statistics on the sample, see the Online Appendix. As with other surveys of its kind, this one over-represents college-educated and white Americans, though we detect no severe partisan or ideological bias.
10 Quinnipiac University Polling Institute 2018; CBS News 2017.
11 See, e.g., Oh and Wu 2018.
12 cf. Kinder and Kam 2009.
13 Both the effect of the FA cue and the extent to which it was moderated by individualism and humanitarianism were very similar regardless of whether one compared *FA* to *control* or *FA+negative* to *negative*, so we lump these conditions together for simplicity.
14 cf. Bloemraad et al. 2016.
15 In the more fully saturated model (see the Online Appendix for full tabulation) that includes controls for all the covariates listed and their interactions with the treatments, the interactions between *humanitarianism* and both the refugee and family treatments remain about the same but the interaction between individualism and the family treatment drops to less than one-third its size in the sparse model reflected in Figure 3.3 (p = .49). Further inspection (results available from the authors) makes it clear that liberal-conservative self-identification is the key control: excluding it from the model but keeping all the other covariates and interactions more than doubles the size of the coefficient on the interaction term between *individualism* and the family treatment and leaves it just short of statistical significance (p = .11). Moreover, liberal-conservative ideology powerfully enhances the effect of the family treatment in this model, with an effect on strong conservatives that is .26 larger than the effect on strong liberals (p < .05).
16 Fitzgerald 1996; Tichenor 2002.
17 For sample statistics, see the Online Appendix.
18 Hopkins, Sides, and Citrin 2019.
19 Kinder and Kam 2009.
20 Key 1961; Zaller 2003.
21 Gallup Organization 2013.
22 ABC News/Washington Post 2013.
23 Gallup Organization 2013.
24 Gallup Organization 2013a.
25 ABC News/Washington Post 2013b.
26 CBS News 2017.
27 NBC News/Wall Street Journal 2017.
28 Pew Research Center for the People & the Press 2017.
29 Gallup Organization 2017.
30 Quinnipiac University Polling Institute 2017b.
31 Quinnipiac University Polling Institute 2017c.

32 Quinnipiac University Polling Institute 2017b.
33 Quinnipiac University Polling Institute 2015.
34 Talev 2015.
35 CBS News/*New York Times* 2015.
36 Pew Research Center for the People & the Press 2015.
37 Quinnipiac University Polling Institute 2017a.
38 Quinnipiac University Polling Institute. 2017d.
39 Shepard 2017.
40 Morning Consult 2017.
41 Of course a major basis for opposition to the travel ban is the idea that it violates the precept of religious freedom and equality. We examine egalitarian values in more depth in the next chapter, when we turn to illegal immigration policy. But recent research by Loren Collingwood and colleagues (2018) strongly suggests that egalitarian values shaped public reactions to this policy as well as people took stock of the arguments that elites put forward.

4 CIVIC FAIRNESS AND THE LEGAL–ILLEGAL DIVIDE

1 Schildkraut 2013.
2 See Tichenor 2002. We will return to the subject of benefits and rights for legal immigrants in Chapter 6.
3 Tichenor 2009.
4 Major news outlets, including the Associated Press, have discarded the term "illegal immigrant" in favor of terms such as "unauthorized" or "undocumented." The Library of Congress faced backlash from Congressional Republicans when it sought to eliminate references to the allegedly derogatory phrase "illegal aliens," the language of US statute, in favor of "noncitizens" or "unauthorized immigrants." See Aguilera 2016.
5 Ngai 2004
6 Merolla, Ramakrishnan, and Haynes 2013.
7 See the transcript to the episode of CNN's *State of the Union* 2017 where Emanuel made the remark."
8 Both of these things were quite important to most respondents, with 68% saying always obeying laws was very important and 73% saying the same of not trying to evade taxes.
9 A disadvantage of this scale is that it is highly skewed. The mean is just shy of .9. Nevertheless, there is substantial variation. The standard deviation is .15. A similar approach was taken by Schuman et al. 1997 in an attempt to ascertain whether some whites opposed laws prohibiting racial discrimination in home sales because of a generalized antipathy to government intervention in private affairs. They used a crude proxy for such antipathy as well – opposition to laws mandating seatbelts – and found a modest correlation.
10 Hetherington and Pérez 2014.
11 Masuoka and Junn 2013.
12 See www.heuni.fi/material/attachments/heuni/reports/6Kngur65P/Appendix_1.pdf
13 Masuoka and Junn 2013.

Notes on pages 94–108

14 Citrin et al. 1997.

15 Valentino, Levy, and Citrin, 2013; see also Pérez 2010, 2016.

16 Valentino, Brader, and Jardina 2013.

17 Pérez 2016.

18 Like any other approach, conjoint has its strengths and weaknesses. For more technical treatments, consult Hainmueller, Hopkins, and Yamamoto (2014) and Bansak et al. (2018). Insofar as some of the methodological issues touch directly on immigration, see detailed discussion of results and robustness tests in Hainmueller and Hopkins (2014) and in Wright, Levy, and Citrin (2016).

19 We opted for this side-by-side format with two profiles at a time simply in order to mimic the look and feel of earlier work on immigration using conjoint analysis (Hainmueller and Hopkins 2014). The idea, as described in Wright et al. 2016, was to maximize comparability with other analyses while adding the randomization of legal status and permitting people to express categorical tendencies.

20 By contrast, debates about legal immigration tend to focus on *how many* immigrants of *which types* it would be beneficial for the country to admit. Few politicians openly advocate "open borders" or a full cessation of all immigrant intakes. Virtually no one advocates a universal right of any and all of the world's people to come to America if they so choose, and no one insists that it is morally incumbent on the United States to take anyone and everyone who lands on our shores.

21 In absolute terms, these acceptance rates do not mean a whole lot since they pertain only to the particular sample of immigrant profiles generated in this experiment, which differs in some critical ways from the pool of legal and illegal immigrants as a whole. For example, a highly inflated 50% of immigrants in the experiment were described as having a poor employment track record when the real rate of immigrant labor force participation is extremely high.

22 These are all based on the logistic regression results, using standard errors clustered by respondent.

23 The interaction between experimental condition (*Legal, Illegal*, or *Dreamer*) and legalism is statistically significant at p < .05.

24 The difference in slopes across conditions is again statistically significant at p < .05.

25 Specifically, we added an interaction between a dummy variable identifying whites and nonwhites to the multivariate model that forms the basis for our probability estimates reported earlier. None of the three-way interactions between legalism or egalitarianism, treatment condition, and this race dummy reached statistical significance even at p < .1.

26 Granted that people may just not be paying attention to the surveys they are being paid to take and that this may lead them to respond "categorically" as well. This *could* explain some baseline level of categorical response, but it cannot explain the large *differences* in categorical response across *Legal, Illegal*, and *Dreamer* conditions.

27 Hainmueller and Hopkins 2014; see also Citrin et al. 1997.

28 This is done for efficiency's sake: it turns out that the attributes exert similar effects on assessments of legal immigrants, illegal immigrants, and Dreamers alike (see discussion in Wright et al. 2016).

29 Citrin, Reingold, and Green1990; Citrin et al. 1997 ; Citrin et al.1997; Theiss-Morse 2009; Wong 2010; Schildkraut 2011; Newman et al. 2012; Hopkins 2015; Citrin and Sears 2014.

202   *Notes on pages 109–117*

30 See, e.g., Ramakrishnan, Esterling, and Neblo n.d.

31 Though Figure 4.9 pools the conditions together, we note that the "penalty" is more or less equal in assessments of legal and illegal immigrants.

32 These results are also similar to those of Hainmueller and Hopkins (2014), who find that Iraqi immigrants are at a disadvantage but that there is minimal discrimination against Latinos relative to whites or Asians.

33 Hartman, Newman, and Bell 2014; see also Kootstra 2016 for a related example outside the United States.

34 Malhotra and Newman 2017.

35 Hainmueller and Hiscox 2010; Hainmueller and Hopkins 2014.

36 If the result is robust, it may simply reflect the well-known finding in social psychology that people hold "positive" individual exceptions to negative stereotypes about marginalized groups in particularly high esteem (see, e.g., Sniderman et al. 1991).

37 Indeed, 14% of whites rate their own group colder than Latinos on the feeling thermometers, while 40% of blacks, 42% of Latinos, and 22% of Asians in the sample rate whites "colder" than Latinos.

38 Specifically, the model is a logistic regression where the dependent variable is whether each immigrant profile is accepted and the independent variables are the randomly varied national origin categories, all four group feeling thermometers, and the interactions between each national origin category and each group feeling thermometer. Predicted probabilities are calculated with all other variables in the model held at their sample means.

39 There are at least two other reasons that this explanation does not pass muster here. Different patterns emerge when the Asian feeling thermometer is used instead. And the influence of both these feeling thermometers is strongly predicated on the legal status of the immigrants involved (over and above explicit national origin information). Whatever its independent role in predicting support for legalization, generalized animosity against "them" and favoritism for "us" does not seem to explain these particular findings.

40 We pool the illegal immigrant conditions for ease of presentation and because results are very similar in both.

41 Research on partisan identification, often treated as a social identity, is an exception. Scholars have vigorously debated over the years about whether partisanship is the "unmoved mover" of political choice (Campbell et al 1960) or a "running tally" (Fiorina 1981) of voters' assessments of each party's performance in office or a heuristic that conveys information about the kinds of policies a candidate will pursue.

42 Schuman (2000) raises a similar point about the items used to measure symbolic racism against blacks and their strong association with support for affirmative action. However, Schuman's critique focuses on nonracial language included in the wording of the symbolic racism items that seem almost to reference affirmative action (e.g., "without help"). Here we are suggesting that the conflation of particular ethnic groups with contemporary immigration means that any attempt to measure attitudes toward these groups is likely in part to capture more general attitudes about immigration.

43 Pérez 2016.

Notes on pages 118–126

44 Hainmueller and Hopkins (2014) also report that ethnocentric and nonethnocentric respondents in their conjoint analysis do not differ a great deal in their valuation of nonethnic attributes.

45 See, for example, Hainmueller, Hopkins, and Yamamoto (2015).

46 Hainmueller and Hopkins 2015; Wright et al. 2016.

47 Abrajano, Elmendorf, and Quinn 2018.

48 Gilens 1999.

49 Pérez 2016, concluding chapter.

50 See, for example, the June 22–24 CNN poll.

51 For the research brief, see Citrin, Levy, and Lenz 2013.

5 CIVIC FAIRNESS AND ETHNIC STEREOTYPES

1 Hainmueller and Hopkins 2014; Wright et al. 2016.

2 Hopkins 2015; Iyengar et al. 2015; Ramakrishnan, Esterling, and Neblo n.d.

3 Pérez 2016.

4 Research indicates that agitated emotional states can engender more ethnocentric reactions to political issues (Banks 2014). To the extent that exposure to questions about admitting immigrants or giving legal status to illegal immigrants makes respondents angry, this effect is built into all of our results. Political junkies, the minions who fulminate in political chat rooms and on message boards, and the small minority of Americans who attend raucous political rallies are probably poorly described by our data – and by most other survey-based generalizations about public opinion. We may also do a poor job describing the state of public opinion in the short run after a major political event. These are standard disclaimers in our neck of the woods, which is not to say that they are unimportant ones. Most research before us that claims the primacy and dominance of ethnic identities in immigration policy opinions relies on research conducted in an ordinary survey context, and to the extent format has varied (e.g., by using video technology or pictures rather than text to manipulate racial cues), there is no consistent evidence that these changes have systematically increased the salience or import of ethnicity (e.g., Valentino, Brader, and Jardina 2013; Hopkins 2013; Abrajano, Elmendorf, and Quinn 2018).

5 For a time, voters in some local Swiss elections were called on to make choices about whether to grant residency to individual immigrants on the basis of information much like that presented in the conjoint. In a clever study, Hainmueller, Hangartner, and Yamamoto (2015) compared administrative records from these elections with survey data based on analogous conjoint designs. They found a close correspondence between the immigrant attributes that voters relied on to make choices in these elections and in their surveys.

6 Some surveys that have asked Americans straight out their preferred level of immigration from Europe, Latin American, and Asia find clear evidence of differentiation by regional background. In the 2000 General Social Survey, about 44% of the sample said the number of immigrants from Latin America should be reduced, similar to the number from Asia, but significantly higher than the 34% that said this about the number of immigrants from Europe. A 2009 Newsweek Poll found that only 20% of Americans thought there were "too many" immigrants coming from Europe, compared to 62% of who thought this about immigrants from Latin America, 35%

about Asians, and 24% about Africans. As this last datum indicates (it strikes us as unlikely that Americans are so partial to African immigrants over Latinos and Asians and on par with Europeans), these comparisons may simply reflect a perception – by 2009 quite a stark misperception – that the great majority of new immigrants were arriving from Latin America. In this sense, the choices people make about individual immigrants may give a better sense of ethnic bias, since the choice about a single immigrant does not so clearly have implications for the broader ethnic mix of immigrants in the country. Some Americans may be intuitive "Huntingtonians" when it comes to immigration, believing that the predominance of immigrants from a single national and linguistic background poses a unique challenge for the engines of assimilation but disavowing any particular hostility toward Latinos. See Huntington (2004, 2009).

7   Masuoka and Junn 2013.
8   Brader, Valentino, and Suhay, 2008.
9   Hartman, Newman, and Bell 2014.
10 Becker 1957.
11 Such differences may exist in reality, or they may rest on distortions, misconceptions, or myths. In the present discussion all that matters is that they are believed to exist and to be significant enough to provide useful decision-making information.
12 See, e.g., Lau and Redlawsk 2006; Druckman, Peterson, and Slothuus 2013; Lodge and Taber 2013.
13 Taber and Lodge 2006.
14 Chavez 2008.
15 Ibid.
16 Once again, as in Chapter 4, we turn up no evidence that support for non-Mexican illegal immigrants is less predictive than support for Mexican illegal immigrants of general opinions about a path to citizenship. This suggests that the predominant symbol respondents are drawing on when they form opinions about a path to citizenship may not be imagined ethnicity but simply the referent "illegal." However, opinions about a path to citizenship in general were significantly less correlated with support for immigrants in the *informed* condition than in the *uninformed* condition. So it appears that the type of illegal immigrant that people conjure when they consider illegal immigration in the abstract more closely resembles the sketchily defined immigrants in the *uninformed* condition than the more functionally assimilated immigrants in the *informed* condition.

6 ASSIMILATION, CIVIC FAIRNESS AND THE "CIRCLE OF WE"

1   There is no dilemma for elements of the "populist" right that have mobilized around the issue, as they have crafted their appeals explicitly around the wholesale rejection of mass immigration.
2   Alba and Nee 2003.
3   See, e.g., Portes and Rumbaut 2006.
4   Though, as we also saw in Chapter 2, majorities have no problem with the retention of private customs, part and parcel of view about assimilation that are largely laissez-faire and pluralistic. The vast majority of the public that sees the introduction of immigrants' "new ideas" as a net positive for American culture (Chapter 1) also

Notes on pages 143–149

indicates that most Americans see assimilation as a two-way street and views some change in the mainstream as salutary (cf. Alba and Nee 2003).

5   Such a process of social recategorization is possible because Americans – unlike, say, the quintessentially "ethnic" nation of Japan – define their national community primarily on the basis of "attainable" rather than "ascribed" characteristics. In other words, Americans understand their national ingroup to include those who were previously outsiders but have adopted mainstream norms, beliefs, and customs.

6   Hollinger 1993.

7   We will not examine public opinion about noncitizens' procedural rights – standing to bring suit, entitlement to equal protection under the laws, due process, and the like. These debates have largely played out in the court system, and have not been central to public debates about immigrants' rights. Rights have expanded dramatically since the 1970s (Fuchs 1990).

8   Hero and Preuhs 2007.

9   Just a couple of examples should suffice here. In 1992, only 21% of respondents to the American National Election Study agreed that legal immigrants "should be eligible as soon as they come here for government services," with 79% saying that "they should have to be here a year or more." In 1994, General Social Survey (GSS) respondents answered a more or less identical question 67 to 33%.

10 See, e.g., Citrin et al. 1997 and Citrin and Sears 2014, Chapter 7; Schildkraut 2011, pp. 118–19; Bloemraad, Silva, and Voss 2016. Schildkraut finds a high level of support for giving legal immigrants access to benefits, but this is based on a survey question that does not stipulate noncitizenship.

11 Zolberg 2006.

12 See Lyons and Green 2016. It should be noted, however, that this measure made no distinction between legal and illegal immigrants.

13 Gonzalez-Barrera 2017.

14 We did not explore shorter lengths of residency because most legal permanent residents must wait at least five years to naturalize.

15 We intended for this cue to signal a cultural orientation apart from the civic fairness requirement to learn English *to the point of self-sufficiency*. Our reasoning was that we had already indicated that the immigrant is employed and gets by. In retrospect, however, we worried that alluding to use of English or native language could also signal functional assimilation in the sense that obtaining proficiency in language may be taken as a marker of potential advancement or long-term prospects to continue to earn one's keep and thus be read as a civic fairness cue. It could also, we realized, be taken as a sign that the immigrant is prepared to participate fully in the political realm. If anything, this confound should *accentuate* the effect of this treatment on policy opinions since it adds a pragmatic and individualistic basis for its influence beyond its implications for cultural "likeness." As it turns out, this treatment had a weak effect on the policy opinions despite its strong effect on horizontal attachment. We are further reassured by the replication of the main pattern of results in a follow-up vignette experiment in which we held language proficiency constant.

16 cf. Wong 2010.

17 Some might object to the strangeness of asking people these kinds of questions about a hypothetical individual. Yet the fact that people *did* score highly here indicates that they are willing to "identify with" even in such an artificial situation.

206   *Notes on pages 151–165*

18   Schildkraut 2005.
19   cf. Wong 2010.
20   Excluding these respondents from the analysis, in case their responses reflect measurement error, does not change any of the results we report here.
21   In the Online Appendix, we also report analyses of the degree to which respondents differentiated between access to benefits based on length of residence among legal immigrants and based on legal status. As we noted previously, the absolute amount of differentiation between these categories of immigrants is far less than across the citizenship divide. We also find no evidence that legalism or egalitarianism predicts what limited differentiation there is. To summarize, naturalization seems to be the barrier that people attend to, and the degree of emphasis they place on it is powerfully shaped by legalistic values and support for equality.
22   Salins 1997.
23   Wong 2010; Citrin and Sears 2014.
24   This question does not distinguish access to benefits from participatory rights but is useful because it allows us to examine which sorts of respondents are most likely to support extending citizenship rights in general to noncitizens.
25   cf. Citrin, Reingold, and Green 1990; Theiss-Morse 2009; Wong 2010; Schildkraut 2011; Wright 2011.
26   What about the other "truly American" items in the GSS? In brief, none of them interacted significantly in a consistent direction with our measure of national attachment (see the Online Appendix). That is, we do not find evidence that *any* of the "truly American" items matter more to those who care deeply about the nation than they do to those who are less strongly attached to it. The closest we come is the "feel American" item. This item predicted opposition to immigration more strongly among those with a strong sense of national attachment than among those with a weak sense of attachment in all three cases, and the differences were large and statistically significant at the p < .1 level in two of the three cases (the rights item is the exception). Thus, it is possible that demanding that true Americans *feel* American influences opinions about immigration policy more strongly among respondents who also feel strongly American, perhaps an indication that ingroup favoritism is at work in that particular case. But when it comes to formal assimilation and functional assimilation, there is no evidence that their influence on immigration policy opinions is any stronger among those with a strong sense of national identity than among those who do not feel strongly attached to America.
27   Norwatesh 2012.
28   cf. Borjas 1999.
29   Harell and Stolle 2010.
30   McLaren 2012; Citrin, Levy, and Wright 2014; cf. Easton 1965.
31   See, e.g., Putnam 2007.
32   Banting and Kymlicka 2017.
33   Wright 2011; Wright and Reeskens 2013; Reeskens and Wright 2013.
34   McLaren 2012; Citrin et al. 2014; Chong and Levy 2018; though see also Kymlicka (2010) for an argument that the scope and substantive impact of this backlash have been exaggerated.
35   Isaacs 1975.
36   "But the stranger that dwelleth with you shall be unto you as one born among you, and thou shalt love him as thyself." Leviticus 19:34.

Notes on pages 166–175

37 Isaacs 1975, p. 213.
38 Alba and Nee 2003.
39 Anderson 1991[1983].
40 Billig 1995.
41 Citrin and Sears 2014.
42 Medina 2013.

7 CONCLUSION

1 Hawking 1998.
2 See, for instance, Lazarsfeld, Berelson, and Gaudet 1948; Berelson, Lazarsfeld, and McPhee 1954; Campbell et al. 1960 ; and Converse 2000[1964]. Tellingly, the main theoretical rupture between the so-called "Columbia" and "Michigan" schools of political behavior concerned neither the fact of what we call "group-centrism," nor the mechanism linking it to attitude and action; rather, it emerged over the question of *which* social groups appeared to matter more.
3 See, e.g., Kinder and Sanders 1996; Peffley and Hurwitz 2002; Tesler and Sears 2010; Tesler 2012.
4 Berinsky 2009.
5 See, e.g., Sullivan, Piereson, and Marcus 1982; Sides and Gross 2013.
6 Campbell et al. 1960; Greene 1999; Green, Palmquist, and Schickler 2002; Mason 2018.
7 Higham 2002[1955].
8 Albertson and Gadarian 2015.
9 See, e.g., Wang 2018.
10 Stephen Morgan (2018) summed up this ambiguity well in a recent working paper: "It is, therefore, unclear how much of Trump's nativism was appealing to white, working-class voters because of its core content. For some voters, it may have been received as an effective demonstration of working-man's bravado, intended as a critique of the excessive 'political correctness' of highly educated elites and the phony politicians that they support." The working paper is available at https://osf.io/preprints/socarxiv/7r9fj/
11 Monmouth Poll 2017.
12 Harell and Stolle (2010) provide a good introduction to this topic, and the recent (2017) volume *Strains of Commitment* edited by Keith Banting and Will Kymlicka provides a variety of points of view from within this broader consensus.
13 A good overview of this literature is available in a recent volume edited by Marc Helbling, called *Islamophobia in the West* (2012).
14 Sides and Gross 2013.
15 Kalkan, Layman, and Uslaner 2009.
16 Wright, Johnston et al. 2016.
17 Specifically, we asked (in sequence) about whether people should be allowed to wear the symbol in question when voting, as a teacher in a classroom, as a student in a classroom, and while walking in the street. For further details on this study, see Wright et al. 2016.
18 Citrin and Sears 2014.
19 Stokes 2017.

208   *Notes on pages 175–184*

20 Trump 2006. This speech was delivered in Greensboro, South Carolina, June 14, 2006. A full video is available at www.youtube.com/watch?v=mf7ed65u8vQ
21 A limitation, at least for our purposes here, is that the vignettes separated immigrants from native-born people but did not specify whether the immigrant had citizenship or not. Based on what we showed in Chapter 6, it makes sense to assume that this distinction matters a great deal. For other details on that study's protocol, see Soroka et al. (2017).
22 Kinder and Kam 2009.
23 Higham 2002[1955]
24 Craig, Rucker, and Richeson 2018; see also Myers and Levy 2018.
25 See, e.g., Lipset 1997; Lipset and Marks 2001.
26 The "burqa ban" in France sailed through both National Assembly and Senate by margins of 335 to 1 and 246 to 1, respectively. Pew surveys from July 2010 showed that more than 80% of French citizens supported the law, as did majorities in Germany, Britain, and Spain. See Widespread Support for Banning Full Islamic Veil in Western Europe 2010.
27 Nicolas Sarkozy Says Islamic Veils not Welcome in France n.d.; France's socialist candidate Francois Hollande says he'd keep "burqa ban" 2012 .
28 Joppke 2004.
29 Howard 2009.
30 See Goodman 2014. Whether multicultural policy is actually in retreat beyond this rhetorical move is a matter of some debate (Kymlicka 2010; Bloemraad and Wright 2014).
31 Ceobanu and Escandell 2010.
32 Citrin and Sides 2008.
33 See, e.g., Sniderman, Hagendoorn, and Prior 2004; Sniderman and Hagendoorn 2009.
34 Hofstadter 1948, viii.
35 See, e.g., Freeman 1995.
36 See Gallup Time Series n.d.
37 See, e.g., Hing 2017.
38 Citrin and Sears 2014.
39 Gallup Time Series n.d.
40 See, e.g., Kopan and Agiesta 2017.

Bibliography

ABC News/Washington Post. 2013a, March. USABCWP.040313.R01C. Ithaca, NY: Roper Center for Public Opinion Research.

ABC News/Washington Post. 2013b, April. USABCWP.041613.R27C. Ithaca, NY: Roper Center for Public Opinion Research.

Abrajano, M., and Hajnal, Z. L. 2015. *White Backlash: Immigration, Race, and American Politics*. Princeton, NJ: Princeton University Press.

Abrajano, M., Elmendorf, C., and Quinn, K. 2018. Labels vs. Pictures: Treatment Mode Effects in Experiments about Discrimination. *Political Analysis*, 26(1): 20–33.

Achen, C. H., and Bartels, L. M., 2017. *Democracy for Realists: Why Elections Do not Produce Responsive Government*. Princeton, NJ: Princeton University Press.

Alba, R., and Nee, V. 2003. *Remaking the American Mainstream: Assimilation and Contemporary Immigration*. Cambridge, MA: Harvard University Press.

Albertson, B., and Gadarian, S. K. 2015. *Anxious Politics: Democratic Citizenship in a Threatening World*. New York: Cambridge University Press.

Allport, G. 1979[1954]. *The Nature of Prejudice, 25th Anniversary Edition*. New York: Basic Books.

Alvarez, M. R., and Brehm, J. 2002. *Hard Choices, Easy Answers: Values, Information, and American Public Opinion*. Princeton, NJ: Princeton University Press.

Americans Stand Out on Individualism. 2016, April 19. www.pewresearch.org/fact tank/2016/04/19/5-ways-americans-and-europeans-are-different/ft_16-04-22_usindividualism/

Amis, K. 1999[1954]. *Lucky Jim*. New York: Penguin Modern Classics.

Anderson, B. 1991[1983]. *Imagined Communities*, rev. ed. London: Verso Books.

Arrow, K. 1972. Some Mathematical Models of Race Discrimination in the Labor Market. In A. H. Pascal, ed., *Racial Discrimination in Economic Life*. Lexington: D.C. Heath, 187–204.

Banks, A. J. 2014. *Anger and Racial Politics: The Emotional Foundation of Racial Attitudes in America*. New York: Cambridge University Press.

Bansak, K., Hainmueller, J., and Hangartner, D., 2016. How Economic, Humanitarian, and Religious Concerns Shape European Attitudes toward Asylum Seekers. *Science*, 354(6309): 217–22.

Bansak, K., Hainmueller, J., Hopkins, D. J. et al. 2018. The Number of Choice Tasks and Survey Satisficing in Conjoint Experiments. *Political Analysis*, 26(1): 112–19.

Banting, K., and Kymlicka, W., eds. 2006. *Multiculturalism and the Welfare State: Recognition and Redistribution in Contemporary Democracies*. New York: Oxford University Press.

Banting, K., and Kymlicka, W. 2017. Introduction: The Political Sources of Solidarity in Diverse Societies. In K. Banting and W. Kymlicka, eds., *The Strains of Commitment: The Political Sources of Solidarity in Diverse Societies*. New York: Oxford University Press, 1–60.

Bargh, J. A. 1999. The Cognitive Monster. In S. Chaiken and Y. Trope, eds., *Dual Processes in Social Psychology*. New York: Guilford Press, 361–82.

Barreto, M. 2017. The Great White Hope: Donald Trump, Race, and the Crisis of American Politics. Talk delivered at APSA Political Psychology Pre-Conference, University of California, Berkeley, August 30.

Barry, B. 2002. *Culture and Equality: An Egalitarian Critique of Multiculturalism*. Cambridge, MA: Harvard University Press.

Bartels, L. M. 2008. *Unequal Democracy: The Political Economy of the New Gilded Age*. Princeton, NJ: Princeton University Press.

Becker, G. S. 1957. *The Economics of Discrimination*. Chicago: University of Chicago Press.

Berelson, B. R., Lazarsfeld, P. F., and MacPhee, W. N. 1954. *Voting*. Chicago: University of Chicago Press.

Berinsky, A. J. 2009. *In Time of War: Understanding American Public Opinion from World War II to Iraq*. Chicago: University of Chicago Press.

Berlin, I. 1997[1979]. Nationalism: Past Neglect and Present Power. In H. Hardy and R. Hausheer, eds., *The Proper Study of Mankind: An Anthology of Essays*. New York: Farrar, Strauss, and Giroux, 581–604.

Billig, M. 1995. *Banal Nationalism*. Thousand Oaks, CA: Sage.

Blalock, Hubert M. 1967. *Toward a Theory of Minority-Group Relations*. New York: John Wiley.

Bloemraad, I., and Wright, M. 2014. "Utter Failure" or Unity out of Diversity? Debating and Evaluating Policies of Multiculturalism. *International Migration Review*, 48(s1).

Bloemraad, I., Silva, F., and Voss, K. 2016. Rights, Economics, or Family? Frame Resonance Political Ideology, and the Immigrant Rights Movement. *Social Forces*, 94: 1647–74.

Bobo, L., 1983. Whites' Opposition to Busing: Symbolic Racism or Realistic Group Conflict? *Journal of Personality and Social Psychology*, 45(6): 1196.

Bobo, L., and Hutchings, V. L., 1996. Perceptions of Racial Group Competition: Extending Blumer's Theory of Group Position to a Multiracial Social Context. *American Sociological Review*, 61: 951–72.

Bobo, L., Kluegel, J. R., and Smith, R. A. 1996. *Laissez-Faire Racism: The Crystallization of a "Kinder, Gentler" Anti-Black Ideology*. New York: Russell Sage Foundation.

Borjas, G. 1999. The Economic Analysis of Immigration. In *Handbook of Labor Economics*. Vol. 3. New York: Elsevier, 1697–760.

Bosniak, L., 2000. Citizenship Denationalized (The State of Citizenship Symposium). *Indiana Journal of Global Legal Studies*, 7(2): 2.

Bibliography

Brader, T., Valentino, N. A., and Suhay, E., 2008. What Triggers Public Opposition to Immigration? Anxiety, Group Cues, and Immigration Threat. *American Journal of Political Science*, 52(4): 959–78.

Brewer, M. B. 1999. The Psychology of Prejudice: Ingroup Love or Outgroup Hate? *Journal of Social Issues*, 55(3): 429–44.

Brewer, M. B. 2007. The Importance of Being *We*: Human Nature and Intergroup Relations. *American Psychologist*, 62 (8): 728–38.

Cable News Network. CNN/Opinion Research Corporation Poll. 2007, June. USORC.062507A.R19. Ithaca, NY: Roper Center for Public Opinion Research.

Campbell, A. L., Wong, C., and Citrin, J. 2006. Racial Threat, Partisan Climate, and Direct Democracy: Contextual Effects in Three California Initiatives. *Political Behavior*, 28(2): 129.

Campbell, A., Converse, P., Miller, W. et al. 1960. *The American Voter*. New York: John Wiley.

Carens, J. H. 1987. Aliens and Citizens: The Case for Open Borders. *The Review of Politics*, 49(2): 251–73.

Carmines, E. G., and Stimson, J. A. 1980. The Two Faces of Issue Voting, *American Political Science Review*, 74(1): 78–91.

CBS News. 2017, August. USCBS.080817B.R37A. Ithaca, NY: Roper Center for Public Opinion Research.

CBS News/New York Times. 2015, December. USCBSNYT.121015B.R56. Ithaca, NY: Roper Center for Public Opinion Research.

Ceobanu, A. M., and Escandell, X. 2010. Comparative Analyses of Public Attitudes toward Immigrants and Immigration Using Multinational Survey Data: A Review of Theories and Research. *Annual Review of Sociology*, 36: 309–28.

Chason, R. 2017. Non-Citizens Can Now Vote in College Park, Md. www.washingtonpost.com/local/md-politics/college-park-decides-to-allow-noncitizens-to-vote-in-local-elections/2017/09/13/2b7adb4a-987b-11e7-87fc-c3f7ee4035c9_story.html

Chavez, L. R. 2008. *The Latino Threat: Constructing Immigrants, Citizens, and the Nation*. Palo Alto, CA: Stanford University Press.

Chong, D. 1993. How People Think, Reason, and Feel about Rights and Liberties. *American Journal of Political Science*, 37(3): 867–99.

Chong, D. 2000. *Rational Lives: Norms and Values in Politics and Society*. Chicago: University of Chicago Press.

Chong, D., and Druckman, J. N. 2007. Framing Theory. *Annual Review of Political Science*, 10: 103–26.

Chong, D., and Levy, M. 2018. Competing Norms of Free Expression and Political Tolerance. *Social Research: An International Quarterly*, 85(1): 197–227.

Chong, D., Citrin, J., and Conley, P. 2001. When Self-Interest Matters. *Political Psychology*, 22(3): 541–79.

Chua, A. 2018. *Political Tribes: Group Instinct and the Fate of Nations*. New York: Penguin Books.

Citrin, J., 2001. The End of American Identity? In S. Renshon, ed., *One America?* Washington, DC: Georgetown University Press, 285–307.

Citrin, J. 2009. Political Culture. In P. H. Schuck and J. Q. Wilson, eds., *Understanding America: The Anatomy of an Exceptional Nation*. New York: Hachette.

Bibliography

Citrin, J., and Green, D. P., 1990. The Self-Interest Motive in American Public Opinion. *Research in Micropolitics*, 3(1): 1–28.

Citrin, J., and Sears, D. O., 2014. *American Identity and the Politics of Multiculturalism*. Cambridge: Cambridge University Press.

Citrin, J., and Sides, J., 2008. Immigration and the Imagined Community in Europe and the United States. *Political Studies*, 56(1): 33–56.

Citrin, C., Levy, M. E., and Lenz, G. 2013. IGS Survey: Californians and Immigration Reform Alternatives. https://escholarship.org/uc/item/903496b4

Citrin, J., Levy, M., and Wong, C. J., 2017. Politics and the English Language in California: Bilingual Education at the Polls. *California Journal of Politics and Policy*, 9(2).

Citrin, J., Levy, M., and Wright, M. 2014. Multicultural Policy and Political Support in European Democracies. *Comparative Political Studies*, 47: 1531–57.

Citrin, J., Reingold, B., and Green, D. P., 1990. American Identity and the Politics of Ethnic Change. *The Journal of Politics*, 52(4): 1124–54.

Citrin, J., Green, D. P., Muste, C., and Wong, C. 1997. Public Opinion toward Immigration Reform: The Role of Economic Motivations. *The Journal of Politics*, 59: 858–81.

Citrin, J., Sears, D. O, Wong, C. et al. 2001. Multiculturalism in American Public Opinion. *British Journal of Political Science*, 31(2).

Clement, S., and Nakamura, D. 2017, September 25. Survey Finds Strong Support for "Dreamers." www.washingtonpost.com/politics/survey-finds-strong-support-for-dreamers/2017/09/24/df3c885c-a16f-11e7-b14f-f41773cd5a14_story.html?noredirect=on&utm_term=.f3ed50a57738

CNN. 2017, May 28. *State of the Union*. Transcript. http://www.cnn.com/TRANSCRIPTS/1705/28/sotu.01.html

Collingwood, L., Lajevardi, N., and Oskooii, K. A. R. 2018. A Change of Heart? Why Individual-Level Public Opinion Shifted against Trump's "Muslim Ban." *Political behavior*, 40(4): 1035–72.

Converse, P. 2000[1964]. The Nature of Belief Systems in Mass Publics. In D. Apter, ed., *Ideology and Discontent*. New York: Free Press.

Craig, M. A., Rucker, J. A., and Richeson, J. A. 2018. Racial and Political Dynamics of an Approaching "Majority-Minority" United States. *The Annals of the American Academy of Political and Social Science*, 677(1): 204–14.

Daniels, R. 2004. *Guarding the Golden Door: American Immigration Policy and Immigrants Since 1882*. New York: Farrar, Strauss, and Giroux.

Dawson, M. C. 1994. *Behind the Mule: Race and Class in African-American Politics*. Princeton, NJ: Princeton University Press.

Dixon, J. C. 2006. The Ties That Bind and Those That Don't: Toward Reconciling Group Threat and Contact Theories of Prejudice. *Social Forces*, 84(4): 2179–204.

Dorf, M. C. 2017, May 16. Is Anti-Immigration Sentiment Anti-Latino? www.newsweek.com/michael-dorf-anti-immigration-sentiment-anti-latino-609485

Dostoevsky, F. 1994[1864] *Notes from the Underground*. New York: Vintage Classics.

Druckman, J., Peterson, E., and Slothuus, R. 2013. How Elite Partisan Polarization Affects Public Opinion Formation. *American Political Science Review*, 107: 57–79.

Easton, D. 1965. *A Systems Analysis of Political Life*. New York: Wiley.

Ellis, C., and Stimson, J. A., 2012. *Ideology in America*. Cambridge: Cambridge University Press.

Bibliography

Enos, R. D. 2014. Causal Effect of Intergroup Contact on Exclusionary Attitudes. *Proceedings of the National Academy of Sciences*, 111(10): 3699–704.

Feldman, S. 1988. Structure and Consistency in Public Opinion: The Role of Core Values. *American Journal of Political Science*, 32(2): 416–40.

Feldman, S., and Steenbergen, M., 2001a. Social Welfare Attitudes and the Humanitarian Sensibility. *Citizens and Politics: Perspectives from Political Psychology*, 366–400.

Feldman, S., and Steenbergen, M. R., 2001b. The Humanitarian Foundation of Public Support for Social Welfare. In J. Kuklinski, ed., *American Journal of Political Science*. New York: Cambridge University Press, 658–77.

Feldman, S., and Zaller, J. 1992. The Political Culture of Ambivalence: Ideological Responses to the Welfare State. *American Journal of Political Science*, 36: 268–307.

Fiorina, M. P., 1981. *Retrospective Voting in American National Elections*. New Haven, CT: Yale University Press.

Fitzgerald, K., 1996. *The Face of the Nation: Immigration, the State, and the National Identity*. Redwood City, CA: Stanford University Press.

Fox News. 2011, December. USASFOX.120911B.R43.Ithaca, NY: Roper Center for Public Opinion Research.

Fox News. 2013, April. Ithaca, NY: Roper Center for Public Opinion Research.

France's Socialist Candidate Francois Hollande Says He'd Keep 'burqa ban'. 2012. https://www.independent.co.uk/news/world/europe/frances-socialist-candidate-francois-hollande-says-hed-keep-burqa-ban-7684105.html

Franklin, B., 1919, January 3. Letter to American Defense Society. https://www.theodorerooseveltcenter.org/Research/Digital-Library/Record/ImageViewer?libID=0265602&imageNo=1

Free, L. A., and Cantril, H. 1967 *The Political Beliefs of Americans: A Study of Public Opinion*. New Brunswick, NJ: Rutgers University Press.

Freeman, G. P. 1995. Modes of Immigration Politics in Liberal Democratic States. *International Migration Review*, 29(4): 881–902.

Freud, S. 1968[1933]. Why War? In L. Bramson and G. Goethals, eds., *War: Studies from Psychology, Sociology, and Anthropology*. New York: Basic Books, 71–80.

Fuchs, L. H., 1990. *The American Kaleidoscope: Race, Ethnicity, and the Civic Culture*. Middletown, CT: Wesleyan University Press.

Gaertner, S. L., and Dovidio, J. F. 2000. *Reducing Intergroup Bias: The Common Ingroup Identity Model*. Philadelphia: Psychology Press.

Gallup Organization. 2013a, April. USGALLUP 13APR09.R01B. Ithaca, NY: Roper Center for Public Opinion Research.

Gallup Organization. 2013b, June. USGALLUP.061913A.R01C. Ithaca, NY: Roper Center for Public Opinion Research.

Gallup Organization. 2017a, January. USGALLUP.020217.R02A. Ithaca, NY: Roper Center for Public Opinion Research

Gallup Organization. 2017b, February 7–12. USGALLUP.021417.R06C. Ithaca, NY: Roper Center for Public Opinion Research.

Gallup Time Series. n.d. https://news.gallup.com/poll/1660/immigration.aspx

Gellner, E. 1983[1996]. *Nations and Nationalism*. Ithaca, NY: Cornell University Press.

Gest, J. 2016. *The New Minority: White Working Class Politics in an Age of Immigration and Inequality*. New York: Oxford University Press.

Bibliography

Gest, J. 2018. *The White Working Class: What Everybody Needs to Know*. New York: Oxford University Press.

Gilens, M., 1999. *Why Americans Hate Welfare: Race, Media, and the Politics of Antipoverty Policy*. Chicago: Chicago University Press.

Gimpel, J. G., and Edwards, J. R. 1999. *The Congressional Politics of Immigration Reform*. Boston: Allyn and Bacon.

Glazer, N., and Moynihan, D. P. 1963. *Beyond the Melting Pot: The Negroes, Puerto Ricans, Jews, Italians, and Irish of New York City*. Cambridge: Massachusetts Institute of Technology Press.

Gonzalez-Barrera, A. 2017, June 29. Mexican Lawful Immigrants among the Least Likely to Become U.S. Citizens. www.pewhispanic.org/2017/06/29/mexican-lawful-immigrants-among-least-likely-to-become-u-s-citizens/

Goodman, S. W. 2014. *Immigration and Membership Politics in Western Europe*. Cambridge: Cambridge University Press.

Gordon, M. 1964. *Assimilation in American Life: The Role of Race, Religion, and National Origins*. New York: Oxford University Press.

Goren, P. 2005. Party Identification and Core Political Values. *American Journal of Political Science*, 49(4): 881–96.

Gottlieb, J., and Maske, M. 2017, September 23. Roger Goodell Responds to Trump's Call to "Fire" NFL Players Protesting during National Anthem. www.washingtonpost.com/news/early-lead/wp/2017/09/22/donald-trump-profanely-implores-nfl-owners-to-fire-players-protesting-national-anthem/

Graham, J., Haidt, J., and Nosek, B. A. 2009. Liberals and Conservatives Rely on Different Sets of Moral Foundations. *Journal of Personality and Social Psychology*, 96(5): 1029–46.

Green, D., Palmquist, B., and Schickler, E., 2002. *Partisan Hearts and Minds*. New Haven, CT: Yale University Press.

Greene, S. 1999. Understanding Party Identification: A Social Identity Approach. *Political Psychology*, 20(2): 393–403.

Greenwald, A. G., and Banaji, M. R. 1995. Implicit Social Cognition: Attitudes, Self-esteem, and Stereotypes. *Psychological Review*, 102(1): 4.

Greer, C. M. 2014. *Black Ethnics: Race, Immigration, and the Pursuit of the American Dream*. New York: Oxford University Press.

Gross, K. A., and Kinder, D. R. 1998. A Collision of Principles? Free Expression, Racial Equality, and the Prohibition of Racist Speech. *British Journal of Political Science*, 28(3): 445–71.

Guryan, J., and Charles, K. K. 2013. Taste-Based or Statistical Discrimination: The Economics of Discrimination Returns to Its Roots. *The Economic Journal*, 123: F417–F432.

Habermas, J. (1994). *Struggles for Recognition in the Democratic Constitutional State*. Princeton, NJ: Princeton University Press.

Hagendoorn, A., and Sniderman, P.M. 2009. *When Ways of Life Collide: Multiculturalism and Its Discontents in the Netherlands*. Princeton, NJ: Princeton University Press.

Haidt, J. 2016. When and Why Nationalism Beats Globalism. www.the-american-interest.com/2016/07/10/when-and-why-nationalism-beats-globalism/

Hainmueller, J., and Hangartner, D. 2013. Who Gets a Swiss Passport? A Natural Experiment in Immigrant Discrimination. *American Political Science Review*, 107(1): 159–87.

Bibliography

Hainmueller, J., and Hiscox, M. J. 2010. Attitudes toward Highly Skilled and Low-Skilled Immigration: Evidence from a Survey Experiment. *American Political Science Review*, 104(1): 61–84.

Hainmueller, J., and Hopkins, D. J. 2014. Public Attitudes toward Immigration. *Annual Review of Political Science*, 17: 225–49.

Hainmueller, J., and Hopkins, D. J. 2015. The Hidden Immigration Consensus: A Conjoint Analysis of Attitudes toward Immigrants. *American Journal of Political Science*, 59(3): 529–48.

Hainmueller, J., Hangartner, D., and Yamamoto, T. 2015. Validating Vignette and Conjoint Survey Experiments against Real-World Behavior. *Proceedings of the National Academy of Sciences*, 112(8): 2395–400.

Hainmueller, J., Hopkins, D. J., and Yamamoto, T. 2014. Causal Inference in Conjoint Analysis: Understanding Multidimensional Choices via Stated Preference Experiments. *Political Analysis*, 22(1): 1–30.

Hajnal, Z., and Rivera, M. U. 2014. Immigration, Latinos, and White Partisan Politics: The New Democratic Defection. *American Journal of Political Science*, 58(4): 773–89.

Haney-Lopez, I. 2003. *White by Law: The Legal Construction of Race*. Cambridge, MA: Harvard University Press.

Haney-Lopez, I. 2014. *Dog Whistle Politics: How Coded Racial Appeals Have Reinvented Racism and Wrecked the Middle Class*. New York: Oxford University Press.

Hanson, G. H., Scheve, K., and Slaughter, M. J. 2007. Public Finance and Individual Preferences over Globalization Strategies. *Economics & Politics*, 19(1): 1–33.

Harell, A., and Stolle, D. 2010. Diversity and Democratic Politics: An Introduction. *Canadian Journal of Political Science*, 43(2): 384–400.

Hartman, T. K., Newman, B. J., and Bell, C. S. 2014. Decoding Prejudice toward Hispanics: Group Cues and Public Reactions to Threatening Immigrant Behavior. *Political Behavior*, 36(1): 143–63.

Hartz, L. 1955. *The Liberal Tradition in America: An Interpretation of American Political Thought Since the Revolution*. New York: Harcourt, Brace.

Hawking, S. H. 1998. *A Brief History of Time*. New York: Bantam.

Haynes, C., Merolla, J., and Ramakrishnan, S. K. 2016. *Framing Immigrants: News Coverage, Public Opinion, and Policy*. New York: Russell Sage.

Helbling, M., ed. 2012. *Islamophobia in the West: Measuring and Explaining individual attitudes*. Abingdon: Routledge.

Hero, R. E., and Preuhs, R. R. 2007. Immigration and the Evolving American Welfare State: Examining Policies in the US States. *American Journal of Political Science*, 51 (3): 498–17.

Higham, J. 2002[1955]. *Strangers in the Land: Patterns of American Nativism, 1860–1925*. New Brunswick, NJ: Rutgers University Press.

Hing, J. 2017, June 29. The Truth about Immigrants and Public Benefits. www.thenation.com/article/the-truth-about-immigrants-and-public-benefits/

Hochschild, A. R. 2016 *Strangers in Their Own Land: Anger and Mourning on the American Right*. New York: The New Press.

Hochschild, J. L. 1981. *What's Fair? American Beliefs about Distributive Justice*. Cambridge, MA: Harvard University Press.

Hofstadter, R. 1948. *The American Political Tradition*. New York: Vintage.

Hofstadter, R. 1955. Review of *The Liberal Tradition in America*, by Louis Hartz. www.nytimes.com/1955/02/27/archives/without-feudalism-the-liberal-tradition-in-america-an.html?mcubz=3

Hofstadter, R. 2008[1952]. *The Paranoid Style in American Politics*. New York: Vintage.

Hollinger, D. 1993. How Wide the Circle of the "We"? American Intellectuals and the Problem of the Ethnos since World War II. *The American Historical Review*, 98: 317–37.

Hood, M. V. III, and Morris, I. L. Give Us Your Tired, Your Poor, ... But Make Sure They Have a Green Card: The Effects of Documented and Undocumented Migrant Context on Anglo Opinion Toward Immigration. *Political Behavior*, 20(1): 1–15.

Hopkins, D. J. 2010. Politicized Places: Explaining Where and When Immigrants Provoke Local Opposition. *American Political Science Review*, 104: 40–60.

Hopkins, D. J. 2015. The Upside of Accents: Language, Inter-Group Difference, and Attitudes toward Immigration. *British Journal of Political Science*, 45(3): 531–57.

Hopkins, D. J., Sides, J., and Citrin, J. 2019. The Muted Consequences of Correct Information about Immigration. *Journal of Politics*, 81(1): 315–20.

Howard, M. M. 2009. *The Politics of Citizenship in Europe*. Cambridge: Cambridge University Press.

Huber, G. A., and Lapinski, J. 2006. The "Race Card" Revisited: Assessing Racial Priming in Policy Contests. *American Journal of Political Science*, 48(2): 375–401.

Huntington, S. 2004. *Who Are We? Challenges to American National Identity*. New York: Simon and Schuster.

Huntington, S. P. 1981. *American Politics: The Promise of Disharmony*. Cambridge: Harvard University Press.

Huntington, S. P. 2009, October 28. The Hispanic Challenge. *Foreign Policy*. https://foreignpolicy.com/2009/10/28/the-hispanic-challenge/

Hurwitz, J., and Peffley, M. 1987. How Are Foreign Policy Attitudes Structured? A Hierarchical Model, *American Political Science Review*, 81(4): 1099–120.

Hyman, H. H., and Sheatsley, P. B. 1964. Attitudes toward Desegregation. *Scientific American*, 211(1): 16–23.

Isaacs, H. 1975. *Idols of the Tribe: Group Identity and Political Change*. Cambridge, MA: Harvard University Press.

Iyengar, S., Jackman, S., Messing, S. et al. 2013. Do Attitudes about Immigration Predict Willingness to Admit Individual Immigrants? A Cross-National Test of the Person-Positivity Bias, *Public Opinion Quarterly*, 77(3): 641–65.

Jacoby, W. G. 2006. Value Choices and American Public Opinion. *American Journal of Political Science*, 50(3): 706–23.

Jacoby, W. G., Searing, D. D., and Tyner, A. H. 2016. The Political Values of Politicians: Stability and Change over Four Decades. Paper presented at the Annual Meeting of American Political Science Association. Philadelphia, September 3.

Jardina, A. 2019. *White Identity Politics*. New York: Cambridge University Press.

Johnston, R., Banting, K., Kymlicka, W. et al. 2010. National Identity and Support for the Welfare State. *Canadian Journal of Political Science/Revue*, 43(2): 349–77.

Joppke, C. 1998. Why Liberal States Accept Unwanted Immigration. *World Politics*, 50: 266–93.

Joppke, C. 2004. The Retreat of Multiculturalism in the Liberal State: Theory and Policy. *British Journal of Sociology*, 55(2): 237–57.

Bibliography

Kalkan, K. O., Layman, G. C., and Uslaner, E. M. 2009. "Bands of Others"? Attitudes toward Muslims in Contemporary American Society. *Journal of Politics*, 71(3): 847–62.

Key, V. O. 1949. *Southern Politics in State and Nation*. New York: Knopf.

Key, V. O. 1961. *Public Opinion and American Democracy*. New York: Knopf.

Kinder, D. R., and Kam, C. D. 2009. *Us Against Them: Ethnocentric Foundations of American Opinion*. Chicago: University of Chicago Press.

Kinder, D. R., and Sanders, L. M. 1996. *Divided by Color: Racial Politics and Democratic Ideals*. Chicago: University of Chicago Press.

Kinder, D. R., and Sears, D. O. 1981. Prejudice and Politics: Symbolic Racism versus Racial Threats to the Good Life. *Journal of Personality and Social Psychology*, 40(3): 414.

Knoll, B. R., and Shewmaker, J. 2015. "Simply Un-American": Nativism and Support for Health Care Reform. *Political Behavior*, 37: 87–108.

Kohn, H. 2005[1944]. *The Idea of Nationalism: A Study in Its Origins and Its Background*. New Brunswick, NJ: Transaction.

Kootstra, A. 2016. Deserving and Undeserving Welfare Claimants in Britain and the Netherlands: Examining the Role of Ethnicity and Migration Status Using a Vignette Experiment. *European Sociological Review*, 32(3): 325–38.

Kopan, T. and Agiesta, J. 2017. CNN/ORC Poll: Americans Break with Trump on Immigration Policy. *CNN*. https://www.cnn.com/2017/03/17/politics/poll-oppose-trump-deportation-immigration-policy/index.html

Krogstad, J. M. 2015, March 10–April 6. On Views of Immigrants, Americans Largely Split along Party Lines. *Pew Research Center American Trends Panel*.

Kymlicka, W. 1995. *Multicultural Citizenship*. New York: Oxford University Press.

Kymlicka, W. 2010. The Rise and Fall of Multiculturalism? New Debates on Inclusion and Accommodation in Diverse Societies. *International Social Science Journal*, 61 (199): 97–112.

Lane, R. E. 1962. *Political Ideology*. New York: Free Press.

Lau, R., and Redlawsk, D. 2006. *How Voters Decide: Information Processing in Election Campaigns*. New York: Cambridge University Press.

Lazarsfeld, P. F., Berelson, B., and Gaudet, H. 1948. *The People's Choice: How the Voter Makes Up His Mind in a Presidential Campaign*. New York: Columbia University Press.

Lenz, G. S. 2012. *Follow the Leader? How Voters Respond to Politicians' Policies and Performance*. Chicago: University of Chicago Press.

Levendusky, M. 2009. *The Partisan Sort: How Liberals Became Democrats and Conservatives Became Republicans*. Chicago: University of Chicago Press.

Lévy, B.-H. 2005, May. In the Footsteps of Tocqueville. www.theatlantic.com/magazine/archive/2005/05/in-the-footsteps-of-tocqueville/303879/

Levy, J. 2017. Against Fraternity: Democracy without Solidarity. In K. Banting and W. Kymlicka, eds., *The Strains of Commitment*. New York: Oxford University Press, 107–26.

Levy, M., Wright, M., and Citrin, J. 2016. Mass Opinion and Immigration Policy in the United States: Re-Assessing Clientelist and Elite Perspectives. *Perspectives on Politics*, 14(3): 660–80.

Lind, M. 2016, September 15. The Open-Borders "Liberaltarianism" of the New Urban Elite. www.nationalreview.com/article/440055/open-borders-ideology-american-urban-elite-threaten-nationalism

Bibliography

Linddara, D. 2018. Migrant Caravans, Trump's Latest Immigration Obsession, Explained. https://www.vox.com/policy-and-politics/2018/4/6/17206042/caravan-mexico-trump-rape.

Lippmann, W. 2011[1922]. *Public Opinion*. Abingdon: Routledge.

Lipset, S. M. 1960. *Political Man: The Social Bases of Politics*. New York: Doubleday.

Lipset, S. M. 1997. *American Exceptionalism: A Double-Edged Sword*. New York: W.W. Norton.

Lipset, S. M., and Marks, G. 2001. *It Didn't Happen Here: Why Socialism Failed in the United States*. New York: W. W. Norton.

Lipset, S. M., and Raab, E. 1978. *The Politics of Unreason: Right-Wing Extremism in America, 1790–1970*. Chicago: University of Chicago Press.

Lodge, M., and Taber, C. 2013. *The Rationalizing Voter*. New York: Cambridge University Press.

Los Angeles Times. 2014, December 21. Editorial: Should Non-Citizens in the U.S. Vote? www.latimes.com/opinion/editorials/la-ed-citizenship-voting-20141221-story.html

Lyons, J., and Green, E. 2016, November 8. S.F. Budget Set-Asides Mostly Pass; Noncitizens May Get a Vote. www.sfchronicle.com/politics/article/S-F-local-ballot-measure-results-Election-2016-10594364.php

Macedo, S. 2011 When and Why Should Liberal Democracies Restrict Immigration? In R. M. Smith, ed., *Citizenship, Borders, and Human Needs*. Philadelphia: University of Pennsylvania Press, 301–23.

MacIntyre, A. 1981. *After Virtue*. London: A&C Black.

Malhotra, N., and Newman, B. 2017. Explaining Immigration Preferences: Disentangling Skill and Prevalence. *Research & Politics*, 4(4): 1–6.

Malhotra, N., Margalit, Y., and Mo, C. 2013. Economic Explanations for Opposition to Immigration: Distinguishing between Prevalence and Magnitude. *American Journal of Political Science*, 57(2): 391–410.

Martin, S. F. 2011. *A Nation of Immigrants*. New York: Cambridge University Press.

Mason, L. 2018. *Uncivil Agreement: How Politics Became Our Identity*. Chicago: University of Chicago Press.

Masuoka, N., and Junn, J. 2013. *The Politics of Belonging: Race, Public Opinion, and Immigration*. Chicago: University of Chicago Press.

McClain, P. D., Carter, N. M., DeFrancesco Soto, V. M. et al. 2006. Racial Distancing in a Southern City: Latino Immigrants' Views of Black Americans. *Journal of Politics*, 68(3): 571–84.

McClosky, H. 1964. Consensus and Ideology in American Politics. *American Political Science Review*, 58(2): 361–82.

McClosky, H., and Zaller, J. 1984. *The American Ethos: Public Attitudes toward Capitalism and Democracy*. Harvard University Press.

McGarty, C., Bliuc, A-M., Thomas, E. F. et al. 2009. Collective Action as the Material Expression of Opinion-based Group Membership. *Journal of Social Issues*, 65(4): 839–57.

McLaren, L. 2012. Immigration and Trust Politics in Britain. *British Journal of Political Science*, 42: 163–85.

Medina, J. 2013, October 7. Veto Halts Bill for Jury Duty by Noncitizens in California. www.nytimes.com/2013/10/08/us/veto-halts-bill-for-jury-duty-by-noncitizens-in-california.html

Bibliography

Mendelberg, T. 2001. *The Race Card: Campaign Strategy, Implicit Messages, and the Norm of Equality.* Princeton, NJ: Princeton University Press.

Merolla, J., Ramakrishnan, S. K., and Haynes, C. 2013. "Illegal," "Undocumented," or "Unauthorized": Equivalency Frames, Issue Frames, and Public Opinion on Immigration. *Perspectives on Politics*, 11: 789–807.

Michels, Robert, 2016[1911]. *Political Parties: A Sociological Study of the Oligarchical Tendencies of Modern Democracy.* Eastford: Martino Fine Books.

Miller, D. 1995. *On Nationality.* New York: Oxford University Press.

Miller, D., and Ali, S. 2014. Testing the National Identity Argument. *European Political Science Review*, 6: 237–59.

Mitchell, A., Kiley, J., Gottfried, J., and Matsa, K. E. 2014, October 21. Political Polarization & Media Habits. www.journalism.org/2014/10/21/political-polarization-media-habits

Mitchell, A., Kiley, J., Gottfried, J., and Matsa, K. E. 2015. On Views of Immigrants, Americans Largely Split along Party Lines. www.pewresearch.org/fact-tank/2015/09/30/on-views-of-immigrants-americans-largely-split-along-party-lines/

Morgan, S. 2018. Fake News: Status Threat Does not Explain the 2016 Presidential Vote. Unpublished working paper. https://osf.io/preprints/socarxiv/7r9fj/

Morning Consult. 2017, June 29–30. National Tracking Poll. https://www.politico.com/f/?id=0000015d-0ea5-d1e3-a97d-5ff5d4dc0001

Muste, C. 2013. The Dynamics of Immigration Opinion in the United States, 1992–2010. *Public Opinion Quarterly*, 77: 398–416.

Mutz, D. C. 2018. Status Threat, not Economic Hardship, Explains the 2016 Presidential Vote. *Proceedings of the National Academy of Sciences*, 115(19): E4330–E4339.

Myers, D., and Levy, M. 2018. Racial Population Projections and Reactions to Alternative News Accounts of Growing Diversity. *Annals of the American Academy of Political and Social Science*, 677(1): 215–28.

Myrdal, G. 1996[1944]. *An American Dilemma: The Negro Problem and Modern Democracy.* New York: Harper & Bros., Transaction Publishers.

NBC News/Wall Street Journal. 2017, August. USNBCWSJ.090617.R24. Ithaca, NY: Roper Center for Public Opinion Research.

Nelson, T. E., and Kinder, D. R. 1996. Issue Frames and Group-Centrism in American Public Opinion. *Journal of Politics*, 58(4): 1055–78.

Neuman, G. L. 1993. The Lost Century of Immigration Law (1776–1875). *Columbia Law Review*, 93(8)1 1833–901

Newman, B. J. 2013. Acculturating Contexts and Anglo Opposition to Immigration in the United States. *American Journal of Political Science*, 57: 374–90.

Newman, B. J., Hartman, T.K., Lown, P.L., et al. 2015. Easing the Heavy Hand: Humanitarian Concern, Empathy, and Opinion on Immigration. *British Journal of Political Science*, 45(3): 583–607.

Newman, B. J., Hartman, T. K., and Taber, C. S. 2012. Foreign Language Exposure, Cultural Threat, and Opposition to Immigration. *Political Psychology*, 33(5): 635–57.

Newsweek. 2009, January. USPSRNEW.011709.R15C. Ithaca, NY: Roper Center for Public Opinion Research.

Ngai, M. M. 2004. *Impossible Subjects: Illegal Aliens and the Making of Modern America.* Princeton, NJ: Princeton University Press.

Bibliography

Nicolas Sarkozy Says Islamic Veils not Welcome in France. n.d. www.theguardian.com/world/2009/jun/22/islamic-veils-sarkozy-speech-france

Norwatesh, A. 2012, March 2. Liberals Need to Choose: Welfare State or Immigration. www.huffingtonpost.com/alex-nowrasteh/liberals-need-to-choose-welfare-state-immigration-_b_1313169.html

Oh, A. H., and Wu, E. (2018, February 1). Why Immigration Advocates Must Take Back the Term "Chain Migration." *Washington Post.*

Orwell, G. 2002[1941]. The Lion and the Unicorn: Socialism and the English Genius. In J. Carey ed., *Essays.* New York: Random House.

Ostfeld, M. 2015. The Backyard Politics of Attitudes toward Immigration, *Political Psychology, 38(1):* 21–37.

Pantoja, A. 2006. Against the Tide? Core American Values and Attitudes toward US Immigration Policy in the Mid-1990s. *Journal of Ethnic and Migration Studies, 32(3):* 515–31.

Paxton, P., and Mughan, A. 2006. What's to Fear From Immigrants? Creating an Assimilationist Threat Scale. *Political Psychology, 27(4):* 549–68.

Peffley, M., and Hurwitz, J. 2002. The Racial Components of "Race-neutral" Crime Policy Attitudes. *Political Psychology, 23(1):* 59–75.

Pérez, E. O. 2010. Explicit Evidence on the Import of Implicit Attitudes: The IAT and Immigration Policy Judgments. *Political Behavior, 32:* 517–45.

Pérez, E. O. 2016. *Unspoken Politics: Implicit Attitudes and Political Thinking.* Cambridge: Cambridge University Press.

Pérez, E. O., and Hetherington, M. J. 2014. Authoritarianism in Black and White: Testing the Cross-Racial Validity of the Child-rearing Scale. *Political Analysis, 22* (3): 398–412.

Peters, J. W., and Parker, A. 2015, November 14. Marco Rubio's History on Immigration Leaves Conservatives Distrustful of Shift. *New York Times.* www.thenation.com/article/anti-immigrant-rhetoric-anti-latino/

Peterson, M. B., Slothuus, R., and Togeby, L. 2010. Political Parties and Value Consistency in Public Opinion Formation. *Public Opinion Quarterly, 74(3):* 530–50.

Pettigrew, T. F. 1998. Intergroup Contact Theory. *Annual Review of Psychology, 49:* 65–85.

Pettigrew, T. F., and Tropp, L. R. 2006. A Meta-Analytic Test of Intergroup Contact Theory. *Journal of Personality and Social Psychology, 90(5):* 751–83.

Pevnick, R. 2016. *Immigration and the Constraints of Justice: Between Open Borders and Absolute Sovereignty.* New York: Cambridge University Press.

Pew Research Center. 2018. Many Unaware That Most Immigrants in the U.S. Are Here Legally. www.people-press.org/2018/06/28/shifting-public-views-on-legal-immigration-into-the-u-s/

Pew Research Center for the People & the Press. 2013, September. USPSRA.062313. R47D. Ithaca, NY: Roper Center for Public Opinion Research.

Pew Research Center for the People & the Press Poll. 2017, February. USPSRA.021617. R35. Ithaca, NY: Roper Center for Public Opinion Research.

Pickus, N. 2005. *True Faith and Allegiance. Immigration and American Civic Nationalism.* Princeton, NJ: Princeton University Press.

Portes, A., and Rumbaut, R. G. 2006. *Immigrant America: A Portrait,* 3rd ed. Berkeley: University of California Press.

Bibliography

Proponents of Cutting the Level of Such Family-Based Immigration Have Often, and Now Controversially, Referred to It as Chain Migration. 2018, February 1. www.washingtonpost.com/news/made-by-history/wp/2018/02/01/why-immigration-advocates-must-take-back-the-term-chain-migration/

Prothro, J. W., and Grigg, C. M. 1960. Fundamental Principles of Democracy: Bases of Agreement and Disagreement. *Journal of Politics*, 22(2): 276–94.

Putnam, R. D. 2007. *E Pluribus Unum*: Diversity and Community in the Twenty-First Century. *Scandinavian Political Studies*, 30(2): 137–74.

Quinnipiac University Polling Institute. 2015, December. USQUINN.122315.R54. Ithaca, NY: Roper Center for Public Opinion Research.

Quinnipiac University Polling Institute. 2017a, January. USQUINN.011217.R50. Ithaca, NY: Roper Center for Public Opinion Research.

Quinnipiac University Polling Institute. 2017b, February. USQUINN.020717.R42. Ithaca, NY: Roper Center for Public Opinion Research.

Quinnipiac University Polling Institute. Quinnipiac University Poll. 2017c, February. USQUINN.022217.R55. Ithaca, NY: Roper Center for Public Opinion Research.

Quinnipiac University Polling Institute. 2017d, March. USQUINN.032417.R53. Ithaca, NY: Roper Center for Public Opinion Research.

Quinnipiac University Polling Institute. 2018, February. USQUINN.020618.R40. Ithaca, NY: Roper Center for Public Opinion Research.

Ramakrishnan, K., Esterling, K., and Neblo, M. n.d. Illegality, National Origin Cues, and Public Opinion on Immigration. Unpublished Manuscript. http://politicalscience. osu. edu/faculty/mneblo/papers/Illegality4Web. pdf

Reeskens, T., and Wright, M. 2013. Nationalism and the Cohesive Society: A Multilevel Analysis of the Interplay among Diversity, National Identity, and Social Capital across 27 European Societies. *Comparative Political Studies*, 46: 153–81.

Rocha, R. R., and Espino, R. 2009. Racial Threat, Residential Segregation, and the Policy Attitudes of Anglos. *Political Research Quarterly*, 62(2): 415–26.

Rokeach, M. 1973. *The Nature of Human Values*. New York: The Free Press.

Roosevelt, T. 1919, January 3. Letter to American Defense Society. www.theodorooseveltcenter.org/Research/Digital-Library/Record/ImageViewer?libID=0265602&imageNo=1

Ross, J. 2015, July 4. Bobby Jindal: The Son of Immigrants and New Champion of the Tough-on-Immigrants Crowd. www.washingtonpost.com/news/the-fix/wp/2015/07/04/bobby-jindal-the-son-of-immigrants-and-new-champion-of-the-tough-on-immigrants-crowd/

Rubin, J. 2017. The Claims of Anti-immigrant Hysterics Are Disproved — Again. www.washingtonpost.com/blogs/right-turn/wp/2017/09/28/the-claims-of-anti-immigrant-hysterics-are-disproved-again/

Salins, P. 1997. *Assimilation, American Style*. New York: Basic Books.

Sassen, S. 2001. Global Cities and Global City-regions: A Comparison. In A. J. Scott, ed., *Global City-regions: Trends, Theory, Policy*. New York: Oxford University Press, 78–95.

Scheve, K. F., and Slaughter, M. J. 2001. Labor Market Competition and Individual Preferences over Immigration Policy. *Review of Economics and Statistics*, 83(1): 133–45.

Shear, M. D., and Alcindor, Y. (2017, October 1). On Dreamers Deal, Democrats Face a Surprising Foe: The Democrats. *The New York Times*.

Schildkraut, D. J. 2005. *Press 'One' for English: Language Policy, Public Opinion, and American Identity*. Princeton, NJ: Princeton University Press.

Schildkraut, D. J. 2011. *Americanism in the Twenty-First Century: Public Opinion in the Age of Immigration*. New York: Cambridge University Press.

Schildkraut, D. J. 2013. Amnesty, Guest Workers, Fences! Oh My. *Public Opinion about "Comprehensive Immigration Reform."* In G. P. Freeman, R. Hansen, and D. L. Leal, *Immigration and Public Opinion in Liberal Democracies*. Abingdon: Routledge, 207–31.

Schildkraut, D. J. 2014. Boundaries of American Identity: Evolving Understandings of "Us". *Annual Review of Political Science*, 17: 441–60.

Schrag, P. 2010. *Not Fit for Our Society: Immigration and Nativism in America*. Berkeley: University of California Press.

Schuck, P. 2007. The Disconnect between Public Attitudes and Public Policy on Immigration. In C. Swain, ed., *Debating Immigration*. New York: Cambridge University Press.

Schuck, P. 2008. Immigration. In P. Schuck, and J. Q. Wilson, eds., *Understanding America: The Anatomy of an Exceptional Nation*. New York: Perseus, 341–74.

Schuck, P. H. 2003. *Diversity in America: Keeping Government at a Safe Distance*. Cambridge, MA: Harvard University Press.

Schuman, H. 1997. *Racial Attitudes in America: Trends and Interpretations*. Cambridge, MA: Harvard University Press.

Schuman, H. 2000. The Perils of Correlation, the Lure of Labels, and the Beauty of Negative Results. In D. O. Sears, J. Sidanius, and L. Bobo, eds., *Racialized Politics*. Chicago: University of Chicago Press: 302–23.

Schuman, H., Steeh, C., Bobo, L. D. et al. 1997. *Racial Attitudes in America: Trends and Interpretations*. Cambridge, MA: Harvard University Press.

Schwartz, S. H. 1994. Are There Universal Aspects in the Structure and Contents of Human Values? *Journal of Social Issues*, 50(4): 19–45.

Sears, D. O. 1983. The Person-positivity Bias. *Journal of Personality and Social Psychology*, 44(2).

Sears, D. O., and Citrin, J. 1982. *Tax Revolt: Something for Nothing in California*. Cambridge, MA: Harvard University Press.

Sears D. O., and Henry P. J. 2005. Over Thirty Years Later: A Contemporary Look at Symbolic Racism. In M. P. Zanna, ed., *Advances in Experimental Social Psychology*. Vol. 37. San Diego: Elsevier Academic, 95–150.

Sears, D. O., Sidanius, J., and Bobo, L., eds. 2000. *Racialized Politics: The Debate about Racism in America*. Chicago: University of Chicago Press.

Shear. M. D., and Alcindor, Y. 2017, October 1. On "Dreamers" Deal, Democrats Face a Surprising Foe: The Dreamers. www.nytimes.com/2017/10/01/us/politics/demo crats-pelosi-schumer-trump-immigration-daca-dreamers.html?mtrref=www.google .com&gwh=08DB7B2A1C2D617B79EE62C32833591D&gwt=pay

Shepard, S. 2017, July 5. Poll: Majority of Voters Back Trump Travel Ban. www .politico.com/story/2017/07/05/trump-travel-ban-poll-voters-240215

Sherif, M., White, B. J., and Harvey, O. J. 1955. Status in Experimentally Produced Groups. *American Journal of Sociology*, 60(4): 370–79.

Sherif, M., Harvey, O. J., White, B. J. et al. 1954. *Intergroup Conflict and Cooperation: The Robbers Cave Experiment*. Norman: Oklahoma University Book Exchange.

Bibliography

Shklar, J. N. 1964. *Legalism: Law, Morals, and Political Trials*. Cambridge, MA: Harvard University Press.

Sidanius, J., and Pratto, F. 1999. *Social Dominance*. New York: Cambridge University Press.

Sides, J., and Gross, K. 2013. Stereotypes, Muslims, and Support for the War on Terror. *Journal of Politics*, 75(3): 583–98.

Sides, J., Tesler, M., and Vavreck, L. 2018, *Identity Crisis: The 2016 Presidential Campaign and the Battle for the Meaning of America*. Princeton, NJ: Princeton University Press.

Skocpol, T., and Williamson, V. 2016. *The Tea Party and the Remaking of Republican Conservatism*. New York: Oxford University Press.

Smith, R. M. 1993. Beyond Tocqueville, Myrdal, and Hartz: The Multiple Traditions in America. *American Political Science Review*, 87(3): 549–66.

Smith, R. M. 1999. *Civic Ideals: Conflicting Visions of Citizenship in U.S. History*. New Haven, CT: Yale University Press.

Sniderman, P., and Hagendoorn, L. 2009. *When Ways of Life Collide*. Princeton, NJ: Princeton University Press.

Sniderman, P. M., and Carmines, E. G. 1999. *Reaching beyond Race*. Cambridge, MA: Harvard University Press.

Sniderman, P. M., Hagendoorn, L., and Prior, M. 2004. Predisposing Factors and Situational Triggers: Exclusionary Reactions to Immigrant Minorities. *American Political Science Review*, 98(1): 35–49.

Sniderman, P. M., Piazza, T., Tetlock, P.E. et al. 1991. The New Racism. *American Journal of Political Science*, 35(2): 423–47.

Sniderman, P. M., Tetlock, P. E., Glaser, J. M. et al. 1989. Principled Tolerance and the American Mass Public, *British Journal of Political Science*, 19: 25–45.

Soroka, S., Wright, M., Johnston, R. et al. 2017. Ethnoreligious Identity, Immigration, and Redistribution. *Journal of Experimental Political Science*, 4: 173–82.

Soto, V. M. 2014, February 24. Would the GOP Contenders Feel the Same about Immigration if the Folks Trying to Cross the Border Were Canadians? www.thena tion.com/article/anti-immigrant-rhetoric-anti-latino/

Stenner, K. 2008. *The Authoritarian Dynamic*. New York: Cambridge University Press.

Stokes, B. 2017. 4. Faith: Few Strong Links to National Identity. http://www.pewglobal .org/2017/02/01/faith-few-strong-links-to-national-identity

Stouffer, S. A., 1955. *Communism, Conformity, and Civil Liberties: A Cross-section of the Nation Speaks Its Mind*. New York: Doubleday.

Sullivan, A. 2017, March. American Wasn't Built for Humans. http://nymag.com/daily/ intelligencer/2017/09/can-democracy-survive-tribalism.html

Sullivan, J. L., Pierson, J., and Marcus, G. E. 1982. *Political Tolerance and American Democracy*. Chicago: University of Chicago Press

Taber, C. S., and Lodge, M. 2006. Motivated Skepticism in the Evaluation of Political Beliefs. *American Journal of Political Science*, 50: 755–69.

Tajfel, H., and Turner, J. C. 1979. An Integrative Theory of Intergroup Conflict. In W. G. Austin and S. Worchel, eds., *The Social Psychology of Intergroup Relations*. Monterey: Brooks/Cole, 33–37.

Talev, M. 2015. Bloomberg Politics Poll: Most Americans Oppose Syrian Refugee Resettlement. www.bloomberg.com/news/articles/2015-11-18/bloomberg-poll-most-americans-oppose-syrian-refugee-resettlement

Taylor, M. C. 1998. How White Attitudes Vary with the Racial Composition of the Local Population: Numbers Count. *American Sociological Review*, 63(4): 512–35.

Taylor, S. E., and Croker, J. 1981. Schematic Bases of Social Information Processing. In T. E. Higgins, C. P. Herman, and M. P. Zanna, eds., *Social Cognition: The Ontario Symposium*, 1: 89–134.

Tesler, M. 2012. The Spillover of Racialization into Health Care: How President Obama Polarized Public Opinion by Racial Attitudes and Race. *American Journal of Political Science*, 56(3): 690–704.

Tesler, M. 2016. *Post-Racial or Most Racial? Race and Politics in the Obama Era*. Chicago: University of Chicago Press.

Tesler, M., and Sears, D. O. 2010. *Obama's Race: The 2008 Election and the Dream of a Post-racial America*. Chicago: University of Chicago Press.

Tetlock, P. E. 1986. A Value Pluralism Model of Ideological Reasoning. *Journal of Personality and Social Psychology*, 50(4): 819–27.

Tetlock, P. E., Kristel, O. V., Elson, S. B., et al. 2000. The Psychology of the Unthinkable: Taboo Trade-offs, Forbidden Base Rates, and Heretical Counterfactuals. *Journal of Personality and Social Psychology*, 78(5): 853.

Theiss-Morse, E. 2009. *Who Counts as an American? The Boundaries of National Identity*. New York: Cambridge University Press.

Tichenor, D. J. 2002. *Dividing Lines: The Politics of Immigration Control in America*. Princeton, NJ: Princeton University Press.

Tichenor, D. J. 2009. Navigating an American Minefield: The Politics of Illegal Immigration. *The Forum*, 7. www.degruyter.com/view/j/for.2009.7.3_20120105083455/for.2009.7.3/for.2009.7.3.1325/for.2009.7.3.1325.xml

Tocqueville. 2000[1835]. H. Mansfield and D. Withrop, trans. *Democracy in America*. Chicago: University of Chicago Press.

Transue, J. E. 2007. Identity Salience, Identity Acceptance, and Radical Policy Attitudes: American National Identity as a Uniting Force. *American Journal of Political Science*, 51(1): 78–91.

Trump. D. 2006, June 14. Speech delivered in Greensboro, South Carolina. A full video is available at www.youtube.com/watch?v=mf7ed65u8vQ

Trump, D. 2018. https://twitter.com/realdonaldtrump/status/1026585401874677760?lang=en

Trump Voters not Bothered by Overtures to Democrats. 2017. www.monmouth.edu/polling-institute/reports/monmouthpoll_us_092017/

United Technologies, National Journal. 2013, June. USPSRA.062413CC.R04. Ithaca, NY: Roper Center for Public Opinion Research.

Valentino, N. A., Brader, T., and Jardina, A. E. 2013. Immigration Opposition among U.S. Whites: General Ethnocentrism or Media Priming of Attitudes about Latinos? *Political Psychology*, 34: 149–66.

Valentino, N. A., Neuner, F. G., and Vandenbroek, L. M. 2018. The Changing Norms of Racial Political Rhetoric and the End of Racial Priming. *Journal of Politics*, 80(3): 757–71.

Valentino, N. A., Soroka, S. N., Iyengar, S., et al. 2017. Economic and Cultural Drivers of Immigrant Support Worldwide. *British Journal of Political Science*. https://doi.org/10.1017/S000712341700031X

Bibliography

Vance, J. D. 2016. *Hillbilly Elegy: A Memoir of a Family and Culture in Crisis*. New York: Harper Collins.

Walzer, M. 1984. *Spheres of Justice: A Defense of Pluralism and Equality*. New York: Basic Books.

Wang, A. B. 2018, May 17. "My Next Call is to ICE!": A Man Flipped Out Because Workers Spoke Spanish at a Manhattan Deli. www.washingtonpost.com/news/business/wp/2018/05/16/my-next-call-is-to-ice-watch-a-man-wig-out-because-workers-spoke-spanish-at-a-manhattan-deli/

Waters, M. C. 1990. *Ethnic Options: Choosing Identities in America*. Berkeley, CA: University of California Press.

Weber, M. 2002[1905]. *The Protestant Ethic and the Spirit of Capitalism and Other Writings*. New York: Penguin Classics.

Wong, C. J. 2010. *Boundaries of Obligation in American Politics: Geographic, National, and Racial Communities*. New York: Cambridge University Press.

Wong, C., Levy, M., and Citrin, J. 2017. Thick versus Thin Assimilation: American Public Opinion about Language and Citizenship. Paper presented at the Annual Meeting of the International Society for Political Psychology. Austin, TX.

Wong, T. 2017. *The Politics of Immigration: Partisanship, Demographic Change, and American National Identity*. New York: Oxford University Press.

Wright, M. 2011. Diversity and the Imagined Community: Immigrant Diversity and Conceptions of National Identity. *Political Psychology*, 32(5): 837–62.

Wright, M., and Reeskens, T. 2013. Of What Cloth Are the Ties That Bind? National Identity and Support for the Welfare State across 29 European Countries. *Journal of European Public Policy*, 20: 1443–63.

Wright, M., Citrin, J., and Wand, J. 2012. Alternative Measures of American National Identity: Implications for the Civic-Ethnic Distinction. *Political Psychology*, 33: 469–82.

Wright, M., Johnston, R., Citrin, J., et al. 2016. Multiculturalism and Muslim Accommodation: Policy and Predisposition across Three Contexts. *Comparative Political Studies*, 50: 102–32.

Wright, M., Levy, M., and Citrin, J. 2016. Public Attitudes toward Immigration Policy across the Legal/Illegal Divide: The Role of Categorical and Attribute-based Decision-Making. *Political Behavior*, 38: 229–53.

Zaller, J. 1992. *The Nature and Origins of Mass Opinion*. New York: Cambridge University Press.

Zaller, J. 2003. Coming to Grips with VO Key's Concept of Latent Opinion. In M. MacKuen and G. Rabinowitz, eds., *Electoral Democracy*. Ann Arbor: University of Michigan Press, 311–36.

Zolberg, A. 1999. Matters of State: Theorizing Immigration Policy. In C. Hirschman, P. Kasinitz, and J. DeWind, eds., *The Handbook of International Migration: The American Experience*. New York: Russell Sage Foundation.

Zolberg, A. 2006. *A Nation by Design: Immigration Policy in the Fashioning of America*. Cambridge, MA: Harvard University Press.

Index

American creed, xv, xvii–xviii, 10, 25, 28, 30, 32, 37, 168, 173, 184. *See also* American ethos; American political culture
American ethos, xvii–xviii, 13–14, 60, 85, 123, 141, 168, 173. *See also* American creed; American political culture
American National Election Study, 2, 6–7, 22, 90–2, 94–5
American national identity. *See* national identity
American political culture, xv–xvi, 13–14
  American exceptionalism, 179
  ascriptive hierarchy in, xv, xviii, 14
  egalitarianism in, 37
  legalism, in, 32–3
  liberal tradition, and, xx, 25, 28, 33, 109
  multiple traditions, and, 14
  Protestant ethic, in, 30
Americanism. *See* American political culture; civic fairness; group-centrism; national identity
ANES *See* American National Election Study
anti-immigrant sentiment. *See* immigration attitudes; nativism
Asians, xix, 93–4
  attitudes of, 94, 105, 134
  feelings toward. *See also* ethnocentrism; prejudice
assimilation, xvii, 143. *See also* American political culture; civic fairness
  American history, in, 28–9, 31–2
  formal. *See* formal assimilation

functional. *See* functional assimilation
multiculturalism, versus, 29
public opinion on. *See* immigration attitudes
thick assimilationism, 28–9
thin assimilationism, xvii
authoritarianism, 26, 89, 157
  measurement of, 91

blacks, xv, 196
  attitudes of, 7–8, 19, 89, 94, 105. *See also* ethnic identity; group-centrism
  feelings toward. *See* ethnocentrism; prejudice
Brown, Jerry, 167
Buchanan, Pat, xix
Bush, George H.W., xix, 186
Bush, Jeb, xx

California Proposition, 187. *See* immigration policy
Cantor, Eric, xx
Carter, Jimmy, 37, 187
Circle of We. *See* national identity
civic fairness, xvii, xx, 9–10, 23 8
  American political culture, and, 13–14
  attitude ambivalence, and, 9–10, 56–7, 62, 73, 86–7
  countries outside the United States, in, 179–80
  dog-whistle, as, 12–13, 35, 177–8
  double-edged nature of, 16–17, 40
  elements of. *See* egalitarianism; formal assimilation; functional assimilation; humanitarianism

Index

civic fairness (cont.)
  ethnic bias, and, 58. *See also* prejudice
  group-centrism, versus, xviii, 10–13, 16,
    20–3, 30, 50–5, 62, 87–8, 95–6, 118,
    124–5, 131–3, 140–1, 147, 158, 160–2,
    170–3
  illegal immigration, and. *See* illegal immigration
  immigration attitudes, and. 170
  issues beyond immigration, and, 14, 51
  liberal tradition, and, 9, 28
  media, in. *See* media, immigration coverage in
  minorities and, 19. *See also* ethnic identity;
    ethnicity
  stereotypes, and. *See* stereotypes
  values underpinnings. *See* egalitarianism;
    humanitarianism; individualism; legalism
Clinton, Bill, 33–4, 145, 186
Clinton, Hillary, 170
constitutional patriotism, 49
Cooperative Congressional Election Study,
    76–7, 79, 148, 153, 155, 157

economic self-interest, xviii, 4, 8, 189
egalitarianism, xv, xvii, xx, 25, 37, 143, 170.
    See also civic fairness; values
  American political culture, in, xv, 37
  ethnicity, by, 91, 93–4
  illegal immigration, and, 37–8, 86–7,
    91–3
  measurement of, 89–90
  moderation by, 102, 156–7
equality of opportunity. *See* egalitarianism
ethnic identity
  blacks, among, 67
  cross-ethnic identity, 5, 7
  group-centric influence on immigration
    attitudes, as, 43–6
  group position/ascriptive hierarchy, as
    expression of, 43–4
  immigration attitudes, and, 6–8
  ingroup love versus outgroup hate, 44–5
  Latinos, among, 67
  linked fate, 44
  measurement of, 67
  moderation by, 72–3
  pan-ethnic identity, 5, 7, 137
  white identity, 17, 72, 190
ethnicity, xv, 5. *See also* ethnic identity;
    group-centrism
  effects of, 109–10, 118, 151
  information cuing, xviii, 62, 97, 130,
    136, 148

ethnocentrism, xvii, 5, 43, 196. *See also*
    prejudice
  attitude ambivalence, and, 5–7
  attitude instability, and, 190
  immigration, conflation with, 139–40
  measurement of, 6, 67, 91, 190
  moderation by, 72, 78–9, 105
European Social Survey, 92

formal assimilation, 9, 28, 31–6, 170. *See also*
    assimilation; civic fairness
  American history, in, 31–2
  categorical response, and, 36, 99, 105–7,
    152–4
  effects of, 100, 149–50, 152, 155–6,
    160–1
  illegal immigration, and. *See* egalitarianism;
    illegal immigration; legalism
  information cuing, 98, 130, 148
  legalism. *See* legalism
  political rhetoric on, 33–5
  political rights and, 35
  public opinion, on, 32, 35–6
Franklin, Benjamin, 42
functional assimilation, 9, 28–31, 62, 125, 170.
    See also assimilation; civic fairness
  American political culture, in, 30
  effects of, 68–9, 108–9
  English language ability, and, 30, 98
  individualism, and, 9, 30
  information cuing, 63, 74, 76, 97, 130, 136
  public opinion, on, 29–31

General Social Survey, 2–4, 22, 88, 159, 163,
    190, 203
group-centrism, xvi–xvii, 5, 42–3
  civic fairness, versus. *See* civic fairness
  economic self-interest, versus, 51
  group interest, xvi
  group position, theories of, xvi, 5, 43–4
  horizontal attachment. *See* national identity
  illegal immigration, and. *See* illegal
    immigration
  immigration attitudes, and, xvii–xviii, 5–8,
    87, 146–7, 169–70
  issues beyond immigration, and, 51–2, 169
  media, in. *See* media, immigration
    coverage in
  national identity, and. *See* national identity
  partisanship, and, 19
  politically constructed, as, xvi
  primordial, as, xvi

Index

public opinion, relationship to, xvi, 169
racial/ethnic identity, and. *See* ethnic identity; prejudice
realistic group conflict theory, and, 5
social identity theory, and, 5, 49
tribalism as, xv
values, interconnectedness between groups/ group identity, and, 14–15
varieties of, xvi–xvii, 5, 11–13, 18–19, 42–50
group position, theories of. *See* group-centrism
GSS. *See* General Social Survey

Henri-Levy, Bernard, 33, 194
heuristics, 10, 20–1, 53–5, 58, 123, 125, 141, 172, 178, 185. *See also* stereotypes
Higham, John, 18
humanitarianism, xvii, xx, 26, 37–8, 143, 170
effects of, 69
family-based immigration, and, 38
illegal immigration, and, 38
information cuing, 64–5, 74, 76
measurement of, 38, 66–7
moderation by, 70–1, 102
refugees, and, 38

illegal immigration, xix, 186
civic fairness, and, 37–8, 86–7, 171
egalitarianism, and. *See* egalitarianism
group-centrism, and, 87, 94, 96, 171
humanitarianism, and. *See* humanitarianism
legalism, and. *See* legalism
immigration attitudes, xviii–xix, 1
abstract restrictivism versus operational openness, 1, 22, 61–2, 74, 171
access to services/benefits, 2, 123, 145
ambivalence in, xviii, 1–4, 62, 83–4, 86, 170
anti-immigrant sentiment, 1, 8. *See also* nativism; prejudice
assimilation, 29–32, 35–6
border enforcement, 6–7, 123
civic fairness, and. *See* civic fairness
consequences of immigration, 4, 184, 189
economic self-interest. *See* economic self-interest
ethnic consciousness, by. *See* ethnic identity
ethnicity, by, 19. *See* Asians; Latinos; whites
family-based immigration, 1
group-centric theories, and. *See* group-centrism
illegal immigration, xx, 1, 6–7, 182–3
immigration level, xix–xx, 1, 4, 6–7, 61, 63, 81, 181–2, 184, 204

immigration policy, and, xix–xx, 180–4
instability of, 4, 83–4, 170
legal immigration, 80–1
legal versus illegal, 22, 86, 121, 171
misperceptions in, 192
multiculturalism, 175
non-attitudes, and, 8–9
non-citizen rights, 2, 146
opinion dikes, in, xx, 182–3
party identification, by, 134–5, 138, 192
pathway to citizenship, 1, 6, 121, 123, 184
permissive consensus in, xx, 181–2
polarization in, 3
prejudice. *See* prejudice
refugees, 1
skills-based immigration, 1
sociotropic motivations, and, xviii, 4–5
threat, and. *See* threat
travel ban, 82–4
immigration policy, xix
access to services/benefits, xix, 12, 145, 182
amnesty, xix, 86
California Proposition 187, xix, 145
coalitions, xx
comprehensive immigration reform, xix–xx, 12, 35, 80, 86, 122, 183
Deferred Action for Childhood Arrivals, 37, 187
Deferred Action for Parents of Americans and Lawful Permanent Residents (DAPA), 34
demographic consequences of, xix
diversity lottery, 187
E-Verify, 6
family-based immigration, 1, 182
green card, 1, 74
H1b visa program, 4
Hart-Celler Act, 74, 187
Illegal Immigration Reform and Individual Responsibility Act, 145, 187
Immigration Act of 1990, 187
Immigration Reform and Control Act, 187
multiculturalism, 183
national origins quotas, 186
non-citizen rights, 12
pathway to citizenship, 35, 122, 183
Personal Responsibility and Work Opportunity Act, 145, 187
political rights, 145–6
public opinion, relationship to, xix–xx, 180–4
RAISE Act, 81
refugees, 1, 182, 187

Index

immigration policy (cont.)
skills-based immigration, 1
travel and refugee ban, 81–2
individualism, xv, xvii, 25. *See also* civic
fairness; values
American political culture, in, xv, 30
functional assimilation, and, 9
information cuing, 74
measurement of, 66
moderation by, 69–72
ingroup solidarity, 47, 172. *See also* ethnic
identity; group-centrism; horizontal
attachment
International Social Survey Programme, 29
Isaacs, Harold, xv, 166
ISSP. *See* International Social Survey
Programme

Jindal, Bobby, 29
Johnson, Lyndon, 186

Key, V. O., xx, 181

latent opinion, 79–80
Latino National Survey, 29
Latinos, xix, 5, 39, 41, 94
attitudes of, 7–8, 19, 72–3, 89, 94, 133,
137. *See also* ethnic identity; group-
centrism
feelings toward, 7, 112–18. *See also*
ethnocentrism; prejudice
immigration, conflation with, 114, 139–40,
151
media, in. *See* media, immigration coverage
in
stereotypes regarding, 6, 23, 54, 87, 130,
151
legalism, xv, 26. *See also* civic fairness; formal
assimilation; values; values
American political culture, in, xv,
32–3
categorical response, and, 36
dog-whistle, as, 35, 87
ethnicity, by, 89, 93–4
formal assimilation, and, 9
illegal immigration, and, 86–7, 89,
92–3
measurement of, 89, 92
moderation by, 102, 156–7
political rhetoric on, 33–5
political rights and, 35
public opinion, on, 36

liberal assimilationism. *See* American political
culture; civic fairness
liberal multiculturalism, 49
liberal nationalism, 49
liberal tradition. *See* American political culture
Lodge, Henry Cabot, 170

media, immigration coverage in, 3, 17, 39–42,
82
civic fairness cues in, coding, 40
content analysis of, 40–2
ethnic cues in, coding, 40
Group-centric versus civic fairness
considerations, relative prevalence of, 41–2
Latinos, in, 39
source variation in, 41
Muslims, 41, 82
Christian identity, and, 175
cultural assimilation, and, 174–5
Muslim exceptionalism. *See* prejudice
stereotypes regarding, 174
Myrdal, Gunnar, xviii, 13, 85

national identity, 5, 46–7. *See also* group-
centrism
achievable (civic) boundaries, 50, 205
ascriptive (ethnic) boundaries, 50
horizontal attachment, 47–50, 54–5, 143,
172
horizontal attachment versus vertical
attachment, 48
measurement of, 159
moderation by, 159, 162
patriotism, 47–8
social identity theory, and, 49
vertical attachment, 47–8, 144
nativism, 12, 109, 184, 187. *See also*
group-centrism; immigration attitudes;
prejudice
American history, in, 12, 18
norms. *See* values

Obama, Barack, 34
opinion dikes. *See* immigration attitudes

patriotism. *See* national identity
Pew Research Center, 66
prejudice, xvii–xviii, 5, 125
anti-black, 45
anti-Latino, 5–6, 12, 19, 44–6, 52–4, 58, 63,
65, 95–6, 112–18, 122, 125–7, 131, 151,
171–2

Index

anti-Muslim, 45, 82–3, 109, 174–7
attitude ambivalence, and, 5–7, 146, 157–8
attitude instability, and, 190
conflation with immigration attitudes, 112–18, 139–40
ethnocentrism. *See* ethnocentrism
generalized versus group-specific, 5, 43, 45
group position/ascriptive hierarchy, as expression of, 43–4
immigration attitudes, and, 11–13, 157–8, 171
implicit, 5, 12, 45, 52, 117–18
information, and, 126–9
measurement of, 91, 190
motivated reasoning, and, 129
social desirability, and, 63, 83, 102, 111–12, 118
statistical discrimination, as, 53, 127, 151, 172
stereotyping, and, 54, 125, 172, 177
symbolic racism, 12, 45–6, 52, 111
tasted-based discrimination, and, 172
taste-based discrimination, as, 53, 125, 127
taste-based versus statistical discrimination, 53–4, 127–9, 131–3
threat, and. *See* threat
progressive's dilemma, 143, 164–6

Racial Prism of Group Identity Model, 44. *See also*; ethnic identity; group-centrism prejudice
Reagan, Ronald, xix, 186
realistic group conflict theory. *See* group-centrism
Roosevelt, Theodore, 29
Rubio, Marco, xx
rule of law. *See* legalism

Smith, Rogers, xv, 13
social identity theory. *See* group-centrism minimal group paradigm, 5
sociotropic motivations, and. *See* economic self-interest; immigration attitudes
statistical discrimination. *See* prejudice
stereotypes, xviii, 11, 20, 27, 125, 170. *See also* prejudice
civic fairness, and, 27, 54, 127

group-centrism, and, 53–4, 127
heuristics, as, 10, 53–5, 58, 123, 125, 141, 172
immigration, prevalence in, 27. *See* Asians; Latinos; Muslims
responsiveness to information, xviii, 12, 23, 172, 176
Survey Sampling International, 35–6, 74–9, 92–7, 106, 111, 130, 139, 156–7

taste-based discrimination. *See* prejudice
threat, xvii, 1, 30, 42–4
Tocqueville, Alexis de, xv, 10, 32–3, 48
tribalism, xv. *See* group-centrism
Trump, Donald, xx, 22, 34, 37, 39, 41, 45, 81–3, 170, 184

values, 10–11, 25–6. *See also* civic fairness
attitudes, link to, 26–7
civic fairness, bases of. *See* egalitarianism; humanitarianism; individualism; legalism
dog-whistle, as, 12–13, 35, 87, 177–8
egalitarianism. *See* egalitarianism
groups/group-identity, interconnectedness between values, and, 14–15
humanitarianism, *See* humanitarianism
illegal immigration, and. *See* egalitarianism; illegal immigration; legalism
immigration attitudes and, legalism, 10–11
individualism. *See* individualism
individual-level inculcation of, 26
issues beyond immigration, and, 51
legalism. *See* legalism
moderation by. *See* egalitarianism; humanitarianism; individualism; legalism
norms, distinction between values and, 192
origins of, 16, 27–8
partisanship, and, 192
symbolic racism, as cover for, 12, 45–6, 52
vertical attachment. *See* national identity

welfare benefits, immigrant access to. *See* immigration attitudes; immigration policy
whites. *See* ethnic identity; group-centrism; prejudice
Wilson, Pete, xix, 145

Books in the series

T.K. Ahn, Robert Huckfeldt and John Barry Ryan, *Experts, Activists, and Democratic Politics: Are Electorates Self-Educating*

Asher Arian, *Security Threatened: Surveying Israeli Opinion on Peace and War*

Jack Citrin and David O. Sears, *American Identity and the Politics of Multiculturalism*

James DeNardo, *The Amateur Strategist: Intuitive Deterrence Theories and the Politics of the Nuclear Arms Race*

Robert S. Erikson, Michael B. Mackeun, and James A. Stimson, *The Macro Polity*

Jennifer Fitzgerald, *Close to Home: Local Ties and Voting Radical Right in Europe*

James L. Gibson, *Overcoming Historical Injustices: Land Reconciliation in South Africa*

James L. Gibson and Amanda Gouws, *Overcoming Intolerance in South Africa: Experiments in Democratic Persuasion*

John R. Hibbing and Elizabeth Theiss-Morse, *Congress As Public Enemy: Public Attitudes Toward American Political Institutions*

John R. Hibbing and Elizabeth Theiss-Morse, *Stealth Democracy: Americans' Beliefs about How Government Should Work*

John R. Hibbing and Elizabeth Theiss-Morse, *What Is It about Government That Americans Dislike?*

Robert Huckfeldt and John Sprague, *Citizens, Politics, and Social Communication: Information and Influence in an Election Campaign*

Robert Huckfeldt, Paul E. Johnson, and John Sprague, *Political Disagreement: The Survival of Diverse Opinions within Communication Networks*

Ashley Jardina, *White Identity Politics*

James H. Kuklinski, *Thinking about Political Psychology*

James H. Kuklinski, *Citizens and Politics: Perspectives from Political Psychology*

Richard R. Lau and David P. Redlawsk, *How Voters Decide: Information Processing in Election Campaigns*

Milton Lodge and Charles S. Taber, *The Rationalizing Voter*

Arthur Lupia, Mathew McCubbins, and Samuel Popkin, *Elements of Reason: Cognition, Choice, and the Bounds of Rationality*

George E. Marcus, John L. Sullivan, Elizabeth Theiss-Morse, and Sandra L. Wood, *With Malice Toward Some: How People Make Civil Liberties Judgments*

Jeffery J. Mondak, *Personality and the Foundations of Political Behavior*

Diana C. Mutz, *Impersonal Influence: How Perceptions of Mass Collectives Affect Political Attitudes*

Michael A. Neblo, Kevin M. Esterling, and David M. J. Lazer, *Politics with the People: Building a Directly Representative Democracy*

Hans Noel, *Political Ideologies and Political Parties in America*

Mark Peffley and Jon Hurwitz, *Justice in America: The Separate Realities of Blacks and Whites*

Efrén O. Pérez, *Unspoken Politics: Implicit Attitudes and Political Thinking*

Markus Prior, *Post-Broadcast Democracy: How Media Choice Increases Inequality in Political Involvement and Polarizes Elections*

Paul M. Sniderman, Richard A. Brody, and Philip E. Tetlock, *Reasoning and Choice: Explorations in Political Psychology*

Stuart N. Soroka, *Negative in Democratic Politics: Causes and Consequences*

Karen Stenner, *The Authoritarian Dynamic*

Susan Welch, Timothy Bledsoe, Lee Sigelman, and Michael Combs, *Race and Place: Race Relations in an American City*

Cara J. Wong, *Boundaries of Obligation in American Politics: Geographic, National, and Racial Communities*

John Zaller, *The Nature and Origins of Mass Opinion*

Alan S. Zuckerman, Josip Dasovic, and Jennifer Fitzgerald, *Partisan Families: The Social Logic of Bounded Partisanship in Germany and Britain*